MOTHERS
AND
DAUGHTERS

MOTHERS AND DAUGHTERS
Loving and Letting Go

EVELYN BASSOFF, PH.D.

NAL BOOKS

NEW AMERICAN LIBRARY

NEW YORK AND SCARBOROUGH, ONTARIO

306.8
B

 NAL BOOKS TRADEMARK REG. U.S. PAT. OFF. AND FOREIGN COUNTRIES
REGISTERED TRADEMARK—MARCA REGISTRADA
HECHO EN CHICAGO, U.S.A.

SIGNET, SIGNET CLASSIC, MENTOR, ONYX, PLUME, MERIDIAN
and NAL BOOKS are published *in the United States* by NAL PENGUIN INC.,
1633 Broadway, New York, New York 10019,
in Canada by The New American Library of Canada Limited,
81 Mack Avenue, Scarborough, Ontario M1L 1M8

Designed by Gene Gardner

Library of Congress Cataloging-in-Publication Data

Bassoff, Evelyn.
    Mothers and daughters : loving and letting go / Evelyn Bassoff.
        p.   cm.
    Bibliography: p.
    Includes index.
    ISBN 0-453-00624-8
    1. Mothers and daughters—United States.   2. Middle aged women-
-United States—Psychology.   3. Separation (Psychology)   I. Title.
HQ755.85.B365   1988
306.8'743—dc19   88-9891
                                                                              CIP

First Printing, October, 1988

1   2   3   4   5   6   7   8   9

PRINTED IN THE UNITED STATES OF AMERICA

For my family:
my husband, Bruce;
my children, Jon and Leah;
and my mother, Helene Silten.

CONTENTS

ACKNOWLEDGMENTS

First, I would like to thank my husband, Bruce Bassoff, for his love, pleasure in my accomplishments, and insistence that we never stop struggling, growing, and changing. I am grateful to him as well for the many hours he spent going over my manuscript, suggesting changes, and pulling me out of holes.

Loving thanks also to my son, Jon, for his tenderness, wit, and understanding; to my daughter, Leah, for her lively spirit and inspiration; to my in-laws, Sylvia and Isidore Bassoff, for their unconditional support and nest away from home; and to my mother, Helene Silten, for having given me roots and then helping me grow wings.

My deep appreciation goes to my dear friends Susan Rosewell-Jackson, Alice Levine, and Judah Levine. With extraordinary gentleness, Susan nurtured the ideas that form this book and, with pots of hot coffee, a fire in the fireplace, Mozart recordings, freshly cut flowers, and warm conversation, also nurtured me on our many "writing retreats" to the Glacier Lodge in Estes Park. Alice not only was instrumental in finding a publisher for the manuscript but, after careful readings of each chapter, made countless helpful suggestions—always with sensibility and sensitivity. And, despite his many professional commitments, Judah was always willing to review the early drafts and to discuss my ideas with respect and enthusiasm.

I was fortunate to have worked with two splendid women at New American Library: Vice President and Publisher Elaine Koster and Senior Editor Alexia Dorszynski. Their responsiveness, encouragement, and suggestions helped to make this project a joyful experience.

A number of my colleagues in the mental health community were most helpful: Reesa Porter, Lee Moyer, Eleanor Mimi Schrader, Donald Williams, Katharine Krueger, Ivan Miller, Lynn Gullette, Jim Brodie, Diane Skafte, Sue Weatherley, Polly Mahoney, Sharon Kornman, and Christina Kauffman. I am extremely grateful for their collegial generosity and invaluable recommendations.

I would like to thank those members of the faculty and staff (past and present) at the University of Colorado in Boulder who supported my research and creative work: Professors Gene Glass, Philip DiStefano, and Richard Turner; the secretarial staff in the School of Education, especially Suzanne Reissig and Sue Middleton; and doctoral candidate Karen Von Gunten. I am also grateful to the many graduate students in the Counseling Program who have stimulated my thinking and enriched my life.

—Evelyn Bassoff
February 1988

PREFACE

Although most love relationships are a coming together, the love relationship between a mother and her adolescent daughter requires that each take leave of the other. Because the mother-daughter bond is so intense, such leave-takings are not usually cordial; rather, they are clumsy, disruptive, bewildering, and, at times, cruel. As psychoanalyst Anna Freud pointed out, few situations in life are more difficult to cope with than the attempts of adolescent children to liberate themselves. While in full agreement with her, I am also learning that few situations in life promise women greater possibilities for achieving maturity, wisdom, and meaningful living.

This book describes how women can become more fulfilled individuals and more loving mothers as they modify their caretaking roles, separate themselves from their daughters, and take increasing control of their own lives.

I have drawn from a rich and varied psychological literature that traces the child's impact on the inner world of the parent. I have also drawn from a less scientific pool of knowledge: our civilization's great fictional literature, especially its myths, folk and fairy tales; their enchanted ladies—ancient Greek goddesses, fairy princesses, even an "evil" stepmother—appear in this book as guides. In addition, in the hope that my own struggles to grow along with my adolescent daughter can benefit other women, I have drawn on my experiences as a mother. But surely my most important sources are the down-to-earth mothers—the married homemakers, working and career women, single mothers, adoptive mothers, and stepmothers who, in the course of psychotherapy, have shared their maternal dilemmas, failures, and triumphs with me. Their stories are the heart and soul of this book and bring to life the theoretical formulations that I present. In order not to violate their confidentiality, I have disguised their identities by changing the details of their situations and, in several cases, combining the histories of two or more women to form composites. Despite these alterations, I believe I have not distorted the essential meaning of their experiences.

My review of the literature in psychology, my lived experience, and my clinical work have all helped me to understand that the developmental tasks of middle-aged mother and adolescent daughter are interrelated. In the saddest circumstances, each undermines and stunts the other's growth; but, in the happiest circumstances, each awakens in the other the courage to meet and master life's challenges. If this book fulfills its purpose, it will help other women find new ways to understand their maternity and its possibilities for individual growth and loving relationship.

MOTHERS AND DAUGHTERS

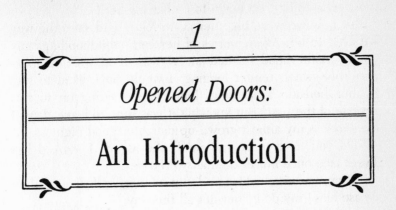

Opened Doors:
An Introduction

MY INDEPENDENT, SOPHISTICATED FIFTEEN-year-old daughter, ill with a case of the flu, came to me one night.

"Mom," she asked sheepishly, "this may sound strange, but could you come to my room and tuck me in . . . the way you used to?"

Touched and surprised, I did what she asked. Then for a few quiet moments, I sat at the edge of her bed, stroking her feverish forehead, remembering how long it had been since she had allowed me to caress her.

Both imperceptibly and suddenly, our relationship had changed. We are a little self-conscious with each other these days, no longer quite in step. I try to reconstruct the events that marked these changes between us. When was it that she had first stiffened as I reached out to hug her? Or rolled her eyes at me in disapproval? When did she first ask me to step out of the dressing room in the department store so she could try on clothes in privacy? When did she first cut me off mid-sentence to dash to the ringing phone? When did almost everything I do begin to embarrass her?

But now we were together again, close and safe, the way we used to be. As memories of her early childhood and my young motherhood flooded me, I was filled with an inexpressibly sweet, tender longing. I would have liked to stay by her bedside for a long, long time, holding on to this reverie of the past. But knowing it was time to leave, I bent over to kiss my almost grown-up daughter good night.

"Do you have to go just yet?" she asked. I stroked her sweet face once more, then answered yes.

"Mommy," she whispered out of her half-sleep, "then please close my door, but not all the way."

Most of life's meaning and beauty are derived from our intimate attachments, yet these attachments also promise frustration, confusion, and sorrow. This book tells the story of the particularly complex love relationship that a woman shares with her adolescent daughter. Maternity has two seemingly opposite aspects: A mother's tasks are to create a unity with her child and then, piece by piece, to dissolve it. Yet, as psychoanalyst Helene Deutsch wrote, most mothers suffer as they cut the psychic umbilical cord that ties them to their children; the wish to preserve this tie is inherent in motherliness and its renunciation is one of the major challenges of motherhood.

My discussion centers on the ways a woman struggles, changes, and grows as she moves toward a state of separateness from her adolescent daughter. Although I am largely concerned with the mother's experience, I will begin by describing the psychology of the adolescent. After all, mother and adolescent daughter influence each other's development; to understand the woman's world, we must also understand the girl's.

The major task adolescents confront is to form an identity separate from that of their parents—a unique, firm sense of self. This process involves discovering their beliefs and values, their wishes, desires, and dreams. They need to find their own way in the world and develop confidence that they are strong enough to survive outside the protective family circle. Ultimately, young women must answer the questions, "Who am I?" and "Where am I going?" To accomplish this task, they need to wrench themselves away from those who threaten their developing selfhood. Almost always Mother is the one most threatening.

Mother is a continual reminder that, not so long ago, these young women did not have a fully separate self but were part of Mother—safe, warm, shielded from danger. Needing to assert their strength and individuality, they must resist the strong temptation to slip back into babyhood, when Mother caressed their bodies, nursed and nourished them, and protected them from all life's hardness. And this is not an easy thing to do. Do we not all, from time to time, still yearn to be mothered in these ways? Moreover, these young women must also escape from Mother's control. Once, not too long ago, Mother had the power to monitor every aspect of her children's lives: the food they took in, their bowel movements, the times for sleep and play. Indeed, at the beginning of life, they did not know where she began and they left off. Mother and child were as one. Now these nearly adult children cannot tolerate the memory of such control but must assert themselves against it: "Leave me alone . . . stop running my life . . I can take care of myself," they insist.

But the truth is that they are not sure they can take care of themselves or that they want to be left alone. At the same time that they scream for independence, they may be secretly longing for the comforts of maternal nurture and the security of maternal control. Despite such longing, they know they must not fall back into Mother's arms, for such a regression threatens their emergence into adulthood and saps their strength. The adolescents caught in these conflicts must learn to defend against the urges to be protected and controlled. In the process of growing up, they must grow

apart from Mother by creating a psychological distance between them. As philosopher Simone de Beauvoir, recalling
her own adolescence, wrote: "I wanted my ramparts to be
impregnable. I was particularly diligent in giving away nothing to Maman, out of fear of the distress and horror of having
her peer into me."

A few years ago, I was counseling seventeen-year-old
Alice through her parents' divorce. Because she believed her
mother, to whom she was devoted, was suffering from extreme loneliness, my young client found it especially painful
to make the necessary emotional break from her and consequently tried to prolong the harmony they had experienced
when Alice was a little girl. As the following vignette illustrates, however, the normal drive to separate from her mother
was compelling and expressed itself seemingly against my
client's will.

One day Alice burned her hand slightly as she was preparing a snack. Automatically, she telephoned her mother
for help. Her mother, accommodating as always, offered
to come home from work and transport Alice to their
physician's office. To both their dismay and surprise, this
offer threw Alice into a rage. After abruptly and rudely
insisting that she did not want Mother to take her to the
doctor, Alice angrily hung up on her. As we talked about this
incident during our therapy session, we came to understand
that on one level this outburst was Alice's way of expressing
self-sufficiency. As soon as she connected with her mother
on the telephone, Alice became angry with herself for
regressing to a state of childish helplessness. She then
misdirected this anger at her mother. Alice's behavior was
simply a tactless way of insisting that she could and should
take care of herself. It was also a way of defending herself
against the tempting ministrations of her mother. As is the
case with all adolescents, a part of Alice longed for the
warmth of her mother's care and comfort, whereas another
part fought against her own childish desires. At another
level, Alice's outburst was a disguised expression of anger

at her mother for their prolonged and threatening close-ness. Despite the trying consequences of the divorce, it was time to loosen their dependent ties to one another.

It may be difficult for mothers to recognize the enormity of their power over their children. How can they possibly see themselves as irresistible seductresses plotting to infantilize their daughters or as power-crazed creatures intent on re-possessing the bodies, minds, and souls of these hapless children? How can they possibly think of themselves in such ways when what they want is simply for their children to become happy, responsible young adults? But although moth-ers may view themselves modestly, the ideal of Mother conveys enormous power, both positive and negative. Mother, or what Mother symbolizes, is indeed a force with which to contend. She is more than flesh and blood; she is a grandiose creation of the human psyche. To realize her enduring influ-ence, women need only remind themselves of the ways their own mothers still affect them. It is common for a competent adult to shrink into a little child in her mother's presence. (I must admit that although I am past forty, when I am with my mother I sometimes feel like ten.)

We should not, however, lose sight of the fact that adoles-cents' hostile distancing from their mothers is usually tempo-rary. Research indicates that relationships between mothers and their adult daughters tend to be close and mutually supportive.[1] It is only after young women are confident of their individuality and secure that they are strong enough to resist being pulled back into childish ways that they can return to their mothers. They return as adults. As a clinical psychologist, I have often been most useful to my adult clients when I have helped them understand that the breach in the relationship with their teenage children is not likely to be permanent. Understanding that mutual expressions of love, respect, care, and appreciation will be possible at a later stage of parenthood can temper the loss they feel. But, in the meantime, during the unsure years of adolescence, young people must erect protective fences and close their doors in order to evolve into adults. To be sure, the fences will be low enough to climb over from time to time, and the doors will not be closed all the way.

Until recently, developmental psychologists implied that while adolescents undergo their dramatic inner changes, their mothers stand by unchangeable, stable, and resolute. Mothers were thought to be a dull backdrop against the action on stage. Indeed, one of the common but false assumptions has been that inner change is a prerogative of the young because adults have fixed personalities. However, just as the adolescent is compelled by inner forces to change, so is the middle-aged mother. Her developmental tasks are no less difficult than those of her child. As a parent she must give up earlier ways of mothering and learn new ones; as an individual she must enlarge her boundaries beyond the home by contributing in new ways to the world through political, social, occupational, or creative activities.

Journalist Ellen Goodman, who often writes about her own experiences of mothering an adolescent daughter, once commented that motherhood is inaccurately depicted as one state, one set of behaviors. Rather, motherhood is composed of many states, and mothering the infant, the toddler, the school child, the adolescent require different behaviors. Goodman described how she automatically reached out for her child's hand as they crossed a busy intersection, forgetting that this child was now a young woman of seventeen. Just as the growing child must relinquish the protective mother of the past, so must the growing mother abandon the idea that she can shield her child from all danger.

Beatrice, a spirited, highly successful client of mine who is a mother of an eighteen-year-old girl, described how anxious she became when her daughter went to a Mexican resort with some college friends during their spring break. Despite the fact that her daughter is responsible and intelligent, Beatrice experienced awful anguish during their separation, imagining that Arielle would end up in a Mexican jail and be subjected to torture. Although she tried to disregard these illogical thoughts, she really believed that her child could be safe only by being near her.

Such anxieties can be explained by theories of human attachment. Ethnologist John Bowlby described how the survival of our species has depended on the closeness of mother and infant. Without mother's all-encompassing care, the helpless small child cannot exist. Infant behaviors, such as crying, fretting, smiling, clinging, and nursing all serve to ensure proximity to the mother. Similarly, the mother is programmed to be close to her baby; when her baby strays beyond a certain distance or calls to her in distress, she will experience alarm, draw near, and retrieve her child. These set patterns of attachment responses do not magically disappear when the baby grows up, and vestiges of separation anxiety may linger for the mother after they no longer serve a purpose. The catastrophic thoughts that plagued my client Beatrice seem, in part, to have been symptoms of this separation anxiety. One of the tasks of mothering the adolescent child is to contain these anxieties and to modify the protective behaviors that were appropriate during earlier stages of mothering.

Another explanation for Beatrice's symptoms derives from the psychoanalytic formulations of Therese Benedek, who explained that each critical period of a child's life revives in the parent related developmental conflicts. As the child encounters the teenage years, for example, the mother will reexperience aspects of her own adolescence. Long-buried emotions and unresolved internal conflicts may now resurface, providing an opportunity to confront and resolve them.

Beatrice and I came to understand that her daughter's anticipated adventures in Mexico revived memories of Beatrice's earliest sexual experiences. During her own coming of age, Beatrice's liberal parents had set few limits for her and, like so many other members of the sixties generation, encouraged Beatrice's sexual experimentation with her peers. But for this young woman sex was not liberating, as her parents imagined, only violating. Arielle's opportunities for casual sex on her Mexican vacation awakened old fears and anxieties in Beatrice, which took the form of catastrophic, violent thoughts—Arielle's subjection to torture in a Mexican jail, for example.

Having to reexperience the conflicts of adolescence during one's middle adulthood may seem like undue punishment. The redeeming aspect, however, is that it provides a second chance to work things through. In Beatrice's case, it encouraged her to understand better her longstanding hostility toward her parents and ultimately to forgive them for their early parental laxness and poor judgment. Also, it encouraged Beatrice to confront her continuing anxieties concerning sexuality. Eventually, she joined a women's group that was dealing with sexual dysfunctions and, with its support, was able to resolve some of her own issues.

In other women, their children's adolescence will revive different kinds of conflict. For example, when my daughter had a medical problem, I became wildly anxious and responded by being overly protective. With the help of a therapist, I came to understand that Leah's situation revived memories of my own frail health. As a young adolescent I was plagued with gastrointestinal problems and was underweight and undersized. Unable to keep up with my more robust friends, I saw myself as weak, unprepared for the world. Until I was able to separate the sickly phantom child in me from Leah, I could not act in a helpfully maternal way toward her; I muddled my anxieties with her real needs. It was only after talking about the vulnerable adolescent girl I still harbored and feeling compassion for her pain that I could release myself from her hold. Having accomplished this, I could respond to Leah's situation appropriately by accepting her physicians' recommendations and by providing the reassurances *she* needed. Healing myself was necessary before I could help heal my daughter.

Whatever developmental conflicts are activated by one's children, their resolution promises higher levels of psychic integration and greater maturity. Author Peter De Vries understood this process when he asked whether any one of us is mature enough for children before the children are born. The wonder of motherhood, he wrote, is not that mothers produce children but that children produce mothers.

Motherly love is not static. To endure, it requires change. In the prenatal stage of motherhood, when the child is a part of the mother's body, motherly love is akin to self-love. Mother and child are as one. Even after birth, mother and child remain extensions of one another by virtue of their exquisite mutual responsiveness. Marshall Klaus and John Kennel, who have studied and written about maternal-infant bonding, point out, for example, that in certain developing nations where the mother still carries her baby on her back, she is expected to anticipate the baby's need to wet or soil and to hold the baby away from her body before it does. Such motherly care implies extraordinary empathy, an awareness of the baby's slightest bodily changes. In our culture as well, most mothers become remarkably attuned to the needs of their young. And mothers are rewarded for this sensitive care by the child's growing adoration of them, which enhances their sense of radiance and power. To their little daughters, mothers are nothing less than goddesses. One of the requirements of maturing maternal love is relinquishing without bitterness this childish idealization.

As children move through adolescence, a mother must accept a less central and glorified role in their lives. In the search for greater selfhood, adolescents will look outside the family for role models and find others to idealize and emulate, most often casting their mothers aside. Motherly devotion at this stage requires the most extraordinary empathy. The mature mother, aware of her adolescent's need for self-definition, must support the necessary separation from her, knowing all the while that by doing so she diminishes her maternal power and importance to the child.

Over the span of motherhood, then, maternal love transforms. In its mature form, it entails an acceptance of diminished status, a giving up of power and control. Recognizing what she is losing, the mother of the adolescent child may suffer from a heavy heart. Nevertheless, she must learn to let go of that earlier time when she was central in her child's life. She too must close doors behind her.

The Jungian scholar M. Esther Harding can help us understand the necessary maternal transformations through her interpretation of certain ancient Greek myths, whose themes are the ritualistic sacrifices of adolescent sons.[2] (I believe the meanings of these myths are equally relevant for adolescent daughters.) According to Harding, the sacrifice of the son occurs not in spite of the mother's love but because of it. It is a necessary condition for the development of both mother and son. She explains that these myths depict the archetypal Mother as two-sided. On the one side, she is compassionate and nurturing, whereas on the other side, she is fierce, withholding, and intolerant of childish dependence. It is the darker side that allows Mother to turn her back on (or symbolically sacrifice) her son so that he can become a strong man and so that she can become a more fulfilled woman. Too much of the lighter side, which is her maternal solicitude and nurture, can undermine her son's passage into adulthood, just as her son's clinging can undermine her passage into greater autonomy. Harding described the necessary maternal transformation as relinquishing the position of superiority as giver. Such relinquishing allows the child to be released from the inferior position of taker. At the same time it allows the mother to be released from her own indulgent tendencies.

A woman who is one-sided necessarily harms the adolescent child, but a woman who can be both soft and hard nourishes this child. We tend, unfortunately, to expect good mothers to be always soothing, yielding, comforting, and giving. We do not understand that mothers who are too eager to take care of their adolescents' needs deprive them of the power of taking care of themselves. Consequently, coddled adolescent children, like all other people who are always on the receiving end, cannot develop a sense of competence and self-sufficiency. They are weakened by their mothers' good intentions.

An example of the way in which too much maternal nurturing can be destructive to a child is the relationship between Pilate and her granddaughter in Toni Morrison's *Song of Solomon*. Although Pilate has great reverence for other people and a deep, genuine love for her granddaughter, her affection is excessive and does not allow the girl to develop the toughness and resiliency to withstand loss and rejection. When the granddaughter is rejected by the man she loves, she is traumatized and incredulous. She also becomes so possessive of the man who rejects her that she tries to murder him rather than let him go. At the end of all this, she dies of her madness—unable to survive the unaccustomed experience of irreversible denial. Ironically, when her grandmother cries out at her funeral, "And she was *loved*," she points to the solicitude that helped destroy her.

Interestingly enough, the man whom the granddaughter loved has himself been overindulged by a mother who nursed him long after it was appropriate. Her feelings of magical power associated with this act of nurturance are expressed in terms of a fairy tale: "She had the distinct impression that his lips were pulling from her a thread of light. It was as though she were a cauldron issuing spinning gold. Like the miller's daughter—the one who sat at night in a straw-filled room, thrilled with the secret power Rumpelstiltskin had given her: to see golden thread stream from her very own shuttle."[3] Named "Milkman" by someone who discovers his embarrassingly long period of nursing, the young man finds that his will to struggle and to define himself in the world has been prematurely sapped. It is only with great difficulty that he is eventually able to set out on the quest that will lead to adult understanding.

Just as pampered (a word that originally meant overfed) children are stunted, mothers who refuse to give up their maternal indulgence fail in their own development as women;

they can relate to others only in maternal ways. A humorous example of this failure is depicted by a character in Bernard Slade's play *Same Time Next Year* who, engrossed in stimulating conversation with her husband's boss during a dinner party, suddenly notices that she has been cutting up the meat on his plate, just as she had been used to doing for her children.

Since many women have had limited opportunity to be powerful in any sphere other than the maternal and have experienced their effectiveness and importance only as mothers, we can understand why they are reluctant to give up their caretaking roles. The hard part for many women who are mothers is to believe that something lies beyond caretaking. Frieda Fromm-Reichmann, the renowned psychoanalyst, put it well: "A door is closing behind us and we turn sorrowfully to watch it close and do not discover, until we are wrenched away, the one opening ahead."

What lies ahead for women is the chance to channel their creative energies in new ways. If they let go of their nostalgic hold on the past, they have the opportunity to enter into a period that the poet Valery has named *le bel aujourd'hui*, which is "the beautiful present." The slackening of maternal caretaking obliges them to devote their energies to new enterprises—professional, creative, political, or social. As their children etch out a personal definition and learn to contribute to the world, so must they. For many women, this will involve searching for a meaningful vocation, a steady purpose.

Recently, I had the pleasure of reading excerpts from the diary of Käthe Kollwitz:

> I do not want to die. . . . I do not want to go until I have faithfully made the most of my talent and cultivated the seed that was placed in me until the last small twig has grown. . . . It is not only that I am permitted to finish my work—I am obliged to finish it. . . . This seems to be the meaning of all. . . . Culture arises only when the individual fulfills his cycle of obligations.[4]

I have helped many women who have come to me for treatment of depression not by administering antidepressant drugs or by imposing lengthy analyses but by encouraging them to find their talents and to recognize that they have something worthwhile to contribute to the world. I have watched women who had been deadened by feelings of inadequacy come alive by discovering meaningful work. As Kollwitz wrote in another section of her diary, for women in their middle years, work becomes everything. Make no mistake, however: Moving from an exclusively maternal role to other roles requires great efforts. All too often, mothers do not feel they have the right to find meaningful work.

In the beginning of this chapter, I described Alice, my adolescent client, and her struggle to grow up. Her mother, however, had an equally difficult time making a transition from one phase of life to another. At the time Alice called her mother to report the minor burn, Claudia was at work. A month after her divorce, she had secured a responsible managerial job in a large firm. Right before Alice's call, Claudia was deeply involved in an interesting new project. Working at her desk, surrounded by co-workers who were gradually becoming her friends, she felt quite happy. Although her recent divorce had left her bereft, at this moment she felt that she would be all right after all. Sadly, her daughter's call undermined this lovely sense of well-being and confidence. As soon as Alice described her mishap, Claudia was overcome by waves of anxiety and guilt. She thought that she had no business being happily at work and that she belonged at home, taking care of her two adolescent children as she had done before the divorce. She even convinced herself that had she been home, Alice would not have hurt herself. It was only after many weeks of counseling that Claudia came to believe that she had a right, even an obligation, to establish a productive work life for herself. After she gave herself permission to enjoy her work, Claudia was able to loosen the ties to her children. Then they could all get on with their lives.

Claudia's anxious responses were not unique. All too often, women do not feel entitled to work and to accomplish in the world. Our culture encourages attitudes of restricted entitlement in women, teaching them to live only vicariously, in the shadow and service of others. Consequently, they may repress their healthy desires to achieve, compete, and assert their self-interest. They are afraid that such autonomy would force them to give up their most important relationships. They do not believe they are entitled to love, be loved, and also have meaningful work.

I have known several women who internalized powerful prohibitions against finding rich, productive lives outside of the family. One of my clients reported that whenever she entertains the idea of becoming a successful professional woman, she is haunted by terrible fantasies of having her children taken away from her. In her heart she believes that being a good mother precludes other roles for her. A colleague, the successful author of two books, confided that no matter where she is or what she is doing, her stomach will cramp and churn at 6 P.M., as if it is reprimanding her for not being home to prepare dinner for her husband and sixteen-year-old child.

What took me by surprise was the realization that I too experience such prohibitions. Because I have combined a profession with motherhood for many years, I smugly believed I had worked out these role conflicts long ago. When I first undertook this book, however, I did everything possible to ensure that it would not get written. Feeling guilty that my profession as a psychologist already took me away from my family, I decided to write at home. During each work session, I left my door wide open so that I would be available if my children needed me for anything. My children, Jon and Leah, are very competent young people, but naturally they responded to this invitation by interrupting me with myriad requests. Between paragraphs I prepared snacks for them and searched for their missing sneakers. Needless to say, I was not a very productive writer. With my husband's loving encouragement, I finally gave myself permission to write my book in earnest and to revel in the passion and joy of creative work. Confident that I was entitled to love, to be loved, and to work, I was able to find a reasonable balance between relationship and accomplishment. Now I could ask my children to respect my need to write without unnecessary interruptions. And without guilt, I decided to close the door to my study . . . but not all the way.

2

Demeter's Story:

Loss and Transcendence

E ACH OF US NEEDS TO LOVE AND TO BE LOVED, yet our intimate relationships, through which these needs are expressed, may confuse and frustrate us. Often we do not know what to expect of others, what to expect of ourselves, or what to expect of others' expectations.

For these reasons, it can be helpful to turn to our civilization's early and enduring sources of wisdom—its myths and fairy tales. In these ancient stories, we find direct and clear explanations of human behavior and relationships. Myths and fairy tales, unlike most other forms of great literature, are not the works of single individuals but are rather the creations of entire cultures, the products of a collective imagination. Elaborated by countless people and passed from generation to generation, these continually unfolding stories describe the crises of human living common to all of us. As Jungian scholars point out, although myths and fairy tales are fantasy, they are nonetheless universally true. They are accurate portraits of the mysterious inner world of our psyches. Long before psychologists discovered how myths and fairy tales enhance self-awareness, artists and poets recognized their explanatory powers. It was the German poet Schiller who wrote that deeper meaning resided for him in the tales told to him in his childhood than in the facts taught by life.

The Homeric "Hymn to Demeter," which dates back to approximately 650 B.C., is the quintessential story of the attachment between a mother and her adolescent daughter. I have chosen to discuss this myth in depth because it illuminates so brilliantly the loss that motherhood inevitably entails and the maternal transformation that such loss makes possible. Because she ultimately creates meaning out of her emptiness, Demeter, the mother goddess, can serve as a guide to her modern, mortal counterparts.

Traditional interpretations of the myth of Demeter and Persephone, who are also named Ceres and Kore, emphasize the nature of the earth's cyclical renewal rather than the nature of loss, grief, and transcendence. For the latter, less conventional interpretation, I am indebted to Jungian writer Polly Young-Eisendrath, whose article "Demeter's Folly" inspired my ideas. Drawing from Charles Boer's and N. J. Richardson's elegant translations from the Greek, I will first tell Demeter's story, then relate her experience of loss and its solutions to those of contemporary mothers.

The story begins as the lovely maiden Persephone is romping with her girlfriends on a flowering meadow of roses, crocus, violets, iris, hyacinth, and narcissus. As she reaches out to pluck a golden narcissus, the earth opens up and Hades, the god of the underworld, leaps forth, lays hold of her, and carries her away on his chariot. Although the great god Zeus ignores his daughter's screams for help, the mother goddess, Demeter, upon hearing the echoes of Persephone's cries, is seized by an awful terror. For nine days and nights she searches the earth and heavens for her daughter, never stopping to rest, eat, or bathe. On the tenth day, she learns that Hades has abducted Persephone to the underworld, where she is to become his bride.

Despondent at the news of her daughter's abduction and imminent marriage, Demeter withdraws from the other gods and, disguised as an old woman, wanders among the earth's cities, finally stopping in Eleusis. Here she is greeted by the daughters of King Celeus and Queen Metanira, who ask who she is. Giving them a false story, she pleads to be taken into their household in order to serve as a nursemaid to the king and queen's infant son, Demophoön. In response to her request, the sisters lead her to the queen's quarters. As Demeter enters, she takes her divine form for a moment, filling the room with her radiance, so that, despite the goddess's dark garments and forlorn countenance, Metanira is convinced of her specialness and receives her graciously. Offering the old woman a good wage, Metanira hires Demeter as a nursemaid and turns her beloved son over to her. Although Demeter is pleased with her new position, she nevertheless rejects the queen's courtesies, refusing to accept food or even to engage in conversation. Only the servant Iambe breaks through Demeter's depression by jesting with her and even makes the sad goddess laugh.

From the start, Demeter loses herself in the role of nursemaid by channeling all her energy into the care of the young prince. Determined to raise him as a god, she anoints Demophoön with ambrosia and deprives him of human food. Suspicious of the strange old nursemaid's ways, one night Metanira spies on her and, with shock, watches as she places the baby in a fire—a ritual meant to make him immortal. At this sight, Metanira, wailing and beating her knees in horror, intercepts Demeter's plan. Furious at Metanira's interference, Demeter, revealing her true identity as a goddess and her intention to make the prince a god, angrily snatches Demophoön from the fire and throws him onto the ground. Condemning mankind for its folly and Metanira for her stupidity, she then commands that a huge temple be built for her outside the city gates. To pacify the enraged goddess,

King Celeus orders his men to begin constructing the temple, according to her instructions, the very next morning. When the temple is at last finished, the goddess Demeter retreats behind its thick walls to mourn, not for the fate of Demophoön, but rather for her own lost child—Persephone.

For a long time, Demeter, the goddess of grain, corn, and bountiful harvests, sits alone with her grief, refusing to function. As a consequence, nothing can grow on earth, nothing can be born. Fields become dry and barren, crops wither, men and animals die. The dreadful famine threatens to destroy everything. Taking pity on humankind, Zeus sends messengers, laden with gifts, to implore his wife to relent, but she angrily rejects their appeals. Demeter poses only one condition: the return of her daughter. At last, Zeus responds to the furious goddess by dispatching Hermes, the messenger god, to Hades to order Persephone's return.

Hades agrees to let Persephone go, but, promising that she will know great honors as his wife, tells her to return to him. To ensure her loyalty, he presents her with—and she does not reject his offer—a sweet red pomegranate seed that will bind her to return to him. Persephone then rejoices at her release and accompanies Hermes on the journey to the upper world. As they approach the temple at Eleusis, Demeter rushes out to embrace her daughter, and the two fall happily into each other's arms. After their joyous reunion, Demeter inquires whether Persephone has eaten anything in the underworld. If she has not, Persephone will be completely restored to her, but if she has, she must henceforth divide her time between Demeter and Hades. Reluctantly, Persephone tells her mother that Hades forced her to eat the pomegranate seed.

Nevertheless, thankful to have her daughter for at least part of the year, Demeter is at peace. Her grief ended, she bestows generous gifts on humankind. The goddess imparts to the princes of Eleusis the ministry of her solemn rites and reveals to them her beautiful Mysteries, which promise a deeper understanding of life and death. Then on her return to Mount Olympus, she revitalizes the entire earth, weighing it down with lush vegetation—flowers, foliage, fruits—wherever she steps. And so, the hymn ends as a new order is established: Persephone becomes queen of the underworld and Demeter takes her place at Olympus as a powerful earth goddess.

Let us now descend from Mount Olympus to earth, from myth to everyday reality, and interpret Demeter's story to deepen our own understanding of motherliness. As I see it, Demeter represents both the nurturing and controlling aspects of motherhood. She is at once a generous, supportive, loyal, and involved mother but also an all-consuming, overprotective one. Because her relationship with her child is primary, she demands exclusive right to this child. When a potential lover wrenches Persephone away from Demeter, she suffers a terrible depression, yet this very suffering forces her spiritual development. It is only after she articulates her loss, grieves for her lost child, and accepts a less exclusive maternal role that Demeter emerges in all her divinity and wisdom as the guardian of the Eleusian Mysteries. In this chapter, I will try to demonstrate how ordinary mothers, not only goddesses, have the opportunity to create personal meaning out of their maternal losses.

Rereading Erich Neumann's monumental work on the female archetype, *The Great Mother*, I came across a plate of an ancient stone relief of Demeter and Persephone. Each is looking knowingly and lovingly into the other's eyes. Indistinguishable from one another, they reflect each other. They are the same. This poignant work of art portrays the unity inherent in the early mother-daughter relationship: one shared life. Indeed, during the first years of their relationship, as the little girl strives to be just like her adored mother, they are as one. I remember when I was a child it was fashionable for mothers and daughters to wear almost identical outfits and how thrilled I was when my mother surprised me with our yellow gingham "mother and daughter dresses." I remember too my own little girl shadowing me, mimicking my movements, and echoing my words as I went about my daily chores.

As the little girl grows into young womanhood, her awakening sexuality threatens the exclusive mother/daughter bond. Perhaps for the first time in her life, a daughter will keep secrets from her mother; she will no longer allow her mother to know her fully. Although the adolescent girl may continue to chatter with mother about friendships, schoolwork, and hopes for the future, she will probably not talk about the powerful sexual feelings that begin to stir her. These are her mysteries—to be shared with girlfriends perhaps—but not with Mother. Ready for a sexual experience, Persephone accepts Hades' pomegranate seed—the sweet, red, juicy seed that symbolizes passion—which unites her to him. However, is it any wonder that when Demeter asks Persephone if she has eaten Hades' "food," Persephone is less than truthful and tells her that Hades *forced* her to eat the seed? Like most adolescents, Persephone cannot acknowledge to her mother her new sexual desire.

Although many mothers will intuitively respect their daughters' secretiveness about sexual matters, others may not. When I was a young woman and in love for the first time, I stayed out very late with my boyfriend one night. The next morning my mother anxiously asked me where I had been and what I had done. My father, who was a very wise man, interrupted her and gently told my mother that such questions could be answered only untruthfully. From that time on, my mother did not ask.

As a young girl passes into womanhood, she leaves the open sunlit world of childhood and moves into the mysterious dark world of love and passion. She leaves her mother behind to meet her lovers. If she is fortunate, her romantic attachments will encourage further growth, but these new attachments may evoke in the mother feelings of great loss, of being cast aside.

As her child turns toward others and away from her, each

woman faces a void, which forces an internal reorganization. For some women, their adolescents' new attachments trigger only mild and transitory depressive symptoms. Moreover, these women may also experience pleasure as their children separate from them—feelings of relief that the heavy obligations of childrearing are ending and happy anticipation of renewed freedom for themselves and new freedom for their daughters. There is no contradiction in their feeling both sadness and happiness. But for other women losing their exclusive relationship precipitates a profound psychological crisis. Like Demeter, they may experience their daughters' falling in love as a falling into hell and be "seized by an awful terror." Let us now explore the circumstances that lead to these detrimental reactions.

Unfortunately, it is all too common for a woman's normal dependency needs to be devalued and unmet. A damaging by-product of the early women's movement is the notion that all forms of dependency are a sign of weakness and a refusal to take responsibility for oneself. But as long as it does not dominate the personality and ensnare others, dependency is a healthy, normal need. All human beings depend on loved ones to care about them, understand them, and support them. The difficulty for women, however, is that from their earliest years, they are taught to be only givers. At the same time that they learn to care for and be responsive to others, they learn to suppress their own wants and wishes—to demand nothing, to withhold criticism, to be quiet. "Don't make a fuss, now; be a good girl," mothers, fathers, and teachers implore. In time these "good" girl children come to believe that they should not expect others to satisfy their psychological needs. Ironically, their sense of emotional deprivation may alert women to the needs of others. Most women I have known nurture others quite naturally; they watch for signs of hurt or want and are always ready to jump in and soothe. But they feel selfish when they ask others to nurture them. Of course, normal yearnings to be cared for and responded to cannot be willed away but must somehow find expression. That many women come to depend primarily on their children for warmth and closeness is not surprising, especially since so many husbands have not learned to nurture well. When their children inevitably turn away from them, these women feel abandoned, deprived, and lonely.

The following case history illustrates one mother's response to loss. I have chosen it because it parallels Demeter's experience and corresponds to the experiences of many women I have known.

Dorothy, a homemaker in her middle years, requested counseling after she discovered that her sixteen-year-old daughter had become sexually active. Elana had been a compliant child, always eager to accommodate her mother, but now Elana refused to end her current love relationship despite her mother's pleas. Dorothy was distraught. Like Demeter, she sank into an agitated depression and was unable to eat, sleep, or rest. Whenever Elana was out on a date with her boyfriend, Dorothy lay awake in terror. To be sure, Elana's sexual activity involved potential dangers— emotional trauma, venereal disease, pregnancy, AIDS. But Dorothy's fear went beyond these real concerns. She was afraid that the docile child whose needs she thought she was meeting so completely was now being stolen from her by this young lover, this "abductor." No longer her daughter's dearest companion or trusted confidante, Dorothy felt alone.

To make sense of Dorothy's anxious reactions to her daughter's affair, we must examine Dorothy's own childhood, which was marred by unfortunate circumstances. Dorothy's unstable mother was unable to care adequately for her, and Dorothy's father had abandoned the family soon after her birth. Moreover, when Dorothy was in grade school, her mother had remarried a man who dominated his wife with an iron hand. What little nurturance Dorothy had received from her mother earlier was no longer possible because the new husband claimed all his wife's attention. Understandably, Elana's romance reawakened feelings of despair and deprivation in

Dorothy. A man was taking away her beloved daughter, just as years before another man had stolen her mother.

As a mother, Dorothy had provided for her daughter what she herself had missed during her own childhood. By striving to anticipate and meet all of Elana's material and emotional needs, Dorothy vicariously soothed the neglected child within herself. It was as if she mothered two children at once—young Elana and young Dorothy. But now Elana didn't want to do things with her mother anymore; the young girl much preferred being with her boyfriend, and even Mother's advice and opinions were no longer welcome. Because Elana insisted that her interests were different from those of her mother, indeed that she was different from her mother, Dorothy felt unimportant to her; she was bereft because she was losing her daughter *and* the good mother invented to love them both.

We can look at Dorothy's experience from a slightly different perspective. Like so many women, Dorothy knew only one way of relating to others and that was by serving them. Her identity and self-esteem derived from her ability to "do" for others. Because Dorothy's own mother had been emotionally needy, we can assume that even as a young child Dorothy learned a caretaking role, becoming mother to her mother. Naturally, Dorothy was filled with anxiety as Elana turned from her. If Dorothy could not be a caretaker, what could she be? Would she be nothing?

Elana's differentiation eventually forced Dorothy to relinquish her doting attachment, which had been her sole way of relating. (Headstrong Elana simply would no longer allow Dorothy the intimacies they had once shared.) But this forced relinquishment caused Dorothy to experience a terrifying sense of loss; it was as if she were being robbed of part of herself. Dorothy's developmental task was to learn new ways of loving and being loved. As feminist psychiatrist Teresa Bernadez put it, what had to be learned was how to function not just in the service of others but in the service of herself *and* others.

Dorothy spent two years in psychotherapy with me. Her feelings of desertion, triggered by Elana's first love affair, were followed by intense anger toward her inadequate mother and then by a period of mourning for past loss—a mourning for the happy childhood Dorothy never had. Only by recognizing how deprived she had been as a child, allowing the buried resentments to surface, and by understanding how unfulfilled childhood needs tainted her present relationships could Dorothy begin to find inner peace. As Demeter knew when she retreated to the temple in Eleusis, mourning for one's losses is necessary before one can live fully in the present.

In time Dorothy stopped seeking gratification through her daughter. Her grief ended, she began to revitalize a tired, mutually unsatisfying marriage and gently taught her husband how to nurture by *telling him* ways he might please her: "You make me feel good when you ask me about my day." "I feel cared for when you put your arms around me and just hold me." "When you suggest that the two of us do something special, I know I'm important to you." In doing this, she gave up the magical idea, entertained by so many women, that if her husband really loved her, he would know intuitively how to express such love. (Men, just like women, must learn nurturant behaviors.) Just as important, she found ways to mother herself by identifying her own needs and, where appropriate, satisfying them. Dorothy began to ask herself "What do I want?" and to honor the answers that came from her heart. As she told me, usually her wants were quite modest and realizable—a soak in a bubble bath, a visit with a friend, an evening all to herself. In time, it became as natural to nurture herself as it had been to nurture Elana.

My clinical experience convinces me that the kinds of deprivation Dorothy suffered are common to many women, although the particular circumstances of deprivation will vary from person to person. Inadequately nurtured as daughters by their parents, emotionally distanced from their husbands as adults, they turn toward their children for the love they desperately miss. When the adolescent children distance themselves, as is only normal, these women are likely to suffer a profound sense of loss. The leave-takings reactivate the sensation of being psychologically abandoned. Yet, by recognizing and grieving for their emotional losses, experienced first as children and now as adults, they have an opportunity to heal themselves at last. It is by persevering through life's necessary pain—not by avoiding it—that one can achieve new solutions and personal transformation.

Not all women are as determined as Dorothy to work through their experiences of loss, and many of them come up with solutions that are considerably less successful. I am reminded of Felicia, a woman in her early sixties, and Gail, her forty-year-old daughter, who came to me for relationship counseling. The pair, who had been living together since the daughter's divorce twenty years before and were extraordinarily dependent on each other, bickered constantly. As a therapist, I am quite used to bickering couples, but there was something odd about the way Felicia and Gail nipped at each other. Gail was extremely critical of her mother—of the way she talked, of the way she looked, even of the TV shows she chose to view. And Felicia complained endlessly about her daughter's inconsideration—her sloppy habits, her unwillingness to share the household chores, her moody spells. What finally struck me was that these two ladies were behaving the way a mother and child behave with one another during the latter's adolescence. Felicia and Gail, so many years off-schedule, were involved in an early separation struggle.

At eighteen, Gail had tried to leave her mother. She rented an apartment, secured a clerical job in a legal firm, and married a co-worker within the year. But from the start, Felicia openly disapproved of her daughter's husband. When, in her second year of marriage, Gail confessed to having marital problems, Felicia assured her that she was welcome to return "home." With mutual relief, the mother and daughter reunited. Quite easily, they resumed their familiar roles:

Felicia, the caregiving mother, and Gail, the eternal child. Over the years, these roles became fixed. True, by holding on to each other, Felicia avoided suffering the loss of her child and Gail avoided the suffering that becoming an adult entails. Yet their lives were stifling and stagnant. Their absolute bond to one another had become a form of bondage.

I was not able to facilitate any meaningful change in their relationship. Both Felicia and Gail were frightened of being abandoned by the other and, consequently, chose to remain together. The most I could do was to teach Felicia and Gail some skills of "conflict management," that is, civil ways of disagreeing with one another. After four weeks, we agreed that it was time to end counseling. With disappointment, I watched Felicia and Gail leave my consulting room. They were holding hands and bickering.

This mother-daughter pair helped me realize the deepest meaning of the word *abandonment*. On the one hand, abandonment describes the terror of being left, but on the other hand, it describes the exhilaration of freedom and spontaneity. If one is to know the joy of living with *abandon*, perhaps one must first face and overcome the terror of *abandonment*. Felicia and Gail were too frightened to risk this terror.

Confronting one's losses does require great courage. Even the goddess Demeter wavers at this requirement. At first, she refuses to make any meaningful changes in her life but instead prefers to soothe her pain by denying the loss that caused it. True, after learning that Persephone is to become Hades' bride, she sinks into a depression and withdraws from the company of the other gods. Like so many of her modern counterparts, however, Demeter aborts the process of grieving before it has a chance to be healing. Perhaps theologian Dorothee Soelle's phrase, a "failure to experience suffering" best describes her early behavior. By hurriedly replacing her lost child, Persephone, with another, the infant Demophoön, the goddess deceives herself into believing that the anguish that loss necessarily imposes can be circumvented.

Moreover, she schemes to transform the human baby into an immortal being, a god. What better way to avoid change than to freeze time? Like her mortal counterparts Felicia and Gail, Demeter refuses to accept the fact that life is transient, that growth requires change. She does not understand that immortalizing a human being ensures stagnation.

Unwilling to suffer the sadness of letting go her earlier role, unwilling to come to terms with the painful reality of loss, unwilling to make internal adjustments, Demeter seeks a regressive solution for her depression. By becoming a caretaking mother again, by appropriating another baby, she will return to a happier phase of her life. Ultimately, Demeter is forced to confront her grief, painful as it is. Her early, misguided effort to cut short her depression by falling into the comfortable but outgrown role of mother/nursemaid is nevertheless instructive. We can learn from her mistakes.

Many women wrestle with the possibility of adopting or giving birth to another child as they anticipate their adolescents' leave-takings. Having a late-life baby may be a joyful event for some women, but if it is an attempt to fill a void by turning back time and avoiding necessary growth and change, it portends psychological problems. Unfortunately, the inherent discomfort of grieving often drives people to form new and premature relationships. Instead of finding internal solutions, they look toward others for shortcut answers and relief.

Just before I turned forty, my husband and I talked about having a third child. He was especially enthusiastic about the prospect. Like him, I often was saddened that our children were taking leave of us, but I was unsure what to do. Did I want a baby? Did I not want a baby? What did I want at this time of my life anyhow? My children's growing up surely reminded me that I was growing older—a fact reinforced by the deepening lines on my face, graying hair, and physicians' warnings about rising cholesterol levels. Like me, most women with adolescents are in their middle years. Suddenly and shockingly we recognize that we are no longer young. (Is it not fitting that Demeter transforms herself into an old woman after her daughter leaves her?) The illusion of immortality and invulnerability that accompanied youth and also, to some extent, our care of the very young, gives way to the sobering realization that life is finite and fragile. Is it any wonder that we feel scared and sad?

For weeks, in a vague but persistent way, the fear of aging and being left behind hung over me. I felt the weight of doors closing in on me. Couldn't I pry those doors open? Wouldn't having another baby allow my husband and me to sneak through the cracks back to a more ebullient time? I did not know what to do. Fortunately I did nothing. I allowed myself to sink into a depression and grieved deeply, painfully, for what I was losing.

During this period of depression, a dream came to me that guided my way. In this dream I found myself at a lovely square in a village in France. I wore a long black dress and held a fish in my arms. My husband was singing to me, imploring me to put the fish in the well that stood between us. But I refused, explaining that the well would no longer contain the fish. The fish then disappeared. I reached for my husband's hand, and we sang a love duet together. When I explored the dream, I realized that it transported me to the very same village square that my husband and I had visited on a holiday after discovering I was pregnant with our first child. How ecstatic we both were and how we frolicked and celebrated that day long past! But in this dream I wore black, the color of mourning. I was grieving for a part of my life that had to die. I would never again be a young mother with a new baby. No, I refused to take the fish (embryo) to the well (my womb). As the fish disappeared (as I let go of the possibility of bearing another child), I took my husband's hand.

The dream made clear that the end of our active parenting could allow for a deepening connection between my husband and me, a renewal of the "twoness" we knew in our earliest years as a couple but had necessarily relinquished when the children came along and demanded our attentions. This is what I wished for and what I wanted to work toward. Out of my emptiness I created a new hope, a new possibility for my future. My grief ended, the symptoms of depression that had weighed me down fell away naturally.

After her efforts to replace Persephone with another child fail, the bereaved Demeter demands that a temple be built for her. By recognizing the need to mourn fully and directly, she is once more freed to behave as a goddess. Discarding the disguise of forlorn agedness, she takes her own splendid form and then retreats to the temple to grieve for her lost, irreplaceable child. Often in the course of psychotherapy, I have watched my clients transform themselves; like Demeter, they become naturally beautiful as they go into themselves— into their own temples—and in this way become themselves. No longer needing to act a part, their faces become radiant and their bodies fluid. It is a terrible strain to hold back emotions: to shut off tears, stifle sobs, or silence screams. Yet many of us are taught to masquerade, to paint a smile over our sadness, to pretend away our sorrows. When we are not able to express our feelings, our faces are masks and our bodies armor. As a therapist, I feel quite triumphant when I can help my clients learn that giving in to their darker feelings does not signify a breakdown but rather the possibility of a breakthrough—a new or deepened understanding—that leads to fuller selfhood.

In her temple, Demeter sits alone with her grief. Wisely she does not permit anyone to coax her prematurely out of despondency, as she permitted the servant Iambe to do earlier. Her grief requires a temporary withdrawal from the social world along with a painful introspection, and the famine she brings about symbolizes the experience of her depression: that state of internal void where everything feels dead. Through my clinical work, I have come to understand how frightened and ashamed people are of depression. For some it evokes sheer terror: "If I indulge such feelings, I will lose all control; I will go crazy." For others it evokes self-reproach: "I get angry at myself for being so weak, such a wimp." Many depressed women are especially afraid of the anger that accompanies their depression. Their fear is understandable because women are taught that anger is an unfeminine as well as a destructive response. And though a woman's expression of anger may indeed feel frighteningly powerful, for it is a wild, primitive outcry, she will probably find that her anger, far from devastating the earth like the goddess Demeter's, releases her from the immobility of her depression and restores her vitality.

Depression is a universal, human response to the myriad losses that assault every life. Yet, sadly, our society derides its expression and berates us for feeling bad. Lesley Hazleton, who has written a highly readable book called *The Right to Feel Bad*, points out that the pursuit of happiness has become a desperate matter: Feeling good is no longer simply a right but a personal duty. What Demeter teaches us is that we must allow ourselves our depressions, bitter as they are, for it is by struggling through them that we learn to adjust to our losses and thereby reach higher levels of selfhood.

Persephone also teaches us that young women must be allowed their depressions, because it is by going deep into one's own underworld that growth and change occur. Mothers who trust their feelings and are unafraid of the darker ones have the splendid opportunity to teach their daughters— their Persephones—the same. To know how to be depressed safely—without acting destructively—is a lesson every adolescent should learn. As Albert Camus wrote, "There is no sun without shadow, and it is essential to know the night."

All too often, however, mothers became unduly alarmed when their daughters are depressed. I recall a case in which a woman was concerned that her adolescent daughter spent long periods of time in her bedroom, where she would wile away hours listening to sad music or simply daydreaming. Not realizing that the girl's withdrawal from the social world allowed her the time to elaborate an internal world, an inner life, the mother prodded her to "snap out" of her mood, to "do something productive." Although the mother's intention was to promote her daughter's growth, she was, inadvertently, stunting it.

I am not suggesting that we turn a deaf ear to a child who cries (or whispers) for help. An adolescent who is overwhelmed by life's difficulties and feels helpless to face them usually requires professional support. I am suggesting, however, that when an adolescent is not endangering herself or others, she has a right to feel and express her sadness—just as her mother has this right. Both adolescence and midlife are times of new beginnings, which necessarily entail mourning for what is past.

As M. Esther Harding writes, "The attitude which says, 'I want to make you happy, to make life easy for you. I want to guard you from every breath of hardship and adversity,' is terrible. It seems so kind, yet it is really cruel."[1] The truly kind mother allows her daughter to be a full person, to suffer as well as to enjoy. She reminds the growing girl that it is necessary to be very sad from time to time and that this sadness should not be hidden by false smiles or stiff upper lips. The wise mother might tell her daughter something like this: "Darling, I see that you are full of anguish. Perhaps it would be helpful to go to your room, close the door behind you, allow your sadness, have a good cry if you will. Later, if you would like, I will listen to you, and I promise not to talk you out of your sorrow or anger. It is a sign of your humanity to have those feelings, and I will never take them from you."

Just as Persephone's retreat to the underworld pushes her evolution, Demeter's own lived-through depression leads to her maternal transformation. Only after her period of mourning, which necessarily involves a reevaluation, is she ready to move into a less engulfing maternal role. Separated from each other—Demeter in her temple, Persephone in the underworld—mother and daughter each undergo transformations as they recognize they must end their shared life. Persephone eats the pomegranate seed that ensures her sexuality and continuing relationship to Hades, and Demeter decides not to stand in the way of her daughter's marriage but to accept her changing relationship with her daughter. Demeter undergoes further transformation. Having released her daughter from their absolute bond, Demeter is able to rechannel her maternal love. She does this by becoming a spiritual mentor to the princes of Eleusis, to whom she now passes on her solemn rites and to whom she reveals her Eleusian Mysteries.

Like Demeter, women must find ways to enable those who follow them. They must not forsake the young who take their leave. The maternal role evolves from one of caretaking to one of guiding the next generation. As their children grow apart from them, many maternal women look outside their families for new and appropriate ways to ensure the welfare of the next generation. These are the women who in their middle years become inspired and inspiring teachers, healers, mentors, social and political leaders.

We should not interpret Persephone's reunion with her mother as a replacement of what has been lost or as a return to an earlier way of being. Rather, it celebrates the coming together of two differentiated women: Demeter, the mature earth goddess, and her daughter, Persephone, the lovely queen of the underworld. In each other's arms, Demeter and Persephone affirm the permanence of their relationship. However, they do not merge but instead mirror the unique person each sees in the other. As I close this chapter, I am reminded of the ancient stone relief of Demeter and Persephone in Erich Neumann's book, which I described earlier. Only now in my imagination, it appears different. I can see two women, a mother and her daughter, looking lovingly into each other's eyes. Each is very beautiful and powerful, and although they resemble one another, each is undeniably herself.

3

Good or Bad Apples:

Mothers and Sex

B Y ALL REASON, AN ADOLESCENT DAUGHTER'S
sexual development should elicit tender feelings in
the mother. It is, after all, a lovely maturational
unfolding. One would expect the older woman to
guide the younger one into womanhood with care and to
celebrate her rite of passage. Yet, many mothers respond to
their daughters' new womanliness with cautious concern,
even dread. In our society the young woman's first menstruation, the menarche, is typically a private and uncelebrated
event greeted by awkward silence. (Indeed, for reasons that
I do not know, the word *menarche* does not appear in most
American dictionaries.) Perhaps we can find out, if we break
this silence, why a young girl's sexual development often
triggers negative feelings and unsupportive behaviors in her
mother, and perhaps we can see how these might be replaced by healthier maternal responses.

Psychoanalytic literature emphasizes the sexual competition between a mother and her nubile daughter. Implicit is
the assumption that such rivalry is natural and consequently

of minor concern. Psychoanalyst James Anthony described this antagonism in the following way:

> The mother/daughter rivalry has its most extreme expression within the setting of the "menopausal-menarche" syndrome, when the mother's waning reproductive life is confronted with the flowering sexuality of the girl. The interaction stirs up considerable anxiety and depression in both, and the nagging relationship of prepuberty is transformed into an open warfare in which the Geneva conventions are abandoned. The father often carries a "diplomatic immunity" in these situations. The bread-and-butter battles are waged between mother and daughter at the same time as the daughter retains her romantic attachment to the father.[1]

Certainly, to achieve selfhood daughters must create a temporary psychological distance from their mothers. And in their efforts to draw away from their mothers, they are likely to draw closer to their fathers, who ideally serve as buffers between them and their mothers. Moreover, the romantic longings that every little girl feels toward her father are reawakened during her adolescence. Part of her, at least, wants to be Daddy's special girl, Daddy's favorite, Daddy's one-and-only. As psychologist Louise Kaplan put it, ". . . the repressed Oedipal fantasies of infancy return in various guises and clamor to reassert their sovereignty."[2]

But although some competition between mother and daughter is inevitable, I do not believe that their *bitter* sexual rivalries are either natural or desirable. Rather, these intense hostilities may derive from a society that demeans women, stunts their psychological growth, and undermines relationships among them. To explain one way mother and daughter may be pitted against each other and the effects of this competition, let me recount a clinical case.

Hesitantly and apologetically, Jessica, an attractive woman in her mid-forties, told me that she was envious of her thirteen-year-old daughter. Next to her pretty, sexy daughter, she felt "all used up and old—like a worn-out shoe." Resentment of her child's new sexuality made her ashamed, and Jessica berated herself for feeling jealous: "I don't want my daughter to look better than me. I don't want her to outshine me. But I hate myself for my meanness. What is wrong with me that I have become such a jealous woman and that I'm envious of my very own daughter?" Bewildered by her hostile feelings, Jessica feared that she could no longer trust her goodness as a mother and therefore the relationship with her only child had become strained and unnatural.

From our discussions, I learned that as a younger woman Jessica had been the object of much admiration and was idealized for her beauty by a host of lovers. Obsessively aware of the physical signs of her aging, she now expected that men, especially her husband, would discount her as she lost her youthful allure. As if to reinforce Jessica's self-devaluations, Andrew, her fifty-year-old husband, did reject her sexually. He initiated sex infrequently, made love to her mechanically, and ogled younger women in her company. A cruel example of his rejection followed a mutually disappointing sexual encounter, when he "jokingly" suggested that he "trade her in for a newer model." What hurt Jessica most (and precipitated the consultation with me) was his excessive admiration of their daughter. Andrew wooed Kathy, even becoming jealous of the boys in whom she was interested. His misplaced affections cut Jessica most deeply on the evening of their twentieth wedding anniversary, for which she had planned an elegant party. Dressed splendidly, Jessica stood before Andrew in hopeful anticipation of his admiration. Without a word to Jessica, he looked past her and, directing his full attention to their daughter, told the young girl how beautiful she was.

But Jessica's low self-opinion derived from more than her husband's cruelties. What soon struck me about this woman was that she talked about herself as if she were a commodity—a toy, a car, or an item of clothing—that could easily be exchanged for some*thing* newer or slicker. Having reduced herself to an object, she could not recognize those intangible human qualities that increase during one's maturity and enhance one's worthiness, qualities like creativity, empathy, intimacy, humor, and wisdom. Like so many women, she measured her worth as a human being largely in terms of her physical attributes, and even in that respect her standards were narrow. To Jessica, only the young were beautiful—an assumption that is, unfortunately, shared by many in our society. Indeed, from the time we are little, we are trained to link beauty with youth and ugliness with age; we believe that pretty maidens are doomed to become repulsive hags. Is it any wonder that older women look upon their bodies with growing horror and contempt? Or that they go to such lengths (from grueling workouts and diets to cosmetic surgery) to create an illusion of youthfulness?

Is it any wonder that, having learned to love only youth, poor Jessica came to despise her aging face and form? How could she appreciate her daughter's flowering when it suggested her own wilting? It is only when the middle-aged woman is confident of her sexual powers and the delights of her mature body that she is able to experience the deepest mutuality with the younger one, in whom passion is first stirring. Depressed and diminished, Jessica could neither guide nor celebrate Kathy's passage into womanhood; it elicited only envy, which her husband fed with his acts of insensitivity.

In reality (a reality Jessica did not understand), the adolescent female does not sexually surpass the healthy middle-aged woman and need not pose a threat. Many distinguished theorists have made the mistake of substituting reproductive capacity for sexuality. Impressive findings from the field of sex research are teaching us that during and after menopause, a woman's sexual capacities do not tend to wane.[3] Indeed, spared the worry of unwanted pregnancies, many women enjoy sex more than ever: Moreover, as they gain confidence in themselves and become more competent in the world, they also become more sexually assertive and responsive.

I am in full agreement with writer Isak Dinesen's assertion that the older woman who is ready to unleash her full strength is the most powerful creature on earth. Dinesen's comment reminds me of a remark by my hairdresser, who, holding on to a strand of my hair with one hand and lifting her cutting shears high over her head with the other, exclaimed with gusto that her forty-five-year-old libido is "hotter than ever before."

Ironically, the middle-aged woman's capacities for sex can be threatening to her male partner, who may defensively sabotage her. I began to understand this dynamic through my couple therapy with Jessica and her husband. Because Andrew was affecting his wife's emotional well-being, I asked him to take part in Jessica's treatment. During an individual session, I learned how insecure he was about his own sexuality and how unprepared he was for the normal sexual changes that accompany aging. He hinted that as he had become older, his sexual performance had flagged—he was no longer the "stud" he had once been, and consequently he brooded over his "diminishing manliness." Early in our discussion Andrew claimed that he had come to dread sex with Jessica because as she had aged, she no longer "turned him on." But later Andrew confided the anguish he experienced on those occasions that he "failed" her sexually. What became evident to me was that Andrew, preoccupied with his waning virility, had projected his own doubts about his sexual desirability onto his wife. He tried to preserve his self-esteem by insisting that Jessica, not he, was the problem. Like the demoralized fox in Aesop's fable, Andrew deceived himself by insisting that the fruits of passion offered by his wife (but beyond his reach) were sour. His dread of being sexually outdone and therefore humiliated by her led him—no doubt unconsciously—to humiliate Jessica by belittling her sexual desirability and by transferring his romantic attentions to his daughter. With his little girl he felt vital, powerful, and sexy. By using his daughter to bolster his self-esteem, however, he not only impaired her healthy development but undermined her relationship with her mother. This seductive father created, or at least exacerbated, the jealousy between Jessica and her child.

Before she is confident enough to engage her young men, an adolescent girl is likely to test out her womanly charms on her father (or father substitute). Should the father value her womanhood at the expense of her mother's, however, the young girl will become confused and frightened. Just as the small boy, struggling through the Oedipal stage, must not believe that he is successfully stealing Mother away from Father, so too the adolescent girl, who is stirred by new and intense feelings of genital desire and an awareness of her own desirability, must not believe that in Father's eyes she is sexually superior to Mother. Such victories are Pyrrhic ones because the weight of illegitimate power crushes the child. Instead, the young girl needs to know that her father, by virtue of his enduring and deepening bond with his wife and his paternal protectiveness, does not wish for sexual favors from his child. It is safe for the daughter to be her father's princess as long as her mother is his queen.

The severe psychological damage for which incestuous fathers are responsible is well documented. From empirical studies, we are also learning that seductive fathers like Andrew, who are not overtly incestuous, also impair their daughters' emotional health. Researchers Judith Lewis Herman and Lisa Hirschman, who conducted controlled interviews with daughters whose fathers had been seductive, concluded that in adult life these women suffered from a confused identity. They were the "good" girls who served and pleased their fathers and, at the same time, the "bad" girls who had come dangerously close to violating the incest taboo and overtaking their mothers. Their dual identities prevented them from developing an integrated sense of self, and they fluctuated from seeing themselves as idealized princesses to seeing themselves as ruthless temptresses. Moreover, their personal relationships were troubled. They tended to overvalue men and to undervalue women—just as Father undervalued Mother. Many years ago, psychoanalyst Karen Horney described the daughters of seductive fathers in the following way: "These women were as though possessed by a single thought: 'I must have a man'—obsessed with an idea overvalued to the point of absorbing every other thought, so by comparison all the rest of life seemed stale, flat, and unprofitable."[4]

As one might expect, Herman and Hirschman found that the daughters of seductive fathers also paid for their special status by suffering the jealousy of their mothers, and that the imposed rivalry between mothers and daughters prevented the latter from realizing their deep longings for maternal nurture. How common and how unfortunate it is that learned sexual competitions also preclude trusting and loving relationships among female peers; all too often, women—adolescent or middle-aged—are ready to sacrifice their friendships with each other for the attentions of men.

In light of Jessica's distorted self-image and her husband's degrading seductive behavior, Jessica's resentment of her adolescent daughter is understandable. Nevertheless, it is terribly sad. Theirs was a costly estrangement. The young girl lost the mother who might have served as her model and guide, and the mother lost the opportunity to accompany her daughter into the next age of womanhood.

Jessica and Andrew dropped out of therapy after a few sessions without explanation. My impression was that Jessica felt hopeless about her situation. Unwilling to threaten her husband, on whom she depended, she was willing (without being entirely conscious of the fact) to sacrifice both her own and her daughter's psychological well-being.

This kind of impasse is well-represented in a volume of short stories about mothers and daughters collected by literary critic Susan Koppelman. Several of these stories depict the ways mothers help socialize their daughters into a society in which they are dominated and coerced by men. Guadalupe Valdes's story "Recuerdo," from which I offer an excerpt, describes the dilemma confronting a Mexican-American mother whose employer wants her complicity in seducing her daughter:

"Maruca is very pretty, Rosa," Don Lorenzo said suddenly.

"Thank you, senor, you are very kind.". . . .

"She will make a man very happy someday," he continued.

"Yes."

"Do you think she will marry soon then?" he asked her, watching her closely.

"No," she hesitated, "that is, I don't know, she . . . there isn't anyone yet."

"Ah!" It was said quietly but somehow triumphantly. . . And Rosa waited, wondering what he wanted, sensing something and suddenly suspicious.

"Do you think she likes me, Rosa," he asked her, deliberately baiting her.

And she remembered Maruca's face, tear stained, embarrassed telling her: "I can't go back, Mama. He does not want me to help in his work. He touches me, Mother . . . and smiles. And today, he put his large sweaty hand on my breast, and held it, smiling like a cow. Ugly!"

"Why, yes, Don Lorenzo," she lied quickly. "She thinks you are very nice.". . . .

"I am much of a man, Rosa," he went on slowly, "and the girl is pretty . . . I would take care of her . . . if she let me.". . . .

"I would be good to her, you would have money. And then, perhaps, if there is a child . . . she would need a house . . ."

. . . "Think about it, Rosita," he said, smiling benevolently . . . "You know me . . ." And Rosa looked at him angrily, remembering, and suddenly feeling very much like being sick.

[On the way home, Rosa muses about her own life: about the small children who are still dependent on her, and about her husband, Pablo, "who had begun to look at Maruca." She decides that it is time for Maruca to leave home.]

And Rosa watched her, then herding the children into the house gently, gracefully; slim and small, angular still, with something perhaps a little coltish in the way she held herself, impatient, and yet distrusting, not quite daring to go forward.

And she thought of Don Lorenzo, and for a moment, she wished that he were not so fat, or so ugly, and especially, so sweaty. But it was an irrecoverable chance! Old men with money did not often come into their world, and never to stay. . . .

"Maruca," Rosa said decidedly, turning to where she sat playing with the baby, "I went to see Don Lorenzo."

"Oh?" There was fear in the bright brown eyes.

"And he wants to take care of you," Rosa continued softly. "He thinks you're pretty, and he likes you."

"Take care of me?" . . .

"He wants to make an arrangement with you, Maruca." Rosa too was afraid now. "He would come to see you . . . and . . . well . . . if there is a baby, there might very well be a house."

"A baby?" The face was pale now, the eyes surprised and angry. "You want me to go to bed with Don Lorenzo?" . . .

"Don't you see, I want you to be happy, to be safe . . ."

"To be happy?" Maruca repeated slowly, as if it had never occurred to her that she was not. "Yes, to be happy." . . . "And sleeping with Don Lorenzo," Maruca asked uncertainly, "Will that make me glad I was born?"

And Rosa looked at her, saw her waiting for an answer, depending on it . . . And she wanted to scream out, "No, no! You will hate it probably, and you will dread his touch on you and his breath smelling of garlic." . . . But the brown eyes stared at her pleadingly, filling with tears, like a child's, and Rosa said quietly: "Yes, Maruca, it will make you happy."[5]

How can we understand Rosa's maternal responses? One might argue that she is protecting her child. By giving the girl to the rich Don Lorenzo, Rosa believes that she has found the only way to spare Maruca from an impoverished life. Selling one's body to a powerful man seems to her a small price for the material comforts he promises. Rosa, herself so powerless, cannot imagine other possibilities for her daughter. Her low expectations and limited vision compel her to pass on this legacy to her female child.

Yet, one might also argue that Rosa sacrifices the child she purports to save. Let us consider the psychological rather than the economic reasons for this sacrifice. Rosa herself is accustomed to sexual exploitation by men. She has worked as a maid and cook for old men with money, whom she describes as "faultless beings who were to be obeyed without question; powerful creatures who had commanded her to come when they needed variety or adventure . . . But only that."[6] The author implies that the very man who now asks for an arrangment with the daughter once used Rosa sexually. By turning over Maruca to Don Lorenzo, Rosa is guaranteeing that Maruca is sacrificed sexually, just as she was. It is reasonable to hypothesize that because she has little regard for herself, Rosa has little regard for the daughter who is so much like herself; self-love, after all, not self-hate, leads to love of others. Like many people who have been demeaned, Rosa ensures the repetition of her humiliation—in this case, against the daughter with whom she identifies.

Psychoanalyst Alice Miller has explained more convincingly than anyone else I know that when victimized people are not able to articulate fully their past sufferings, they will act out these sufferings in active or passive ways against themselves or others; they will repeat, in a tragically compulsive way, the hurt they were made to endure.[7] Although

Rosa is not actively abusive toward Maruca, by pandering for her she effectively breaks her will, just as her own will was broken when she was forced to prostitute herself.

All too frequently, my most wounded clients demonstrate such destructive repetitions: The woman who, as a child, was abused by her parent marries a man who brutalizes her and her children; the woman whose vitality was choked by a stifling marriage partner encourages her daughter to settle into a similarly deadening arrangement; the woman who as a child was repeatedly raped by her father picks up men at bars and takes them home to bed. Some readers will no doubt wonder why it is that victims, who understand suffering too well, continue to inflict emotional pain against themselves and others. One reason may be that victims compulsively repeat tragic situations in a misguided effort to remedy them. So, for example, the daughter of an abusive father may marry a man like him because she is motivated by the unconscious idea that by virtue of her love she can heal the damaged husband, who represents the damaged father she failed to heal. Of course, she only transports the family sickness from one generation to the next; most likely her cruel husband will not soften in response to her love but will, instead, victimize their own unfortunate children, just as she was victimized by her father. It is likely that, at an unconscious level, Rosa also believes that some good will come from Maruca's repetitions. Although Rosa's sexual favors to old, rich men were never rewarded with love, perhaps Maruca's will be; perhaps this time it will turn out differently; perhaps Maruca's triumph can vindicate Rosa.

But wounded women do not heal by surrendering themselves or their daughters to those who will hurt them again and again. In order to become healthy, wounded women must give words to their past suffering and these words must be taken seriously. Only after remembering, talking about, and grieving for the injustices done to them are they free from compulsively reenacting them and perpetuating their suffering. The outcry of the ever-growing numbers of women that are making public their histories of sexual abuse is, to my mind, a hopeful sign. After women's massive psychic wounds are exposed, they can begin to heal.

Rosa's sexual experience as a woman and consequent response as a mother are more common than we would like to think. Although its form may vary, sexual exploitation has been carried from one generation to the next, across cultures and economic strata. As Rosa shows, one way women have perpetuated this exploitation is by turning out (blatantly or subtly) their adolescent daughters to the men who will take care of them in exchange for their sexual services. They have encouraged their daughters to become showpieces in order to entice men to marry them.

Not surprisingly, many adult clients in my practice express great rage toward the mothers who sacrificed them, ostensibly for their own good. A middle-aged client told me with pent-up bitterness that her mother had encouraged her to have her nose shortened when she was a teenager to make herself more attractive to boys. Another remembered how mother worried that her daughter's extraordinary scholastic achievements would be threatening to potential boyfriends and advised her to concentrate less on her studies. Women with eating disorders often report that it was their mothers who encouraged them to go on their first diets—for some women, in fact, these diets (usually futile and frustrating attempts to conform to current standards of beauty) are the activities shared with their mothers they remember most vividly.

I cannot in good conscience absolve myself of such destructive maternal behaviors. I recall with shame the night of my daughter's first school dance, when I encouraged her to wear an outfit that would make her look sexier. As a young woman, I had derived my personal power almost exclusively from my sex appeal and had measured it by the number of male admirers I could collect. Unaware of the harm I was doing, I tried to empower my child by marketing her sexuality as I had learned to market mine. In my naïveté,

I did not see that my daughter, like many of her generation, can experience power in healthy ways. Her security and self-esteem do not depend on attracting a man who will, in exchange for sexual favors, take care and approve of her. A gifted and accomplished young actress, Leah fantasized about being in the limelight rather than of waiting in the wings for a powerful man. To her credit, she chose to wear her most comfortable clothes to the dance despite my misguided entreaties. Relinquishing my supportive role, I had almost become my daughter's agent instead of her guide.

Perhaps no literary work depicts this maternal failure more candidly than does the Brothers Grimm's well-known fairy tale "Snow White." No doubt one of the reasons this tale has endured for centuries is that it suggests a pattern of mother-daughter relationship that feels familiar to us. It rings true. Most interpretations of this fairy tale emphasize the development of its heroine, Snow White, but my interpretation focuses on the plight of the (step)mother, the "wicked" queen (who is more accurately a suffering queen). Because fairy tales view the world from the perspective of their heroes and heroines, we see the queen through Snow White's eyes; but this perspective is not necessarily distorted. A daughter watches her mother carefully and can often reflect her inner world quite accurately. When the queen wants to know the truth about herself, she turns to her magic looking glass and sees her daughter's "fair" face, which sheds light on the darker, troubled aspects of the mother hidden from view.

As readers will recall, the crisis for the queen and Snow White begins with the young girl's budding sexuality. When the magic mirror proclaims that Snow White is even fairer than the queen, the queen becomes so envious that she vows to destroy the girl. (In some versions of the fairy tale, moreover, the father is drawn to the beautiful adolescent, and his transgression arouses the wife's jealousy, which is what occurred with my client Jessica and her daughter.) After a failed attempt to have a huntsman kill the girl and bring back her heart, which might be interpreted as the mother's attempt to consume her daughter's vitality, the queen takes matters into her own hands. She disguises herself as an old peddler woman and sets out to locate her daughter, who has found shelter with seven dwarfs—undersized men who make no sexual demands on the girl.

As a peddler (one who sells wares), the queen mother takes on the role of a panderer or pimp (one who sells girls). She tempts Snow White with three offerings: stay-laces, a decorative comb, and a red apple, each of which is meant to make the young girl sexually marketable. All these devices almost kill her. The stay-laces of a corset, which exaggerate a woman's curves, bind the girl's body so that she is unable to breathe; the comb, which creates an alluring coiffure, poisons her; and the red apple, which symbolizes premature and thus forbidden knowledge about sex, suffocates her. Twice the helpful dwarfs are able to rescue Snow White. They cut away the laces that have shut off her breath, and they draw the tainted comb from her hair. But they cannot revive the young girl after she has ingested her mother's poisoned food, food the mother herself shares with her. What the fairy tale teaches us is that a mother's marketing of her daughter's sexuality exploits her. Traditionally rationalized as the only way to ensure the daughter's success in a world where sex promises power, such coercion effectively kills the girl's spirit. It is only when Snow White herself coughs up the poisoned morsel of apple she was cajoled into swallowing that she awakens from her deathlike sleep and is ready to enter into a love relationship with her prince. In other words, it is often necessary for daughters to cough up or unlearn the harmful information their mothers shared with them.

Women—mothers and daughters—must unlearn the idea that their value as human beings is measured in terms of their sexual allure and that they are marketable sex objects; but this is not an easy thing to do. We are bombarded by myriad messages, especially through commercial ads, suggesting that a woman is no more than the sum of her erotic

parts—slender legs, firm buttocks, rounded breasts, sensuous lips, and shaded glances.

I am grateful to my daughter who, by refusing to "fix
herself up" for the purpose of catching a young man's attentions, as I suggested she should, helped me realize that a
female must never allow herself to become a sex object. Leah
is a good teacher. However, I am reminded of another girl
who tried but failed to teach her mother the same lesson.
Becoming aware of the indignities she suffers as a young
woman, the teenaged Madge in William Inge's play *Picnic,*
struggles to explain her sense of exploitation to her mother,
Flo. Madge asks what good it is to be pretty and Flo replies
that pretty *things* are like flowers and sunsets and rubies and
that pretty girls serve as billboards, reminding the world
that life is good. Reflecting on her mother's explanation,
Madge tells her that she doesn't like to be looked at all the
time and that, as a person, she gets lost in all this. Flo,
unable or unwilling to understand her daughter's plea for
respect, can only admonish her for talking selfishly.

Just as women must unlearn the idea that they are mere
objects, women must also unlearn the idea that their aging
bodies are unattractive. I confronted this idea in myself
several months ago when a friend and I attended a workshop
conducted by a woman in her fifties. "She must have have
been beautiful *when she was young,*" he whispered in my
ear, and I readily agreed. Fortunately, my friend's comment
and my response to it disturbed me and left me with a
lingering feeling of discomfort. Hours later I understood
why: This gray-haired, full-bodied woman, who did not pretend to look younger than her years, was radiant at the
moment, but because she was an older woman neither of us
could see this.

Happily, I am beginning to see with clearer eyes. I have
just returned from a trip to England, where I spent many
days wandering through London's National Gallery. My most
vivid recollections are of Rembrandt's portraits. These are
not the smooth, innocent faces of maidens but the rich,

wrinkled, experienced (and beautiful) faces of aging men and women. Although I used to be pleased when people told me that I look younger than my age, these portraits have helped me appreciate the newly forming lines and crevices of my forty-two-year-old face, which is the face my experiences have painted, the face I have *earned*.

Just as the healthy adolescent girl eventually comes to welcome her changing body, with its rounded breasts and curves, so the middle-aged woman can eventually accept her new form. But, before such a welcoming of the new occurs, both adolescents and middle-aged women may cling for a time to the old forms they are outgrowing.

In Lass Halström's Swedish movie *My Life as a Dog*, for example, we witness a pubescent girl's valiant but futile fight against her changing body. Resenting the budding breasts that prevent her from competing against the boys in the boxing ring, she tries to hide them by binding her chest with a cloth. It takes time for this girl, who is a tomboy and a Peter Pan refusing to grow up, to relinquish the boy-child body that allowed certain advantages for the woman's body that promises new but yet unknown joys.

Similarly, the middle-aged female may struggle against accepting her new, mature appearance. When I go shopping for clothes, I still stop at those racks that hold the flowered "junior" dresses with their low-cut bodices, tight-fitting waistbands, and full skirts, which I used to love to wear. Sometimes I even try them on, only to have the mirror-on-the-(dressing room)-wall tell me that such girlish clothes are no longer appropriate. Then I move on to the racks that hold the tailored dresses, which as a middle-aged woman, I have grown into. Slowly, somewhat fearfully, certainly awkwardly, I am letting go the image of the young woman I was for the older woman I am becoming.

I am learning that *both* Snow White and her mother can be fair and lovely. A vital middle-aged woman is no less beautiful than a vital young woman. She is simply beautiful in a different way. Art historian Merlin Stone's description of an aging British Columbian Earth Mother comes to mind: "Her face carved with the intricacies of the art of the finest sculpture . . . grew rich with wisdom lines," as does a passage from May Sarton:

I mind certain physical deteriorations, but not *really*. And not at all when I look at the marvelous photograph . . . of Isak Dinesen just before she died. For after all we make our faces as we go along, and who when young could ever look as she does?—The ineffable sweetness of the smile, the total acceptance and joy one receives from it, life, death, everything taken in and, as it were, savored— and let go.[8]

It will require an enormous effort to unlearn obsolete ideas and to see women as full of metamorphic interest. It is only when women begin to value themselves as whole beings (rather than as ornaments or fetishes) who change naturally and beautifully over time that they will be capable of nurturing their daughters' and their own growth.

In the happiest cases, the girl's passage into young womanhood inspires an equally important passage into mature womanhood for her mother. I was able to observe this process in my client Miriam. When her oldest daughter graduated from high school, Miriam, whose interests had centered around the home and family, turned to me for career counseling. "Last summer," she explained, "Sandra and I flew all over the country to look at colleges for her. I loved being part of her adventure, but I must admit I was envious too. I want an adventure of my own. It is as if little wings are sprouting from my sides, and I am almost ready to fly."

When I asked Miriam if anything was stopping her from trying out her wings, she told me that she worried that her personal ambitions might undermine her marriage. Having suffered the heartbreak of one divorce, she did not want to jeopardize the current relationship with her kindhearted but rather possessive and traditional husband. Miriam's concerns were quite realistic; husbands may be threatened as their wives divert energy from them to the outside world, and many marriages are rocked as partners change roles. Research findings demonstrate that women who pit their needs to nurture others against their needs to assert themselves succumb to depressions.[9] Ultimately, a woman's sense of completeness depends on her ability to integrate nurturance (tenderness, connectedness, loving softness) with healthy aggression (success, ambition, and achievement). But this can be an overwhelming task. I have spent many hours in therapy sessions with women who were trying to find this balance—between the need to be adventurous and the need to love.

During our discussions, Miriam weighed the risks of upsetting her marriage against the risks of thwarting her growth and eventually decided to pursue her own interests. She applied to the local university (as it happened, the same one in which her daughter was now enrolled) to work toward a degree in English literature. As I have witnessed many times, an adolescent daughter, so full of hope and ambition, can be an inspiration to her mother. Sandra's leave-taking was the impetus for Miriam's new adventurousness. Miriam abandoned herself to her studies with fervor, but she found, to her delight, that this abandonment did not impair her marital relationship. In fact, she found that for the first time she was able to make love joyfully and spontaneously with her husband.

From what I could tell, Miriam's new sexual vitality derived from her growing self-esteem and individuality. A woman who is sure of herself is not afraid of losing her self-identity and is consequently free to give herself fully to her lover. Confident of her wholeness, her separate identity, she is able to merge with her lover because she knows all the while that she will emerge from lovemaking intact. Since she cannot be possessed, she has no need to put up defensive walls to protect her boundaries, and her lovemaking can be spontaneous and unguarded.

Originally the term *virgin* signified unmarried, not sexually inexperienced, and referred to a woman's independence. An unmarried woman could be her own mistress, whereas a married one was the property of her husband. The task of the middle-aged mother is to strive toward a state of virginity in the original meaning of the word, of liberation, of self-possession. Paradoxically perhaps, it is the self-possessed woman rather than the overly dependent one who is more capable of a vibrant sexual relationship.

Having met her goals in therapy, Miriam and I agreed that it was appropriate to terminate our relationship. Months later, however, as I was strolling across campus, I caught a glimpse of Miriam and Sandra. Carrying armloads of books, they were rushing to their separate classes, and as they crossed paths each blew a kiss in the other's direction. I could not help but smile, knowing that the apple this mother and daughter shared was not poisonous like Snow White's but good and sweet instead.

In "Snow White" the stepmother is destroyed by her envy of her daughter. The story ends at Snow White's wedding—the rite of passage that dramatically marks the separation between parent and child—where the queen, who is immobilized by her anger and terror, puts on red-hot iron shoes, in which she dances to her death. Envy is a normal human emotion. It is not evil for the older generation to admit some envy of the younger one for its vigor and seemingly endless opportunities. Through grieving, however, mature women are able to accept their lost youth and move on. A woman (like Miriam) who is herself growing and changing is not as likely to experience the emotional deprivation that feeds envy. The queen's tragedy is that she cannot overcome her envious rage. Her self-centeredness fixes her in one place. Although she dies in a frenzy of motion, she is unable to move. Her failure is that she does not grow, does not change; she undergoes no transformation as woman or mother. A mature counterpart would take pleasure in the unfolding beauty, power, sexuality, and creativity of her children. She would "kvell"—a Yiddish word that signifies the unrestrained joy that a parent feels as she witnesses her child's budding and blossoming.

As I indicated in the first chapter, the conflicts involved in each critical phase of the child's life revive similar conflicts in the parent. As a young girl matures sexually and begins to date, she is likely to bring to the surface unresolved sexual issues for the mother. In Francis Ford Coppola's fanciful movie *Peggy Sue Got married,* forty-two-year-old Peggy Sue, a mother of two teenagers who is newly separated from the husband who was her high school sweetheart, returns to her past to relive her eighteenth year. Surprisingly, she makes only one major change in her life: She initiates a night of passionate love with the sexiest boy in the senior class. For Peggy Sue, there are no negative consequences for enjoying the adventure she missed twenty-four years before—because everything is possible in the movies. But in real life, this may not be the case. An adolescent's sexual awakening may arouse in the mother dormant longings, which she may act out vicariously or directly in maladaptive ways.

New love is of course magical; under its spell one's whole being is illuminated. The luckiest women witness their daughters' new loves with full hearts and few regrets. Rogers and Hammerstein's sweet song "Hello Young Lovers," from *The King and I,* comes to mind. Because she once had a great love of her own, middle-aged Anna is able to bless a young couple in love. Less fortunate women, however, may respond to their daughters' romances with growing envy.

We have all known mothers who live vicariously through their sons and daughters. Often a woman's overinvolvement in her children's social life is an attempt to make their romances her own. Having to live for their mothers as well as for themselves, however, is far too heavy a burden for all young people. The most spirited adolescents will rebel against such maternal overinvolvement, but the more accommodating ones will, at considerable expense to themselves, try to meet their mothers' expectations. Child psychoanalyst Donald Winnicott has explained that people who strive to meet the expectations of others may become "false selves." In their efforts to please, they relinquish their own wishes and will; their life force diminishes.

Similarly, a mother who looks to her children to supply her missing experiences is ultimately disappointed. She is especially vulnerable because her happiness lies not with herself but with her child, whom she cannot control completely. As research in the field of female developement is beginning to demonstrate, lack of control over one's fate may be a major precipitant of psychological illness among women.[10] A woman whose fulfillment depends on the success of another is inherently not in control of her life.

Rather than live out their sexual desires vicariously, some middle-aged mothers become sexually adventurous themselves in reaction to their daughters' initiation into sexual life. These young Aphrodites arouse in the mother a longing, even a desperation, to recapture (or perhaps know for the first time) that rapturous feeling of falling in love. A single woman, for example, may discount the people and activities that she once valued—good friendships, work, creative activities—as she frantically pursues romance. I knew a woman who squandered her savings on an operation to lift her breasts, on a faddish wardrobe, and a Club Med vacation in her determination to have as much "fun" as her popular eighteen-year-old daughter seemed to be having. A married woman, on the other hand, may become less tolerant of her husband's familiar but perhaps too predictable loving; she may wish to flee from his comfortable arms into those of a new exciting lover. It is not uncommon that a middle-aged woman's sexual and romantic cravings are so intense that they drive her to risk all, even to jeopardize the stability of her family life.

Naomi, who had been a faithful wife and a devoted mother, described her clandestine love affair as an escape from human ordinariness. In her lover's bed, she was no longer a conventional homemaker but, instead, a powerful sex goddess. Like Peggy Sue, her counterpart from the silver screen, Naomi had suppressed her sexual wishes during adolescence and early adulthood. A shy girl who had been humiliated by a speech defect, she had rarely dated. The young man who became her husband, himself inexperienced, was her first lover and still compared unfavorably with her secret partner, who was a skilled and practiced lover.

It is not surprising that Naomi's extramarital affair eventually caused her anguish, which convinced her to seek counseling. She described being overcome by waves of anxiety, especially during periods of solitude. Moreover, even with her lover she felt on edge, and her agitation often spoiled their lovemaking. Anxiety may indicate a contradiction in a person's value system; it is a symptom of inner struggle. Naomi's bouts of anxiety, which fortunately were too distressing to ignore, forced her to confront the impossibility of leading two lives simultaneously—one as family woman, the other as clandestine lover—and to choose to be with her husband or with her new partner or with neither of these men.

As she explored the reasons for initiating a love affair, she began to understand that in part her sexual adventure was an attempt to compensate for an unexciting adolescence: to become, twenty years too late, a wild, sexually free teenager. With considerable sadness, she realized that she did not love her lover. Instead, she loved the feeling of being sexually desired by him and affirmed in this new way. Like an infatuated adolescent, Naomi looked at her lover more to see her lovely reflection in his eyes than to see him.

Naomi also began to understand that in an illusory way this affair renewed a closeness with her seventeen-year-old daughter. Stirred by her passions, she felt more identified with Elaine, who was herself sexually active. Now Naomi could imagine what it was like for her daughter to experience the excitement of new sexual love; now she could share her secrets after all! Although Naomi never told her daughter about her love life, she really wished to do so. In her fantasies, she could see them sitting cross-legged on her daughter's bedroom floor, whispering and giggling about the details of their sexual escapades. By becoming an adolescent herself and friend to her adolescent daughter, Naomi imagined that she could recreate the mother-child unity that is inevitably dissolved with the passage of time.

Unlike Peggy Sue, we cannot turn our clocks back to return to earlier periods of our lives. When our children reactivate the inner conflicts we failed to reconcile in our youth, we must confront them as adults. Inevitably this includes mourning for our missed opportunities—including our sexual ones. Naomi, who continues her psychotherapy, knows that the earlier solutions for the boredom and longing that plagued her were regressive ones, and she is trying to find more appropriate ways to feel good about herself. As her understanding of her daughter's and her own need to separate deepens, she is consciously loosening their ties. With feelings of both relief and loss, moreover, she has ended the affair, which was so special in the beginning but ultimately became dissatisfying. As she sorts out her values, goals, and needs, Naomi must also decide whether she wants to remain with her husband—and, as she says, this may be the most difficult dilemma she has ever confronted.

Naomi's in-progress story reminds me of another in which a daughter's sexual development awakened not longing but fear. Frances had been sexually abused by an alcoholic father and mistreated by a callous husband, who abandoned her and their two small daughters. Quite understandably, she generalized the hatred she felt toward these men to all men, and had rejected sexual intimacies since her early thirties. Hardworking and devoted to her daughters, she enjoyed a harmonious relationship with them through their latency. As might be expected, however, the older daughter's sexual development triggered a crisis. Unlike the women who try to make their nubile daughters sexually marketable, Frances did all she could to suppress Kate's new womanly loveliness and her interest in sex. Frances would not allow Kate to use

makeup or to wear attractive clothes; she imposed strict curfews and shut down the girl's natural curiosity about sex.
One afternoon, for example, she took Kate to a movie which,
unknown to Frances, was sexually explicit. The love scenes
disturbed Frances so much that halfway through she yanked
Kate from her seat and, shaking all over, drove the girl
home. Henceforth Frances made sure that Kate went only to
family movies. To Frances's despair, Kate began to disobey
her; flaunting her defiance of her mother, she applied heavy
makeup, dressed seductively and, before turning fourteen,
became sexually active. A school counselor referred the mother
and daughter to me after Kate had become pregnant.

Psychoanalytic scholars have taught us that children act
out their parents' repressed wishes. The sensitive child, so
exquisitely attuned to the needs of the parent, will live out
that part of the parent's life that is unlived. She will resurrect what her mother has tried to bury. In her poem "Black
Mother Woman," Audre Lorde speaks of this:

> *I cannot recall you gentle*
> *yet through your heavy love*
> *I have become*
> *an image of your once delicate flesh*
> *split with deceitful longings. . . .*
> *But I have peeled away your anger*
> *down to the core of love*
> *and look mother*
> *I Am*
> *a dark temple where your true spirit rises . . .*
> *I learned from you*
> *to define myself*
> *through your denials.*[11]

Through her inappropriate and premature sexual attachments, Kate was living out Frances's fiercely repressed longings for emotional and sexual intimacy. Loving her mother—as
all daughters want to do—she was fulfilling Frances's uncon-

scious wishes and secret dreams: defining herself through the older woman's denials.

Frances was a conscientious client. Motivated by her maternal devotion toward both her daughters, she was determined to change her destructive behaviors and spent years in group and individual therapy to this end. Although she was terribly afraid of being hurt again, Frances realized that she did want to love and be loved by a man. Eventually she opened her heart to a gentle, sensitive man, with whom she allowed a sexual relationship to develop—and Kate, who was then nineteen, heartily approved of and lovingly supported this attachment. I am sure it was a great relief to know that now she no longer had to live out her mother's unlived life—Mother was doing just fine on her own.

It is interesting to compare Frances's successful love relationship with Naomi's unsuccessful one. Naomi's affair, like most adolescent ones, was volcanic, intensified by many ups and downs. Moreover, its very illicitness stimulated a great deal of excitement. Before their final breakup, several tearful separations were followed by passionate reunions. But, as Naomi herself came to realize, she and her lover used each other to enhance themselves, to experience the "highs" that accompany romance; they never learned to care deeply for one another. Frances's love relationship, on the other hand, is quiet and predictable; and because it is based not on self-interest but rather on concern for the other, it endures. "Jim is good to me, and I can say that I'm good to him. We have fun together; sex is never mean and aggressive, it's sweet and playful. But I know that even when I'm not fun—when I'm grouchy or I look kind of dowdy—Jim still loves me. And Jim doesn't have to be a superman either. When he's feeling low or even when he flops sexually with me, I can take him in my arms and comfort him." I suspect that ordinary human relationships such as this one are really the most special. I suspect as well that women who are fortunate enough to know such relationships are in a good position to act as guides to their adolescent daughters who are embarking on their own amorous and sexual adventures.

Recently, I read Merlin Stone's account of an ancient Panamanian rite of passage.[12] When a girl had her first period, the older women of the tribe escorted her to a sacred hut—"the shrine of female puberty"—which stood amid a grove of saptur trees. Instructing the young one to lie on the earth near the shrine, the women gathered about her in a "Ring of Protection," tossed sacred soil upon her, and through prayer evoked the spirit of their Goddess Mu, the Blue Butterfly Lady. Then the women painted the red juice of the saptur, which symbolized menstrual blood, on the young girl's face, chanted their blessings, and honored her with a dance of new womanhood. After this, they led her into the shrine, where they cut her hair—in Stone's words, letting "the black ribbons of her hair fall upon the earth, as her childhood falls from her." When the girl emerged from the shrine as a grown woman, the older women presented her with a felled saptur and a name, which belonged only to her and was not to be revealed to others.

In today's complicated world, mothers and daughters do not have such splendid rituals. Unlike the simple, ancient Panamanian tribeswomen, we sophisticated women are often confused and tentative as we lead our own daughters into adulthood. But we can still be their guides. When we become conscious of our motivations, when we refrain from repeating the destructive behaviors of our mothers and resolutely look for better paths to follow, when we go forward with love relationships despite our fears of being hurt by them, we are pointing our daughters toward positive directions as well.

At our best, we are changing, growing women, and the apples we offer our daughters are still ripening.

4

Love's Hard Service:

Mothers of Troubled Girls

WRITING IN A PRIVATE JOURNAL SHORTLY before her death, the Jungian analyst Florida Scott-Maxwell questioned why love is equated with joy when it is so much else: "hard service," for example, "full of small and great pains."[1] No one will understand this sentiment better than the mother of a deeply troubled adolescent. Rather than joyful, her maternal love may be anxious, confused, frustrated, and guilty—as well as brave and hopeful.

Few in the mental health field have listened to the stories of these women. All too typically, professionals who treat disturbed adolescents exclude their worried mothers. A colleague of mine, who specializes in adolescent psychiatry, uses the term *parentectomy* to describe the routine procedure of "cutting away" parents from adolescents in treatment. And because mothers, more than fathers, are considered the cause of their children's difficulties as well as obstacles in their treatment, they are the ones more likely to be shut out. To be sure, well-meaning and sensitive therapists may exclude them to assure the adolescent clients' absolute confidentiality. Nevertheless, exclusion from their children's treatment, for whatever reason, deprives mothers of the compassion they deserve and the guidance they almost certainly require in their trying circumstances.

In addition to having few supports, few places to turn for solace, mothers of troubled adolescents are hurt by many dearly held but faulty ideas about good mothering. Quite typically, idealized, grandiose expectations of mother love interfere with the down-to-earth, disciplined mothering that their adolescent daughters require. For example, one expectation is that a *good* mother protects her child against life's hardness—its frustrations, losses, and despair. Like the good fairies who presented Sleeping Beauty with gifts of endowment, mothers commonly believe they can bless their daughters with everlasting health, beauty, charm, and goodness. When they do not protect their daughters from the tragedies that are part of the human condition, these mothers are likely to suffer from guilt and frustration. As Marge, the mother of a seventeen-year-old drug abuser, despairingly asked, "How can it be that despite all my concern and my good intentions Lisa is so miserable? It all seems terribly unfair. Mothers who are much less devoted than I am have happy kids. Am I just cursed? Do I lack a special something that other mothers have?"

Marge's personalization of Lisa's problems is not unusual. When I tell a woman that her daughter has an emotional disorder, her first response is likely to be "How did *I* fail her?" and her second, "How can *I* make her well again?" We have invested maternal love with an enormous amount of power—the power to save and the power to heal. A sweetly poisonous Victorian verse reminds us:

Don't poets know it better than others?
God can't be everywhere: and so, invented Mothers."[2]

But such maternal power is illusory, and this illusion causes much unnecessary suffering. Not only does it lead to a sense of maternal inadequacy but, in some cases, to a sense of maternal destruction. For surely, if mothers believe they have the power to make their children happy, they will also believe that they have the power to bring about their children's ruination. In keeping with this belief, mothers hold themselves responsible—and are held responsible in the court of public opinion—for any number of afflictions, from allergies to autism, that strike young people.

Through the 1970s, the years I attended graduate school, I recall, for example, how clinicians engaged in the treatment of schizophrenia pointed an accusing finger at the mothers of young people with this affliction. They labeled them "schizophrenogenic mothers"—literally, "schizophrenia-producing mothers"—and insisted that their intrusive, overprotective, dominating maternal style *caused* their children's sickness. The schizophrenogenic mother turned out to be a phantom. When researchers looked for her, she was nowhere to be found; their studies could not demonstrate a significant relationship between overbearing mothering and schizophrenic disorders in children. As accumulating evidence supported a neurological rather than a psychological explanation for the origin of schizophrenia, fewer fingers pointed accusingly at Mother for willfully causing her child's terrible affliction. Still, I suspect many people (mothers included) continue to assume that a woman has the power to bring about her children's happiness or unhappiness and is accountable for events that are, in reality, beyond her control.

Certainly mothers affect their young; certainly hostile or apathetic or narcissistic mothering has negative, sometimes disastrous, effects. But a mother's influence—for good or bad—is tempered by other influences in the child's life. Even a newborn is not a blank tablet but rather a person with a unique temperament, a given predisposition, specific endowments and limitations; and, surely, an adolescent is shaped by many people besides her mother—father, teachers, peers, and media personalities.

Professor Jerome Kagan has argued convincingly against

the over-empowerment of mother love, comparing it to "the potency attributed in other societies at other times to spirits, loss of soul, sorcery, sin, gossip, God, and witchcraft. . . ."[3] He points out that a mother's way of loving is only one of many influences to which a child is exposed. He also points out that children, depending on their nature and circumstances, will interpret their mothers' behaviors toward them in various ways.

I have noticed that although one child may thrive under the care of a strict and demanding mother, for example, another may come to feel incompetent or even unloved. And it is always interesting to me how siblings living with the same parents under more or less the same conditions turn out so differently from one another. Unfortunately, we have no way of telling how an individual child will respond to one kind of upbringing versus another. We are always using hindsight to make our judgments.

When a mother, upon being told that her daughter is emotionally troubled, asks me how she failed this child and what she needs to do to make her well, I answer, "Perhaps *you* did not fail your daughter, and perhaps *you* cannot make her well."

The following clinical case illustrates how a woman's well-meaning attempts to protect her daughter against hardship actually had the opposite effect. Because it also illustrates how mother love can and does grow and change in response to a child's crisis, I hope it will help those readers who are entangled in dysfunctional relationships with their troubled youngsters.

Diana, an eighteen-year-old, had enjoyed a normal childhood and early adolescence. Openhearted and generous, she drew people to her and had a wide circle of friends. More social butterfly than bookworm, Diana nevertheless had always performed quite well in school. When she went off to college, no one had any reason to suspect that her life would not continue on its smooth path. During her freshman year, however, she experienced the first of many manic episodes. During these attacks, this ordinarily pleasant girl became loud, agitated, and explosive. As if driven by dark, untamable forces within her, she would lose all reason and go on wild rampages. These bouts of mania cursed her young life: She failed courses, lost friends and jobs, and, from time to time, got into trouble with the police for her disorderly conduct. Periods of deep depression, during which Diana felt hopeless and even suicidal, usually followed the manic outbreaks. Quite appropriately, Diana turned to her mother, Helene, for solace.

But Helene wanted to do more than provide comfort. She was determined to eliminate her daughter's pain—somehow. Having heard about my work with adolescents, she telephoned long-distance to request that I take on Diana as my client and offered to pay for her daughter's treatment. I agreed to meet with Diana and, feeling very comfortable with one another, we began our counseling relationship.

I counseled Diana for six months before I met her mother in person. Nevertheless, Helene was present *in spirit* (as mothers of most of my female clients tend to be) at many of our sessions, and through her daughter's descriptions I came to know a little about her. Born into a wealthy and distinguished family, Helene had married well and had gracefully settled into the routine of homemaking and mothering three sons and a daughter—Diana, the youngest. Interestingly, although Diana shared many vivid recollections of Helene as mother, she could not form a clear picture of Helene as wife. According to Diana, her mother's relationship to Walter, a well-known economist, seemed cordial enough but remained somewhat distant. For example, Diana could not remember her parents doing things as a couple or even hugging and kissing one another. Walter was absorbed in his work, Helene in their magnificent home and the children. But, according to Diana, although the children were her mother's major interest, when it was time for each to leave for college, Helene let them go with her blessings. As long as the boys and Diana led successful lives, she seemed content with her own. And, for their parts, the four children continued a warm relationship with their devoted mother even after they left home. Until Diana's mental crisis, life for this upper-middle class family had run a smooth course.

I think that Helene first hoped that with psychological treatment Diana's affliction would be quickly cured. But this was not the case. As I explained to Helene in a telephone conversation, with self-discipline and the help of prescribed drugs, Diana could eventually learn to control her illness; however, she would not be able to rid herself of it. Helene did not take this news well, fighting against the reality that her daughter would have to struggle harder than most other young people to lead a fulfilled and dignified life.

What became clear to me over the next months was that if she could not prevent Diana's manic and depressive episodes, Helene was determined to minimize their consequences; if Nature had robbed Diana of certain advantages, Helene would make compensation. An old folk tune describes this spontaneous wish of every parent to fix what goes wrong in her child's life. In this song, the parent tenderly promises replacement for everything that might disappoint: the mockingbird that doesn't sing, the diamond ring that turns to brass, the shattered looking glass, even the billy goat that runs away. "The Mockingbird" became Helene's lullaby.

Diminished judgment is one of the symptoms of a manic outbreak. During these episodes Diana often squandered the money her friends foolishly lent her, but she was never accountable for these debts. She simply reported to her mother the amount to be returned, and Helene promptly mailed the sum to her. Unable to hold the part-time jobs that would have provided her with spending money, Diana complained that she could not afford new clothes. Again, Helene accommodated her daughter, and so Diana appeared for her sessions always stylishly dressed: "Care packages from home," she would explain with some embarrassment.

Hush, little baby, don't say a word.
Momma's gonna buy you a mockingbird.
And if that mockingbird don't sing,
Momma's gonna buy you a diamond ring.
And if that diamond ring turns to brass,
Momma's gonna buy you a looking glass.

Although she was adept at rationalizing, in her heart Diana knew that she would have to cope with her illness and to take responsibiltiy for her life, just as other eighteen-year-olds take responsibility for their lives. She also knew that she could not use her mother as a stay against her own disorder but had to struggle toward self-sufficiency. Although separating from mother—refusing her infantilizing care—is more difficult for someone who is physically or psychologically handicapped, it is not less necessary. In time, Diana responded to her mother's misguided generosity not with gratitude but with growing hostility. Her mother's gifts of love made Diana feel like a pitiful charity case. It is a fact of human nature that we tend not to like people who obligate us to them, and Helene's benevolence created in her daughter an oppressive feeling of indebtedness. Still, Diana was not yet strong enough to refuse her mother's material offerings and her overprotection.

What Helene, who was without a doubt well-intentioned and loving, did not realize was that hidden in every "care package," every gift of love, were insidious messages: "Mother does not believe you can take care of yourself" and "Mother must always take care of you because you are sick and vulnerable." Weakened by her decreasing self-confidence, Diana became more and more dependent on Helene—and more and more resentful of her. Mother and daughter now called each other daily, unaware that their umbilical telephone cord was strangling them both. And I, as therapist, was ineffective in loosening their symbiotic knot. How could Diana refuse her mother's care, as I urged her to do, when Diana believed she could not survive without it?

Most of us have had terrible experiences that turned out to be blessings in disguise. For Diana, a near-tragic accident was such a blessing. During a manic episode Diana took off in the middle of the night and, driving at far too high a speed, overturned her car. Although she suffered only a few bruises, the car was damaged beyond repair. Helene's immediate response was to ship her own car—a polished black Cadillac—to Diana.

And if that looking glass becomes broke,
Momma's gonna buy you a billy goat.

At first Diana felt glad that, once again, her mother had rescued her. Soon, however, this feeling changed. Driving the Cadillac, Diana began to feel increasingly uncomfortable. Indeed, on college streets dotted with bicycles and brightly painted compact cars, Diana's huge, black-finned sedan was very much out of place—just as she was. One day Diana burst into our session and sobbed, "I understand why I hate that Cadillac so much, why I can hardly breathe when I am in it. It is as if I am the chauffeur of my own hearse. . . . I believe I am dying."

Now, for the first time, Diana accepted the fact that she was being killed by her mother's solicitude, that each time she accepted her "care package" she died a little more. And this insight, painful as it was, moved Diana to make changes in her life. As she said, "I don't want to feel like a spoiled little rich girl driving around in Mommy's fancy car anymore." To my relief, Diana was getting ready to grow up. "And if that billy goat runs way," Momma, *mustn't* buy me another one someday."

It was not long after this shift that Diana suggested she invite Helene to meet with us. Diana, who had in a recent phone conversation already indicated to her mother the difficulty in their overly close relationship, wanted to explain in person why she would no longer welcome her mother's protection. Helene readily agreed to fly in for a meeting.

I took an immediate liking to Helene, who was a down-to-earth and open person. After we got through our introductions and some small talk, she began: "On the telephone last week, Diana told me that we're too close, that I do too much for her, that I am always rescuing her. I want both of you to know that it's not easy to admit that my love has hurt my daughter because my greatest wish has always been to make the children happy, never the opposite. On the plane trip out here, I did a lot of thinking, as you can well imagine. What I want to tell you is that I'm ready to change. If my past behavior toward Diana has made her life worse, I absolutely must change."

Diana accepted her mother's offer to change. The three of us then negotiated some conditions. Diana would commit herself to working at a part-time job—no matter how routine and undemanding. She would then be able to pay a portion of her expenses, including my fee, which I would lower to accommodate her small income. We also agreed that it was not feasible for Diana to be suddenly and completely cut off from her parents' support but that it was essential for her not to depend on it unconditionally or interminably; for example, Helene promised to continue tuition payments only as long as her daughter took her college work seriously. Finally, Diana and Helene contracted to limit their phone conversations to one or two per week. For her part, Helene left our session with the understanding that her own life would be changed by the elimination of Diana as the "problem" that absorbed her.

In a published letter to her own adolescent daughter, sociologist Jesse Barnard wrote that she was learning not to be a "spontaneous mother," who follows her impulses and jumps in with both feet to solve her child's problems. Rather, for her daughter's good, she was trying to keep her hands off and let her work things out herself. Helene, as well, could no longer be the spontaneous mother but was required to temper her maternal generosity. The spontaneous mother, contrary to what we have been taught, is not always the good mother.

Diana relinquished not only her mother's protective care but, after two more years of therapy, mine as well. From time to time, she calls or writes to me. She still struggles to control her mental illness but, more often than not, is a responsible, productive young woman. To my delight, one day I also received a long letter from Helene. She wrote that with the help of a supportive psychotherapist, she was making a good life for herself. Without Diana to preoccupy her, she was forced to fill the gaps in her life and was now involved in community service with wayward adolescents. Moreover, she and her husband were beginning to mend their own relationship, which had worn thin through years of neglect. In a postscript, she added,

> Before and during Diana's crisis, I was a professional mother. Diana and you forced me to change professions, and I am a better woman for this. Of course, I cannot say that life has become a bed of roses. Sometimes, I still ache for Diana and for the other troubled people I work with. But like my daughter, I am also growing up. I am learning to come to terms with a more realistic world. I am learning that mother love cannot shield children from pain and that the good and innocent are not spared suffering.

Helene's story reminds me of political activist Rose Chernin's more tragic one, as portrayed by her daughter Kim Chernin in the biography *In My Mother's House*. Rather than a psychological illness, Rose had to confront her daughter's catastrophic physical illness. At a time when treatment for cancer was still unsophisticated, she was told by a physician that her adolescent daughter was suffering from Hodgkin's disease: "I thought, he has given me my death sentence. I sat there and felt I was dying. Then I realized it was even more than that. I was going to lose Nina and survive!"[4] Like Helene, she felt that she had to do something to help her daughter: "It is your own child, she looks at you so reproachfully, as if you ought to be able to help. You feel that there must be something, there must be. But you can't find it. You sit there, you keep trying but you can't find the thing to do."[5]

Perhaps the most frustrating act of love is *not* to do something for the child in pain; perhaps the most disciplined act of love is simply *to be with* the suffering child. Sometimes the most loving maternal message is, "I know you are suffering a great deal, and even though I cannot make your unhappiness go away, I am here to listen to you tell me about it, if this is what you want to do." I have had the privilege of knowing one woman who was capable of such love. For days and nights Ann stayed by the bedside of her son, who was dying from AIDS. Instead of holding out to him the fraudulent promise of cure, she simply assured him that she would not draw away and that she was not afraid of his pain. When his tired, tortured body finally gave out, Ann was holding his hand.

I do not presume to compare my maternal experiences to those of Helene, Rose, or Ann; up until now I have been spared the great pains of mother love. But when my adolescent children experience the small pains of growing up, I have learned that it is best to offer them a listening ear rather than an instructive word. Having the opportunity to "unload" their sorrow seems to lighten it for them, and allowing myself to listen to it without necessarily solving it makes me lighter too. A verse from a poem by Rosalie Sorrels comes to mind:

> *What can I say, but that it's not easy?*
> *I cannot lift the stones out of your way,*
> *And I can't cry your bitter tears for you.*
> *I would if I could, what can I say?*[6]

---

6. Excerpt in Tillie Olsen, *Mother to Daughter, Daughter to Mother* (London: Virago Press, 1983), p. 12. Copyright © 1974 by Rosalie Sorrels. All rights administered by Music Management, P.O. Box 174, Pleasantville, NY 10570. Used by permission.

The great task for mothers of adolescents is to disengage over time from their daughters' lives and to be born into their own. Despite their maternal crises, neither Helene nor Rose withdrew from the world. Helene involved herself in community service, and many months after her daughter's death Rose resumed her political activities:

"Nina's death could not be altered. But there was still so much in the world that needed changing. . . . Nina was dead. But the world continued and I had to go on with it. . . . I could have died then, I could have killed myself, but I didn't. I went into the struggle. I went back into life. . . ."[7]

Nor did they sever the ties with their daughters: Helene noted that sometimes her heart still ached for Diana, and Rose remarked, "We had no time to get used to the idea she was dying. I have not got used to it yet. Thirty years have passed and the idea still haunts me."[8] Yet both women eventually separated themselves from their daughters' lives sufficiently to lead their own full ones.

Although for most mothers of adolescent daughters separations are difficult, they are especially hard for mothers of troubled adolescent girls. I have noticed that when their daughters are in crisis, some women suddenly lose all sense of boundary and merge with them. One particular clinical case illustrates the difficulties that such a merger may present.

Lena, a corporate executive and the mother of a sixteen-year-old girl, was in therapy to explore the reasons for the collapse of her marriage and the possibilities of her new single life. A woman who rarely asked for help, Lena was remarkably controlled and composed. Therefore, I was taken aback when she called for an emergency appointment. She came to our session in tears and between great sobs talked about shoplifting and about being arrested and humiliated by the police. Her story made no sense to me: How could it be that this high-functioning, upstanding woman was stealing lipsticks and earrings from a department store? Had I misjudged her so badly?

It was only after many minutes had passed that I realized Lena was talking about her adolescent daughter, not about herself. She had identified with her daughter Lilly's recent experience to such an extent that neither she—nor I—could tell who was who: Lilly's crime became Lena's. Over and over, Lena lamented, "Why did this awful thing happen to *me*?" and "What will people think of *me*?" This mother's overidentification with her daughter had two negative effects. On the one hand, Lena—ashamed, humiliated, and self-blaming—suffered for a crime she did not commit on the other, preoccupied with her own emotions, she could not offer Lilly appropriate maternal guidance.

As is the case for so many mothers, Lena believed that others held her accountable for her daughter's behavior; Lilly's shortcomings then became public testimony of Lena's shortcomings. I do not think that Lena's assumptions were unusual. From the time they first bring their babies home from the hospital, most mothers are plagued by thoughts that they are solely responsible for their child's adjustment in the world and that others are judging them by this adjustment. (Indeed, each time I am called to my children's schools for conferences I wait apprehensively for the verdict of my innocence or guilt as a mother: "Mrs. Bassoff, you have obviously done a splendid job raising this wonderful child," or "Your child seems to be having some serious problems. Tell me, what is going on at home?") Bearing responsibility for all her daughter's actions, Lena naturally blamed herself for the the shoplifting; it was *her* crime, evidence of *her* failure as a good mother, and good enough cause for the imagined public outcry against her.

Overwhelmed by feelings of humiliation, Lena could not for quite some time focus on the meaning the shoplifting and consequent arrest held for her daughter. She could not appreciate how different her daughter's emotional experience was from her own. For example, Lena told me that the night after the incident, she was unable to get any rest. Assuming that Lilly must be awake, she went into her bedroom only to find the girl sleeping peacefully. Standing watch over her sleeping daughter, Lena wondered, "How could this be? How can Lilly be fast asleep when I'm a bundle of nerves?"

The psychiatrist Heinz Kohut has pointed out the destructive potential of the mother who fails to demarcate her emotional experience from that of her child. Absorbed by her own tensions and moods, she may impose these on her daughter's experience—infect it, if you will, with her own anxiety. Similarly, she may be overly responsive to the emotions in the child that correspond to her own while neglecting those that do not. Although such a mother may appear to be concerned and involved with her troubled child, she is not attuned to her, and her faulty maternal perceptions may lead to inappropriate maternal responses. This seemed to be true of Lena.

Lena's therapeutic tasks were fourfold: to relinquish the belief that she was accountable for her daughter's behavior; to differentiate her experience from that of her daughter; to understand the meaning of her own experience; and to find appropriate ways to respond to her troubled daughter. Lilly's wrongdoing unloosed for Lena feelings of inadequacy and shame, which she had previously covered up. Now, for the first time, she was able to acknowledge how important it was that others found no flaws in her and how hard she had to work to present a perfect image of an upstanding and correct woman, a perfect mother with a perfect child. She had believed that others would scorn and humiliate her if they were privy to her human inadequacies or to those of her daughter, whom she saw as an extension of herself.

My suspicion is, although I never met Lilly, that by shoplifting she was in one way colluding with her mother's unlived or repressed side—the "bad girl" who was kept under raps by the "good girl" and was never given the chance to cause a ruckus. At her own considerable expense, Lilly gave her upstanding mother the opportunity to express herself vicariously. Rather than despise her darker side, Lena, through therapy, learned to accept it with a certain compassion and good humor. It has been my experience that when a woman welcomes her feelings—even the embarrassing or nasty ones—instead of locking them away in a dark secret place, they become much more cooperative. They no longer pounce on her unexpectedly or misbehave to get attention or intrude upon relationships when they should not. Knowing they are recognized, they have no further need to tyrannize her.

I often tell my new clients that they might conceive of psychotherapy as a grand dinner party to which they are to invite all the feelings that inhabit their inner worlds. Each of these feelings must be treated hospitably, as a hostess treats a guest; each deserves to be attended to. I remind my clients of the fairy tale "Sleeping Beauty" in which the king and queen's decision to exclude from their feast the thirteenth fairy caused her to act in an outrageously destructive manner, and I implore them not to shut out even one "guest" from their "party."

As Lena became more aware and accepting of her own feelings, she also became more respectful of her daughter's individuality and could better appreciate their similarities *and* differences. Her boundaries, which had been blurred, were now more clearly drawn. "Owning" her feelings, she no longer burdened her daughter with them.

As it turned out, Lena learned that Lilly's shoplifting had not been an isolated incident. Indeed, the young girl was in the habit of stealing. Once Lena was able to disidentify from her daughter, she responded in an appropriately parental way by setting the limits, providing the emotional support, and securing the psychological help Lilly required. Moreover, it was my impression that as she learned to accept her own demons, she was also more tolerant of Lilly's flaws. No longer ashamed of her daughter, she was able to say to me, "Lilly is just a lovable girl who happens to have serious problems." The hard service of mothering a troubled teen-ager is somewhat softened by tolerance.

Misperceiving the troubled child, as Lena did at first, may lead to faulty maternal responses. With an inaccurate under-standing of the adolescent's problem, the mother will not be in a position to guide her. I do not want to imply, however, that it is desirable for a mother to insist on fully understanding her troubled daughter's inner world. If they are to separate from one another, mother and daughter must keep many of their experiences from each other. The truly empathic mother will respect her daughter's right to privacy; the empathic maternal response may be *not* to know rather than to know the child.

Understandably, the mother of an adolescent in crisis, in an effort to protect her from more pain, may feel compelled to find out exactly what is going on with her, to know what she is doing and even what she is thinking. I cannot say when appropriate concern becomes unwelcome intrusive-ness, only that there is a fine line between the two that must not be crossed and that discovering this line is one of the arts of good mothering. Those who are too quick to interfere in their daughters' lives might benefit from the wisdom of the Jungian writer Irene Claremont de Castillejo:

Parents . . . tend to see the defects and to believe they know the complexes of their children; but if they are wise they will remember that they do *not* know the innermost truth of their children's souls. We do *not* know the destiny to which another has been born. We do not know where he is to rebel, which mistakes he is to make. Perhaps some idiosyncracy or some failure to fit into society may be that child's particular contribution to the world, which should not be cured but fostered.

We may see the mistakes of the young but if we are wise we must also learn to be blind; to know and yet *not* to know is one of the paradoxical secrets of relationships.[9]

An unhappy adolescent girl may create in her mother a great urgency not only to know everything that is going on with the girl but to fix what is wrong in her. Certainly there are adolescent crises that demand decisive parental activity, and the mother who does not move quickly to secure professional help for a daughter who is endangering her own or other people's safety is negligent. It may be, however, that we, members of a society that overvalues "taking action," sometimes intervene where we should not. We seem intent on dissecting, analyzing, and reconstructing our children's lives. I suspect that our Western culture's emphasis on *doing*, encourages many mothers to intrude unnecessarily in their daughters' lives. I suspect as well that we are too eager to find adolescent pathology where none exists.

D. T. Suzuki, the Zen master, once contrasted the action-oriented view of the Western world with the more contemplative one of the Eastern world through the interpretations of two poems. The first, by the Romantic English poet Tennyson, reads:

> *Flower in the crannied wall*
> *I pluck you out of the crannies;—*
> *Hold you here, root and all, in my hand.*
> *Little Flower—but if I could understand*
> *What you are, root and all, and all in all*
> *I should know what God and man is.*

The second, a seventeenth-century verse by the Japanese poet Basho reads:

> *When I look carefully*
> *I see the* nazuna *blooming*
> *By the hedge!*

Although the Eastern poet contemplates the *nazuna* and lets it be, the Western poet insists on an active relationship with the little flower: He plucks it out of its sheltered growing place to analyze it "root and all," to *use* it to enhance his own power of understanding. Unwittingly, through his attempts to know the little flower, he kills it. Basho's verse describes a tender, unobtrusive relationship between the poet and the *nazuna* plant. He does not wish to examine it, the way Tennyson must examine his little flower, but only to observe and delight in this living thing as it is.

Following Basho's way, we Westerners might do well to observe sometimes from a distance rather than to act impulsively to change what is. We might be able to help our troubled children pass through their pain by allowing them to experience it and by accepting these young people the way they are.

A short anecdote illustrates how one mother assumed a benign, nonintrusive relationship with her daughter. Millie, the mother of a restless, rebellious seventeen-year-old, explained her decision not to intervene in the following way: "Joan is a smart girl, but she's decided to drop out of high school. She just hasn't found a comfortable niche for herself yet. I know she's struggling through something hard, and I think it's best for me not to interfere with this struggle. Of course, I would feel relieved if she agreed to see a counselor, but she doesn't want to and since she's not doing anything dangerous, I won't force her. Joan wants time and space to figure things out for herself. This is her way, and who is to say that it is wrong?" Millie, it seems to me, is exceptional in her ability not to presume that she must fix her daughter's life; in similar situations other mothers might blame themselves for their daughter's unhappiness and set out to reverse it against her wishes.

The ideal of the good mother who should always heal her child's wounds has another corollary that I would like to elaborate upon: The notion that the good mother should tolerate any and all of her unhappy daughter's behavior— even when this behavior is abusive, even when the mother is made the daughter's whipping post.

When I asked one of my clients, an intelligent, highly

educated woman, why she allowed her daughter to shout abuses at her, she answered that perhaps this was the "healthiest" way for the girl to express her anger. This woman believed that the child was healing herself by hurting her mother and that it was her maternal obligation to be used in this way. Another client, the parent of a fourteen-year-old girl who was using drugs heavily and stealing from her parents' bank account to pay for them, reported that when her daughter flung obscenities at her or pushed her around, she responded by turning the other cheek. This misguided woman did not acknowledge that her passive mothering was damaging her child and eroding her own dignity; on the contrary, she thought of herself as almost saintly, saying, "I suppose my only fault is that I'm too good to my daughter."

The assumption that the "good mother" accepts outrageous behavior from her child is taken to its extreme in the poem, "The Severed Heart" by Jean Richepin, translated by the Spaniard J. Echegary, winner of the Nobel Prize for Literature in 1904.

> *There was a young man loved a maid*
> *Who taunted him, "Are you afraid,"*
> *She asked, "to bring me today*
> *Your mother's head upon a tray?"*
>
> *He went and slew his mother dead*
> *Tore from her breast her heart so red*
> *Then towards his lady love he raced*
> *But tripped and fell in all his haste.*
>
> *As the heart rolled on the ground*
> *It gave forth a plaintive sound.*
> *And it spoke, in accents mild:*
> *"Did you hurt yourself, my child?"*

In a very interesting paper, professors of psychiatry Henry Harbin and Denis Madden, who have extensively studied battering adolescents, maintain that inevitably one or both parents of the abusive child have abdicated the parental, or executive, role. They report that most of these parents shy away from being in charge and turn over their parental power to the adolescent child, who is too immature to assume it. The child may consequently manifest a grandiose sense of self along with an inflated sense of entitlement and try to bend the weak parent to her will. Or, in a frustrated attempt to punish the parent for being ineffective, the child may become increasingly abusive to her.[10]

One of the dearly held beliefs about the good mother is that she is always gentle, never powerful. It may be the fear of assuming legitimate power that holds women back from being appropriately parental—setting limits, enforcing rules—with their misbehaving adolescents. Yet every adolescent daughter wants her mother to be strong. I am in full agreement with poet and author Adrienne Rich's assertion: "A mother's victimization does not merely humiliate her, it mutilates the daughter who watches her for clues as to what it means to be a woman. Like the traditional foot-bound Chinese woman, she passes on her own affliction. The mother's self-hatred and low expectations are the binding-rags for the psyche of the daughter."[11] Moreover, no guilt is heavier than that incurred by the daughter who has lashed out at and further weakened her mother. The adolescent daughter who prods and pushes and provokes her mother is asking her to be firm: to stand up to her, to refuse to be exploited by her. She is offering her the opportunity to become the self-respecting, commanding woman whom she wishes to emulate. Should the mother fail to assume her rightful authority, she betrays both herself and her daughter.

The woman who is really a good mother, rather than the idealized version of the good mother, is one who does not have an inflated view of her maternal rights or powers and, even in the face of her children's great pains, can stand back to allow them to lay claim to their own lives. Moreover, she is a woman who, because she respects all life, including her own, will not tolerate verbal or physical violence against others or herself.

The good mother is also a woman who takes *reasonable* responsibility—without indulging in excessive guilt or self-recriminations—for her maternal failings and does not shirk from their effects. "Is there any stab as deep as wondering where and how much you failed those you loved?" Florida Scott-Maxwell wrote in her diary.[12] To this let me add, is there any balm as healing as taking *reasonable* responsibility for one's failures?

Several years ago, I counseled a girl who had just attempted suicide. During the course of therapy, it became clear that an early abandonment by her mother had contributed to the girl's depression. When Dawn was just five, she was left with her father for two years so that Judith could pursue graduate studies out-of-state. One can assume that Judith's abrupt leave-taking precipitated a sense of overwhelming loss for the child who suddenly felt motherless. Little Dawn could not, of course, appreciate her mother's reasons for going away—the young woman's desperation to break out of a stifling domestic life that was strangling her vitality; her frantic fear that unless she found a way to satisfy her cravings for intellectual stimulation, she would die inside. No doubt, all the little girl could understand was the pain of longing for Mother and the feeling of being unsafe without her. Sixteen-year-old Dawn swallowed fifty aspirin after her boyfriend broke up with her. The sudden ending of a love relationship, which for every teenager is a deep wounding, nearly became a fatal event for Dawn because it reawakened the unbearable sensations associated with her mother's abandonment years before.

After meeting several times with Dawn and Judith, I was convinced neither had come to terms with the effects of their premature separation and that until they did neither could be at peace with herself or with the other. What was required of Dawn in therapy was finally to release the tremendous store of rage she held against the mother who had left her. What was required of me was the skill to help Dawn let loose this rage in a safe and nonabusive way. What was required of Judith was the strength to face, without excuses or distortions of the truth or an indulgent guilt, her early maternal failing and make a long overdue apology to her daughter. Accomplishing these tasks, I was confident that Dawn and Judith could begin to mend their relationship. And, in fact, this is what happened. As Judith opened herself to her daughter's anger and apologized for having abandoned the five-year-old child who had trusted and depended on her, a great burden no longer strained their relationship. Eventually, through their individual therapies, each would also find a new inner peace. As psychoanalyst Alice Miller explains, mothers who acknowledge their maternal wrongdoings to their mature children help them "to live not *against* but *with* their past"[13]—and I strongly suspect that these mothers themselves learn to do the same.

Mothering requires mourning. As she watches her daughter grow up, each mother also looks back on the childhood years, which cannot be relived. If she does not deny painful realities, she knows that, despite all her good intentions, at times she was unfair to her daughter, and that it is too late for these injustices to be undone. This, however, is no cause for despair. One has to experience failure as well as success for one's life to be whole. In fact, failure, not perfection, motivates us to grow and change. Like Judith, the women who come to accept their mistakes and their failures, moreover, are better able to accept those of their daughters.

Separations, always difficult for mothers of teenage girls, are especially difficult when the girls are emotionally troubled. Yet these separations can promote a woman's growth by forcing her to replace the unworkable and naive notion that mother love is all-powerful or all-accepting with more realistic expectations. As she casts aside the inflated Victorian stereotype of the godlike mother, a woman has the chance to become a down-to-earth good mother as well as a more knowing human being. Relinquishing false or illusory maternal power, however, is not equivalent to assuming a posture of maternal helplessness or weakness as is the tendency of abused mothers. The mothers whose stories I have related, particularly Helene and Lena, became stronger people as a result of their separation struggles. As they turned their daughters' lives back to them, these women took more responsibility for their own.

Although they pretend to be strong, individuals who are domineering and fight against relinquishing control of others tend to be insecure. In order to ward off the catastrophes that they experience as imminent, they insist on controlling everything and everyone. Releasing the adolescent daughter, especially the troubled one, to her own life necessitates a growing self-confidence and confidence in the world on the part of the mother. She is required to develop the trust that her daughter will find her own way in the world. The most generous gift of maternal love may be the messages: "Mother has trust in your ability to live your life well" and "Mother has faith in your ability to cope with the troubles that come your way." In my experience, such messages are often self-fulfilling prophecies. And sending such messages often helps the daughter behave in ways that make trusting her easy to do.

Earlier in this chapter, I explained how the lullaby "The Mockingbird" reflects the spontaneous wish of most parents to protect their children against life's small and great tragedies. Now another song, "Scarlet Ribbons," which I sang to my little daughter at her bedtimes, keeps playing in my head. In this song, a mother overhears her daughter praying at bedtime for scarlet ribbons for her hair. Because it is very late and the village stores are closed, the mother cannot find a way to buy these ribbons for her daughter. Throughout the night, she aches in anticipation of the young girl's disappointment, but, just before the break of dawn, she peeks into her daughter's room and, to her wonderment, discovers a gay profusion of lovely scarlet ribbons lying at the foot of her daughter's bed. The sweet lyrics reassure me that daughters are not as dependent on their mothers as we mothers sometimes think. In their own way (a way that may remain mysterious to us), they reach out to take from the universe what they need.

5

Momma's Body, Momma's Food:

Eating Disorders*

MOTHER LOVE BEGINS WITH THE GIVING OF food. Nuzzling in Mother's arms, taking in her body and warm milk, the newborn daughter first tastes the closeness of human relationship. From infancy through childhood and adolescence, she will be succored, soothed, and sustained by the food Mother offers. Indeed, Mother's protective love and her food may be indistinguishable from one another: The darling daughter is mother's "honey" . . . "sugar" . . . "sweetie pie" . . . "dumpling" . . . "pumpkin" . . . and "apple of my eye." If, as she approaches womanhood, this daughter rejects mother's love-food by starving herself or vomiting it up, we must ask about their relationship: "What is going wrong *between* mother and daughter? What is the starving girl hungering after? What is she communicating to mother through her illness?"

---

*I am grateful to the graduate students in the spring 1987 seminar in counseling at the University of Colorado, whose ideas about anorexia and bulimia stimulated many of my own.

Rather than perpetuating the tradition of blaming mother for the daughter's affliction, we will do best by understanding the mutual victimization of mother and starving daughter. More than other mental illnesses, the eating disorders seem to express the shared despair of women, which is passed from mother to daughter to mother.

As early as the seventeenth century, doctors had documented what were then rare cases of self-starvation or anorexia nervosa; today cases of anorexia nervosa (also called anorexia) and the related illness bulimia nervosa (or bulimia) have increased at such an alarming rate among Western women, especially adolescents, that clinicians suggest an epidemic. A heavy-set nineteen-year-old client recently told me, "If this new diet doesn't work, I guess I'll try bulimia." At the dinner table last night my daughter casually mentioned that several of her friends would like to have "the guts" to become anorexic. A graduate student of mine, who titled her research paper "Today's College Women: Daughters of the First Generation of Weight Watchers," provided evidence that over 20 percent of college girls are bulimic. In *The New York Times*, I came across a study of nearly 500 San Francisco school children, which found that almost 50 percent of the nine-year-old girls and 80 percent of the ten-and eleven-year-old girls were on diets.[1]

The anorexic girl may consciously refuse to eat or may alternate long periods of starvation with episodes of binging and purging. Obsessively—through diet and exercise—she pursues thinness, often to the point of emaciation. Starved, malnourished, sometimes skeletal in appearance, this young woman, believing that she is enviably and exquisitely thin, responds with an air of indifference to those who beseech her to eat. Addicted to the intoxicating highs of her fast, she lives in a dream world and, unencumbered by weight, experiences the illusion of exhilarating freedom and, for a time, limitless energy. "I felt so powerful when I did not eat—so *deliciously* in control," a young woman recovering from anorexia told me. "Like some supernatural being, I could live on air. And, even better, by virtue of my self-imposed starvation, I was defying everyone—even Mother Nature herself."

The bulimic girl, who is more implusive and more guilt-ridden than her anorexic counterpart, replaces self-starvation with overeating and purging. She gorges herself, then induces vomiting or uses laxatives to rid herself of the massive amounts of food gobbled down in shame and disgust. "I am up to 44 laxatives a day," a college girl whispered to a counselor-in-training, who is a student of mine, during an initial psychiatric interview.

But anorexia and bulimia are two forms of defense against the same terrible and overriding fear of fatness and consequently of womanliness. Fatness (softness, fullness, roundness) and womanliness are, after all, inseparable. Indeed, the female body must accumulate a critical level of fat before it can carry out its mature function of reproduction, which is announced by the menarche and affirmed each month by menstrual bleeding. The young girl with an eating disorder has a phobic fear of her own developing femaleness: She is afraid of the woman she is becoming. By starving herself, she engages in a desperate struggle—sometimes to the death—against the adult female body that is "consuming" her: the body she has inherited from Mother.

Recently, I spent an hour in session with the parents of a girl who does not eat. They explained that Joyce had been a wonderfully charming child—talented, bright, the apple of their eye—but was now uncommunicative, perfectionistic, driven, and, paradoxically, preoccupied with food while she starved herself. They told me, for example, that she had spent all of a Sunday preparing an elaborate meal for the family, watched them as they ate, then slipped into the kitchen to take for herself one leaf of lettuce dipped in mayonnaise and bounded away for a six-mile run to burn off the meager calories she had allowed herself.

A few days after the session with her parents, I met with Joyce. On first impression, she looked to me like a little bird, so small and delicate, but, at the same time, she seemed removed, unapproachable, even forbidding. Her eyes darted from contact with mine so that, in my disconnection from her, I became disoriented; we seemed to be floating in air together, never touching. I did not believe that she would ever allow me to know her or to affect her, but, from the start, I sensed that Joyce would affect me. I often learn important lessons about human nature from my most dysfunctional clients. Coming to understand Joyce's dramatic symptoms, I also became sensitive to the way they reflected our society's (and my own) hidden sickness. Just as the punk kids who shave their heads and mutilate their bodies are a symbol of the violence that is rampant in our lives, Joyce's self-starvation called attention to the emotional hunger endemic among today's women. The sentiments of Angelyn Spignesi, who writes about eating disorders from a Jungian perspective, seem especially fitting: "We are grateful, in a sense, for the symptoms of the starving woman and for the way they have refused to be stifled or cured. . . . They will not let go of her, and through her the culture. . . . There is something here demanding recognition."[2]

Some clinicians (I among them) suggest that the anorexic and bulimic girls' acts of self-abuse may be expressions of their mothers' covert feelings of worthlessness. The younger woman manifests physical symptoms for the older woman's psychological sickness—her low self-esteem and feelings of inferiority. While the older woman has learned to live out her suffering silently, her symptomatic daughter dramatically calls attention to woman's collective despair. By the extreme misuses of her body, the girl with an eating disorder unwittingly forces all women to reexamine their own feelings about their bodies.

It has always been through her body—her surest, sometimes only, tool of power—that woman has negotiated the world. Whereas a man typically derives his sense of well-being from his accomplishments, a woman's self-esteem—even in today's consciousness-raised world—depends in great part on her feelings of physical attractiveness. But the development of a positive body image is extremely problematic for contemporary women. Since the 1960's the cultural standard to which they have tried to conform has been one of thinness—a thinness so remarkable that it is, more often than not, outside their reach.

Nuzzling her newborn daughter in her arms, offering her body along with her warm milk, the woman who became a mother in the sixties or seventies may very well have been on her first serious diet. Perhaps, too, she was already restricting her daughter's eating to spare her from fatness. Influenced by models in fashion magazines and on television commercials, who were flaunting long-legged, small-breasted slimness, she was no doubt learning to despise her new ample, soft, voluptuous Mother's body. This young mother had two possible courses to follow: to resign herself to her normal motherly but clearly devalued form or to force it to meet the cultural standard of ultra thinness.

Most women chose (and are still choosing) the latter course. But despite promises made to them by the diet and fitness industries and despite their own heroic efforts to lose weight, they failed (and continue to fail) to achieve the sleek, designer bodies so valued in the marketplace. And with these failures, women have come to hate their bodies. It comes as no surprise that researchers who conducted a survey on body image for *Glamour* magazine reported that close to 90 percent of the young women who responded thought their mothers disliked their own bodies. Just as middle-aged women have learned self-contempt, their adolescent daughters, similarly influenced by the powerful messages of the media, may devalue their mothers' appearance and, in fact, become afraid of taking after them.

My client Claire, an attractive, plump woman in her early forties, noticed that eleven-year-old Sara, who was beginning to mature physically, left the dinner table each night without touching her plate. She had lost the roses from her cheeks, seemed tired and was prone to all sorts of infections, but the family physician could find no medical explanation for her failure to thrive. Worried and confused, Claire went to her child after dinner and, once again, asked her why she was eating so poorly. At first the girl turned away from her mother, insisting with her usual impatience that she was eating well. But Claire demanded a more truthful answer. Bursting into tears, the girl cried out, "Don't you see, Mom, I'm not eating because I don't want to grow up to look like you."

The smiling, skinny girls in tight jeans and tank tops who flit across television screens or peer out from the pages of fashion magazines sell an insidious message along with their products: "Life is fun and exciting only for those who look like us." How could Sara love her Mother's body—the pattern for her own—when it suggested limited chances for happiness?

Not uncommonly, a daughter is discouraged from loving her mother's body by the mother herself. I attended a dinner party some months ago where I met the mother of one of my daughter's classmates. As we chatted about our girls, this woman, who has a stocky build, sighed, "I pray each day that my daughter hasn't inherited my fat, ugly body; you can fix a crooked nose with a surgeon's knife, change eyes from gray to violet with colored lenses, but there's nothing to be done with a big body." The woman who dislikes her body necessarily influences the daughter to do the same and becomes an anti-model by teaching this daughter to be unlike her. Like the media's sleek models, she too conveys the message to her daughter that the chosen ones are thin, while adding another: "Don't—whatever you do—turn out like me."

Yet every daughter wishes and needs to admire her mother. Devaluing Mother inevitably damages the daughter's sense of well-being. Contrasting with Sara's rejection of Claire, writer Adele Wiseman portrays a more fortunate daughter's admiration of her mother—before society has had the chance to invalidate it:

I must be very young; my mother is still singing, all the time. I am the third of four living children, but at this moment we are alone. I play beside her on the couch while she dusts the sunroom windowsills. There are five round-arched windows. The woodwork is tawny, red gold. When my Mother sings the neighbor comes out of his house and into our yard and stretches himself out on the lawn. I gaze at her fine, pink face, glowing in the window light. Her dark hair has small, tight tight waves. They glow in the light. Everything glows. I am aglow with the rapture of the revelation that she is the most beautiful in the whole world, my mother. I am too young to ask, "Why me? How come I am chosen?" I belong to what is given. It is an intensely aesthetic pleasure, experienced, thank goodness, before the pinched and crabbed world with its penny-ruler measurements interposed its decrees that her nose is too long, her eyes too deeply set, baffling the child's intuitive perceptions, my unerring love.[3]

I am not suggesting that the daughter idealize mother. As healthy little girls grow up, they learn to love their mothers as human beings rather than as models of perfection. I am suggesting, however, that when mother and daughter devalue the mother, they forfeit what psychotherapist and researcher Susan Rosewell-Jackson calls the sense of "female continuousness" that allows them to delight in each other and consequently in themselves. "I think my life began with waking up and loving my mother's face," Mirah says in George Eliot's *Daniel Deronda*.

Unlike the healthier daughter who takes in her mother's body and gladly identifies with it, the anorexic daughter rejects it outright. Reactively, she cultivates her ultra-thin, anti-mother body, seemingly in compliance with our culture's mandates. Yet, by carrying the feminine ideal of thinness to a grotesque extreme, she makes a mockery of these standards of beauty. Like Victor Frankenstein's monster, she is the idea of her inventors—the geniuses of the diet/fitness/fashion industries—gone out of control. "Look," her body speaks, "I am even better than you thought possible: bonier, flatter, lighter, more boyish—hardly woman at all." As she flaunts her sad little body, the anorexic daughter moves all women to question the values that they have accepted too easily. She moves them to ask, "Isn't the compulsion to achieve slimness out of control for me, too?" It is easy for us to condemn the old Chinese tradition of binding the young girl's feet in the name of beauty, until they became too atrophied to support her. But it is harder to reject our culture's pressures to subject women to diet after diet, to programs of obsessive exercise, even to surgery—in the name of beauty.

Three times a week I swim laps in a local indoor pool. I do so in part for enjoyment but mostly to "stay in shape." After a session with Joyce, my anorexic client, I automatically headed for the pool. But because the day was clear and balmy, I resented having to work out indoors. Then a simple idea came to me: "I *don't have to* work out." Letting go of my obsession, I did instead what I wanted; I took a lovely leisurely walk in the sunshine— not in the name of shapeliness but rather in the name of well-being. Without being aware of it, my young client had changed me.

The anorexic girl's obsessions and preoccupations around dieting and exercising encourage all women to look with fully open eyes at their self-abusive ways and to reevaluate their unkind, often cruel relationship to their own bodies. In her book *Feeding the Hungry Heart*, Geneen Roth includes her client Rachel Lawrence's recollection of the frantic measures to lose weight that controlled the women in her family, the women whom she emulated. I am presenting an extended excerpt from this essay because it portrays with uncommon candor the sickness of dieting that grips countless women—mothers and daughters—and is often the forerunner of bulimia.

It will help you to understand if I tell you about my family. Every Sunday my family would gather at our

grandparents' farm for lunch. Grandmother would prepare large meals with the help of her two daughters,
Rosemary, my mother, and Linda, her sister. They
cooked luscious dinners Southern style. . . . The meal
was cooked and served by the three women and eaten
by the men and children. The women did not sit down
to dinner with us but stood in the back of the kitchen,
talking, eating furtively, waiting on us. They ate from
plates the size of cup saucers. . . .

On these Sundays I listened to a long progression of
new diets, from the three Oreo cookies a day, protein
only, carbohydrate only, grapefruit before every meal,
to my aunt's spit-out plan, her alternative to swallowing
excess calories. I assumed this was the way every woman
lived and ate. The alternative, they assured me, was
mounds of flesh on their bones. . . .

There were several doctors in my family, one of
whom staggered into the profitable sideline of helping
women lose weight. He began giving my mother and
Linda shots containing the urine of pregnant cows. This
would, he said, speed up their metabolism, and they
would lose weight rapidly. He cautioned them not to
exceed five hundred calories a day and to eat no sweets,
not even a stick of gum. The gum, he said, would set up
a craving for sugar. To maintain their weight they had to
stay on a low-calorie diet during the week, but on the
weekends they could eat anything and everything they
wanted. Many weekend nights my mother called to me
from the kitchen, pleading with me to help her stop
eating. She would yell, "I am devouring everything in
sight!" I thought then that she was kidding.

Her sister, my aunt, grew more anxious about main-
taining her appearance as time went by. She took me on
her rounds of drugstores, sending me in to pick up
prescriptions from suspicious druggists for diet pills,
laxatives, and enemas. I was only nine or ten, but I
understood her despair, her shame, and especially her

sense of need. She bought thousands of dollars' worth of clothing and cosmetics until her parents were forced to close out charge accounts and tear up credit cards. She became too thin, losing her luscious breasts and hips, by alternately starving and gorging herself, vomiting anything she ate for fear of becoming fat and therefore unwanted. In the height of her despair she lit cigarettes and burned holes in her skin to prove her ugliness.

I began to develop breasts and hips but stayed adolescent-thin; food was not a problem but a pleasure. I was determined to transcend the women in my family; I had paid close attention to their ongoing pain and frustration. . . . Yet, the confused feelings that accompany burgeoning womanhood, and the conflict between my personal desires and my family's obsessions overwhelmed me. My vital feeling about being a woman contrasted sharply with what I saw in life: the thwarted desires, smothered potentials and constricted, empty lives of the women around me. I withdrew and dove into food. In three weeks' time I had gained twenty pounds. My debutante "coming out" ball followed close on the heels of my sudden "fleshing out." I grew too fat for my dress. I habitually bought grocery sacks of food—Oreo cookies, Sara Lee brownies, Twinkies, Fritos—and stuffed them voraciously down my throat. I became panic stricken; I felt I was smothering. I read *Cosmopolitan*, diet guides, *Mademoiselle*, anything I could find that would tell me how to lose weight. I became determined to learn how to diet. I did learn, and learned so well that I then became terrified to stop. I dieted two years straight; two years of shutting down my sensory awareness. I tried not to smell food, taste food or be tempted by its color, texture or consistency. I tried to kill my needing or wanting *anything*. I felt dead; but I was thin—very, very thin.[4]

The abuse of the womanly body through fanatical dieting is often accompanied by an overvaluation of the male one, which is by nature angular, flat, and muscular. In *The Obsession: Reflections on the Tyranny of Slenderness,* Kim Chernin tells of the growing fascination of and wish to emulate a boy's beauty that accompanies the derogation of her own body.

> Now, I reverted to a fantasy about my body's transformation from this state of imperfection to a consummate loveliness, the flesh trimmed away, stomach flat, thighs like those of the adolescent runner on the back slopes of the fire trail, a boy of fifteen or sixteen, running along there one evening in a pair of red trunks, stripped to the waist, gleaming with sweat and suntan oil, his muscles stretching and relaxing, as if he'd been out there to model for me a vision of everything I was not and could never be. I don't know how many times this fantasy of transformation had occupied me before, but this time it ended with a sudden eruption of awareness, for I had observed the fact that the emotions which prompted it were a bitter contempt for the feminine nature of my own body. The sense of fullness and swelling, of curves and softness, the awareness of plenitude and abundance, which filled me with disgust and alarm, were actually the qualities of a woman's body.[5]

For the anorexic girl, maleness is associated with the power, strength, and freedom denied femaleness. By fanatically subjecting her body to grueling programs of exercise, by burning off every pound of fat so that she cannot grow breasts or fleshy hips or cannot menstruate, the starving adolescent strives to turn her body male. The bulimic girl too, by taking in great amounts of food and then violently expelling them, expresses the confusion of her identity as a woman; craving the food that symbolizes Mother in all her plenitude, she is at the same time repulsed by it.

Starving girls speak through their symptoms to tell us that being masculine in this culture is, after all, preferable to being feminine, and research on sex roles supports their conclusion. Study after study suggests that masculine women, who are competitive, assertive, ambitious, and forceful, are esteemed more than their gentle feminine sisters.[6] By rejecting her womanliness, the anorexic girl merely exaggerates—carries to grotesque extreme—the common belief that masculine characteristics are more valuable than feminine ones. Similarly, by binging and purging the bulimic girl reflects the discomfort that many contemporary women feel about their femininity. As Kim Chernin writes in *The Hungry Self: Women, Eating, and Identity*:

And so we leave home, we leave the apron and the sack dress behind, we put on blue collars and hard hats and tailored executive suits. We roll up our shirt-sleeves as the boys do and settle into work in their sphere, where certain qualities are admired, other traits abhorred. We are sensitive to these distinctions—newcomers always are. We keep our eyes open. Our ears take in the subtle communications a more secure person could afford to miss. And now we take ourselves in hand, tailoring ourselves to the specifications of this world we are so eager to enter. We strip our bodies of flesh, our hearts of overflow of feeling, our language of exuberant and dramatic imprecisions. We cut back the flight of fancy, make our thought rigorous and subject it (this marvelous rushing intuitive leaping capacity of ours) to measures of demonstration and proof, trying not to talk with our hands, trying hard to subdue our voices, getting our bursts of laughter under control.[7]

In many ways taking our places in the masculine world is exhilarating—in the energies it liberates, the opportunities it opens. But it has its costs. Allow me to digress and reflect on my own experiences. My mother is very feminine—soft, yielding, non-competitive. When I was a young woman I was determined not to become like her; I wanted instead to "make something of myself," to strive and achieve. But in my eagerness to avoid the traps of tradition that held her back, I abandoned her world absolutely. Along with Professor Higgins of *My Fair Lady* I thought a woman should be more like a man. My driven, on-the-run anorexic client Joyce makes me uneasy because she reminds me of myself; she, too, is alienated from her feminine spirit.

The feminine spirit is, above all, one of nourishment. It is not surprising that many of the vivid memories I have of the women who cared for me—my mother, my grandmother, my favorite aunt—take me back to their kitchens. I see my mother's love in the bowl of fresh strawberries and sour cream that she offered me the day I came home from summer camp sweaty, mosquito-bitten, tired. I feel my grandmother's nurture in the cup of homemade chicken soup (spirals of gold—"wedding rings," she called them—floating on top) that she fed me after the two of us ran home in a summer storm from the neighborhood movie house. I know my aunt's unstinting generosity in the assortment of desserts: *petits fours, strudels, sacher tortes* spread out each Sunday afternoon on a table that I decorated with a glass filled with flowers. As a little girl, I was pitifully thin, but the Viennese women in my family were sensuous, full-breasted, voluptuous presences. They seemed at home in their bodies and in their womanhood. They liked to prepare foods and to share them. We were not well off financially, but I remember that the refrigerator was always full. "*Ess,* dahlink, eat," they crooned as they savored the food placed before us.

My son and daughter do not know the delight of discovering on Sunday afternoons the table spread with assorted desserts. In our house on Sunday afternoons—as in many of today's homes—each has a project or activity; we grab a bite as we rush to do this or that. Of course, I would not want to give up my worldly ambitions and spend my life only in the service of others. I insisted on surpassing my mother's traditional life for good reasons, and it is to her credit that she did not try to hold me back. However, in empowering myself I have followed masculine models almost exclusively, unwittingly giving up the sensual delights and the *art* of my feminine heritage. I abandoned too easily the world of women, which succored, soothed, and sustained me, for the world of men, which challenges me, to be sure, but is sometimes a little too cold and too rational for my temperament. Although she is unaware of it, my client Joyce moves me to rediscover my feminine ties—the old world I left behind as I set out to discover the new one. The form such rediscovery may take remains unclear to me, but the task to develop valued feminine models of living for my daughter and me is compelling.

Through her symptoms, the girl with an eating disorder acts out the ideals of her culture: its idealization of slenderness, masculine beauty, and masculine power. However, anorexia and bulimia are more than responses to the demands of society at large. They are complicated syndromes with many tangled roots. It is precisely because they are the effect of many causes and the solutions to many problems that they are so tenacious, so resistant to cure. In some cases they are manifestations of the adolescent girl's inability to separate from her mother and to become a person in her own right.

At first glance, the anorexic girl appears to have mastered separation from her mother—with a vengeance. She does not want to look like her mother; she does not want her mother's food; she excuses herself from the family at mealtime; she may, in fact, leave the family realm completely to go off to Europe or to an out-of-state college, for example. But her emancipation is both forced and false. In fact, her attempt to live apart from her family—to wrench herself free from it—may precipitate the crisis of self-starvation. Although the seeds of their illnesses were planted before the actual leave-taking it is not uncommon for young girls to become anorexic or bulimic shortly after leaving home.

The anorexic girl's defiant tactics to separate from her

mother ultimately fail to transform their relationship just as the girl's extreme efforts to take charge of her body through dieting ultimately fail to provide her with any real sense of self-control. When we look closely at the anorexic girl, we are likely to find an adolescent who is afraid of relinquishing her early ties to her mother and who is very much out of control.

In those cases where the illness progresses, we witness her physical and emotional regression. She is not the independent, arrogant young woman she seems at first glance but rather a desperately frightened little girl who wants but does not know how to separate herself from Mother. Clinicians often remark how much younger than her years the anorexic patient looks. Suppressing menstruation as well as the development of secondary sex characteristics—breasts, hips, roundedness—through self-starvation, she has prevented her passage from girlhood to womanhood. The effects of starvation are a stunting of physical and emotional growth: as long as she does not become a woman, the anorexic girl continues as her mother's little daughter. In the worst cases, she may even regress to an infant-like state. Nurses who treat hospitalized anorexic girls report that they often find them curled up in the fetal position. Because they refuse to feed themselves, moreover, they must be fed—just as infants are fed.

In her way the bulimic girl too expresses the simultaneous wish for oneness with and separation from her mother. She takes in great amounts of food to soothe her emotional neediness, much as a babe finds comfort by taking in her mother's milk. But indulgence in such foods shames and disgusts her so that she is forced to expel the foods that symbolize Mother. Marion Woodman, who has written several books about eating disorders, reports that the foods typically injested during binges are cereals, sweets, and milk products. What strikes me is that these are the foods we feed babies, and I wonder if they are not somehow symbolic of the bulimic girl's yearning for early mothering. The connection between hunger for food and hunger for Mother is touchingly portrayed in an essay included in Roth's *Feeding the Hungry Heart*:

> My hunger has a name; it has a face, a personality of its own. My hunger is a child who lives inside me. I call my hunger Molly. Around her small body, I've grown longer, developed breasts, a woman's face. But she is the beginning. When I close my eyes, I see her clearly: she is five or six years old, thin and wraithlike. Her hair is brown, uncombed and stringy. Her mouth remains open, wanting, and her hands reach out, pleading. She cries one word, like a doll that you turn upside down, and this she repeats over and over. Mama. Mama.[8]

Psychotherapists offer many explanations for the failure of mother/daughter separation. Some maintain that women who as children were deprived of nurturant mothering continue to cling to their mothers in the hope of receiving their love; when the mother continues to disappoint them, they turn to food or drink as compensation. As one of my clients put it, "I need my mother's approval. When I don't get it, I eat a quart of Häagen-Dazs. Then, for a little while, I don't feel so empty inside."

Kim Chernin suggests that bulimic or anorexic young women sabotage their separation and differentiation from mother because they fear surpassing her, leaving her behind. Having more opportunity than Mother (as is the case for this new generation) and being able to accomplish more than Mother create feelings of debilitating guilt in the younger woman that lead to her pathological solution. The girl who becomes obsessed with food brings her development to a halt; she has no time to invest in classes or in career; the rituals of eating, fasting, and exercising occupy all her time and ensure that she will not surpass her mother's achievements.

My clinical experience supports Chernin's hypothesis. I have worked with many girls and women who suffer because they secretly believe that their successes in the world betray their mothers and are testimony to their mothers' failures. My young female clients, as well as those in middle-age, find many ways to hold themselves back in an effort to avoid the terror of transcending their mothers' lives. Eighteen-year-old Donna, the first woman in her family to go to college, became so obsessed with dieting and fitness that she had little time for studying; the hopes for her bright academic future dimmed as she sabotaged it. During our session, she told me that she felt out of place at college and would drop out. She was haunted by the fear that if she earned a degree, her mother would resent her and exclude her from the family. Another client, forty-three-year-old Edna, whose traditional mother was obese as well as agoraphobic, gained twenty unwanted pounds during the time she was interviewing for jobs in the corporate world. She told me about a dream she had: Her mother was lying in a crypt from which she beckoned to her with outstretched hand. As she took hold of the hand, it pulled her down. She tried to lift her mother from the crypt, but her heaviness made this impossible. Exhausted, Edna lay beside her mother.

The suffering of the anorexic or bulimic girl draws attention to the damage that an entangled mother/daughter relationship may precipitate. It is every mother's great task to encourage her daughter to move on—to grow apart—and to assure her that this movement is not a betrayal. There is no one right way for a woman to help her teenage daughter separate from and surpass her. Each mother, I am convinced, must find her own solutions.

In my own life, I am finding several opportunities to encourage my daughter's growth apart from and beyond me. Recently, sitting in the back seat of the family Toyota, I watched as my husband instructed Leah, who had just gotten her learner's permit, to operate the clutch and shift. Embarrassed as I am to admit it, I cannot drive a car with a standard transmission without rolling down the slightest incline or stalling at every second red light. But after just thirty minutes at the wheel, Leah could move smoothly from one gear to the next. Winking at her, my husband teased me about her easy handling of the car compared to my clumsiness. As my daughter turned back to look at me, I caught in her expression a hesitancy and discomfort. In that instant I knew she was wary about outdoing me. "Leah," I said emphatically, "I think it's absolutely terrific that you'll be a much better driver than me. I am so proud of you." Knowing I was sincere, her face lit up and she continued her lesson with admirable self-confidence. I, in turn, felt aglow and self-satisfied. I had given my daughter my blessing to pull ahead of me, and she had accepted it.

Unfortunately, when a woman believes that her life is unfulfilled and unlived, she may not have the capacity to take pleasure in her daughter's successes. One of the requirements of the proverbial "good mother" is that she sacrifice her own life for the sake of her children's well-being. Sadly, however, many women who carry out this mandate become embittered and envious rather than contented. Knowing they squander their precious talents, they find it too difficult to encourage their own daughters to make the most of theirs. Their daughters are a painful reminder to them of what they are giving up. Although these deprived mothers may borrow their daughters' achievements, the vicarious pleasure derived from these accomplishments is never enough.

Paradoxically, it is not the woman who sacrifices herself for another who is most capable of generous giving but rather the woman who joyfully lives in the present. Perhaps the greatest gift that women can give their daughters is to take precious care of their own lives—to develop their natural talents and to honor the opportunities that come their way. By so doing, they become vital models for their children as well as full women in their own right. Children need not feel guilty when they ask for themselves what their mothers feel deserving enough to take. The mothers of adolescents with eating disorders (but really the mothers of all adolescents) nourish their daughters most when they also nourish themselves. By filling themselves, they help their daughters do likewise.

Hiroka, an exquisitely beautiful and brilliant high school senior whom I treated several years ago, suddenly stopped eating after her application for admittance to an ivy league college was accepted. Within a month, her weight dropped to such a dangerously low level that I was forced to hospitalize her. I came to understand that Hiroka's wonderful opportunities wracked her with guilt because they brought into contrast her mother Natsu's bleak existence. Natsu, who grew up in Japan, felt ashamed that her English was not fluent; consequently, she rarely ventured out into American society. Cloistered in the family's cramped apartment, unstimulated and unchallenged, she succumbed to pathological depressions that, unlike normal depressions that lead to new growth, debilitated her.

I began meeting with Natsu and discovered that she was talented both as a water colorist and as a poet but had stopped painting and writing shortly after emigrating to the United States. It did not take much encouragement from me to persuade Natsu to pick up her brush and pen once more. Natsu astounded me with her lovely paintings and elegant haiku, blossoming with images of colored flowers. My appreciation prompted Natsu to introduce her work to the town's community of artists and poets, which responded enthusiastically. Not surprisingly, Natsu blossomed, much like her painted flowers, and as she did, her daughter recovered. At Hiroka's graduation, Natsu presented her with a water color of two full blooms on separate stems of the same plant—flowers growing apart but still a part of each other.

Natsu helped me understand, once again, that a mother's growing sense of selfhood is the ground from which the daughter's selfness emerges. More beautifully than anyone I know, Tillie Olsen, in her novel *Yonnondio*, elaborates this truth:

We'll set awhile. My head is balloony, balloony. Balloony." She staggered, put her arms around Mazie, sang:

O Shenandoah I love thy daughter
I'll bring her safe through stormy water

smiled so radiantly, Mazie's heart leapt. Arm in arm, they
sat down under the catalpa. That look was on her mother's
face again, her eyes so shining and remote. She began
stroking Mazie's hair in a kind of languor, a swoon. Gently
and absently she stroked.

Around the springs of gray my wild root weaves,
Traveler repose and dream among my leaves

her mother sang. A fragile old remembered comfort
streamed from the stroking fingers into Mazie, gathered to
some shy bliss that shone despairingly over suppurating
hurt and want and fear and shamings—the Harm of years.
River wind shimmered and burnished the bright grasses,
her mother's hand stroked, stroked. Young catalpa leaves
overhead quivered and glistened, bright reflected light
flowed over, "lumined" their faces. A bee rested on Mazie's
leg; magic!—flew away; and a butterfly wavered near,
settled, folded its wings, flew again.

I saw a ship sailing

her mother sang,

A sailing on the sea

Mazie felt the strange happiness in her mother's body,
happiness that had nought to do with them, with her;
happiness and farness and selfness.

I saw a ship a sailing
And on that ship was me.

The fingers stroked, spun a web, cocooned Mazie into
happiness and intactness and selfness. Soft wove the bliss

round hurt and fear and want and shame—the old worn fragile bliss, healing, transforming. Up from the grasses, from the earth, from the broad tree trunk at their back, latent life streamed and seeded. The air and self shone boundless. Absently, her mother stroked, stroked unfolding, wingedness, boundlessness. . . .[9]

It is by dreaming their dreams that women breathe magic into their daughters' worlds; it is by sailing their ships that they bring their daughters "safe through stormy weather." Out of the happiness that is born of their selfness, they are able to spin the cocoons—the second wombs—from which their daughters emerge intact, with selves of their own, and, like butterflies unfolding wings, take their own flight.

Earlier I remarked that the starving girl's acts of self-abuse are often overt expressions of the mother's covert feelings of worthlessness. Similarly—happily—the daughter's fullness is often an expression of the mother's, as the story of Hiroka and Natsu and the blissful moment shared by Mazie and her mother show. Another pair, Demeter and Persephone—who face many of the same difficulties that plague contemporary mothers and their starving daughters—illustrates how mother and daughter help feed each other through their individual growth. In Homer's "Hymn to Demeter," which I discussed at length in the second chapter, the terrible famine that starves the planet earth comes to an end only as both goddesses, each in her own way, move to higher stages of feminine development.

Docile and compliant Persephone, who insisted on a childlike relationship with her mother, is forced into womanhood by the abductor Hades. Much like her anorexic counterparts, she first resists growing up. Pulled into the underworld (which symbolizes the dark, inner world of the self), compelled to mourn for her lost maidenhood, Persephone succumbs to depression—a depression that ultimately transforms her from girl to queen. Previously nourished by her mother's love-food (remember that Demeter is the goddess of grain), she comes to accept a different kind of love-food: a man's love-food, represented in the myth by the red pomegranate seed. (Red is the color of blood—the blood spilled during the menstrual period and during the first sexual intercourse.) By taking the red food offered by Hades, Persephone accepts her status as an adult sexual woman—as every healthy maiden eventually does. Only after she has accepted her womanhood is she free to end the enforced separation from her mother. Similarly, the anorexic girl must gradually accept her womanhood, which will allow her to take nourishment from a lover or husband in the future. Moreover, it is when she is secure in her womanhood and sexuality that a daughter is best able to initiate a supportive, warm, spontaneous relationship with her mother.

Persephone's journey into the underworld forces Demeter's own transformation. When she is at last ready to grieve for the lost (exclusive) relationship with her daughter, Demeter has a magnificent temple built to which she retreats. In the symbolic language of the psyche, a temple signifies a woman's body. In her identity as mother goddess, Demeter did not celebrate her sensuality or sexuality. Similarly, in our times we split motherliness from sensuality and sexuality, as if these qualities are somehow incompatible. "The Madonna and the whore" idea expresses the artificial separation of feminine spirituality from the female body. But just as her daughter Persephone learns to accept her new womanliness, Demeter learns to honor her female body. And is not Demeter's task a task for mortal women as well? In her magnificent temple—in her body—Demeter heals herself, thereby ending the dreadful famine that starved the earth. Reunited with her own body, Demeter may reunite with Persephone. Their enforced separation comes to an end as each woman accepts her sensual, sexual femininity—her wonderful woman's body.

The woman who honors her body indirectly blesses her daughter's. She teaches the young girl that it is quite natural to love one's body and consequently to treat it with respect.

And it is not only the long-legged, small-breasted body that is lovable. One has only to visit an art museum to appreciate the infinite variety of female beauty. Modigliani celebrates the elongated oval form, Renoir the squat round one; Klimt's model is delicate and angular, Moore's massive and muscular. Certainly, we would do well not to judge beauty with "our penny ruler measurements," as Adele Wiseman put it.

But broadening the standard of feminine beauty is not enough. As long as women and men look upon the female body as an object or fetish to be admired or toyed with, they will continue to demean it. Anorexic and bulimic girls are able to torture their bodies because they have made *things* out of them; they have objectified themselves. Demeter's magnificent temple is so much more than the representation of body as object; it is also a repository of her feelings, emotions, sensuality, sexuality, and spirituality. It is where she goes to grieve and to be reborn; it is, as my psychologist friend Lee Moyer says, "her sacred precinct." Loving and honoring one's body goes beyond admiring its surfaces and requires, rather, a deep respect—even awe—for what Marion Woodman calls "this magnificent creation. . . . [our] greatest gift, pregnant with information . . . grief . . . and joy."

We mortal mothers can learn from the goddess Demeter. We have allowed others to dictate the worth of our bodies and have not stopped our daughters from doing the same; in the process our bodies become objects to others and to ourselves. It is time to live in our bodies fully, to make them our own, and to take pleasure in them. I recall, with great delight, a client of mine who had no trouble loving her body. Pointing to her large thighs, she exclaimed, "I guess some people would call them 'thunder thighs' but I love these legs of mine; they've taken me all over America, Europe, Asia; they've carried me to the peaks of the highest mountains. What more could I ask of them?" And I recall my favorite aunt's reply when as a young girl I despaired that I was not pretty enough, "But, Evi, every woman becomes beautiful when she is herself."

*   *   *

Angelyn Spignesi is right. We owe a debt of gratitude to the starving young girls who stubbornly refuse to go away. They force us to attend to problems we might otherwise ignore and challenge us to begin remedying these *in our own ways*. My client Joyce affected me. Her frenetic pace and drivenness reminded me that my own life was not in balance: As I marched to the quick rhythms of the good old boys' brass band, I stopped hearing the soft sounds of my mother's lullabies. I do not yet know how to achieve a perfect balance between masculine and feminine ways of being, but at least I can begin to test some possible solutions.

Tomorrow I have no appointments scheduled with clients, no university class to teach. I had planned to do some necessary revisions on the early chapters of this book, but I have changed my mind. Instead I will go to the butcher's to buy a fresh chicken and to the green grocer's for carrots, celery, onions, and fresh dill. Strawberries are very expensive this time of year, but since my daughter loves strawberries, I will surprise her with a pint. In this town there is a European bakery that makes lovely cakes and tarts; I will buy some for me and my family to share and set them out on the kitchen table, which I will decorate with a glass of flowers from the garden (the newly sprouted daffodils and tulips which, in my busyness, I had failed to notice and delight in). In the afternoon, I will invite my son and daughter to make chicken soup with me; maybe, just maybe, they will have the time and inclination.

The day after tomorrow I will return to the word processor, my manuscript, my professional responsibilities—a little more nourished, a little more in balance.

6

Stirring the Oatmeal:

Mothers as Wives

IN ADOLESCENCE LOVE OFTEN BUDS. IN MIDLIFE—
for the fortunate ones—it blooms. Sadly, current divorce
rates show that love between men and women does not
grow profusely in today's America. Frequently, married
love dies before reaching full maturity so that it is, as D. H.
Lawrence wrote, an arrest of spring in which May does not
dissolve into June, the hawthorn petal does not fall for the
berrying.

By anticipating death in the process of budding, many of
my adolescent clients have become cynical about heterosexual love. To ward off the disappointment they believe is
inevitable, these young people reject feelings of tender love.
A girl of nineteen, who is in treatment to work through her
parents' divorce, told me that she did not want to become
involved in a meaningful relationship with a boy because it
could end only badly. On the graffiti-covered walls of the
ladies' rooms on campus, I see, instead of the traditional
Cupid's hearts that frame young lovers' initials, denunciations of heterosexual love: "Trust no man, not even a

brother/If women must love, let them love one another";
and "A woman needs a man about as much as a fish needs a
bicycle." For many teenagers, beneath the appearance of
social openness—easy friendships and casual sex—is a bed-
rock of mistrust. The Simon and Garfunkle song "I Am a
Rock," written for a generation of flower children, plays well
for its progeny—the many young people who build their
walls and fortresses so deep and mighty that none can pene-
trate them and who, like rocks, harden themselves against
the pain of love.

Hurt and confused by their troubled or failed marriages,
many of my adult female clients are as wary of heterosexual
relationships as are their daughters. Not so long ago, these
women thought they knew what love and marriage promise,
but now they are unsure. Nevertheless, most still want to
believe that it is possible for love between men and women
to grow over time, for their daughters to develop enduring
relationships that will enhance rather than diminish them.
They want to be able to guide them toward loving relationships and, in many cases, to find such paths for themselves.
What women often ask of me and what I hope to provide in
this chapter through the interpretation of clinical, personal,
and literary examples are ways to understand married love
and to nurture its growth—even in a hard and rocky climate.

Marriages seem particularly vulnerable to breakdown during those stressful years when one's children are passing
through adolescence. Difficulties that were glossed over in
calmer times may now surface and even explode. Yet, a
marital crisis does not have to doom a relationship. It can
also cause a couple to grow—to move from one plateau to
another.

Jungian writer Robert A. Johnson describes a story that
illustrates how growth sometimes comes about only as a
result of painful jolts: When the first elephant was born into
captivity, the other elephants in the compound tossed it
from one to another. The zookeeper was horrified because
he thought they were killing the baby, but they were only

making it breathe so that it would live and thrive. At each stage of their development, but particularly during adolescence, children (much like the elephants Johnson describes) seem to toss their parents around and unbalance them. Although such upheaval is most unpleasant, it creates movement and ideally leads the parents to more solid ground.

The story of the Konner family illustrates how a normal young adolescent precipitated a crisis in her parents' marriage, which forced them to make needed changes. I will tell this story in some detail because its basic patterns are repeated in so many other contemporary families. Moreover, because the Konners saw themselves through their crisis, their solutions may serve as models for others.

Richard and Denise Konner, an attractive couple in their middle thirties, requested counseling to help them decide whether their embittered, embattled marriage was worth saving. At our first interview, they explained that theirs was a traditional arrangement. Although she had taken part-time jobs from time to time, Denise had mostly stayed home to care for Jo, who was born within the first year of their marriage and had just turned fourteen, while Richard established himself in academia as an administrator. Until recently the family functioned with little outward strife. For Richard, who was naturally high-strung and nervous, Denise's easygoing household had been a haven of sorts, but that haven was increasingly threatened by fractiousness and disorder. Both Denise and Richard agreed that Jo, who through her childhood had been a quiet, sweet-natured, and compliant child, had set the household topsy-turvy. Seemingly overnight the docile little girl transformed herself into a defiant young teenager. Moody and ill-mannered at home, she stayed out with her new junior high school friends past her curfew, and sometimes overslept and arrived late at school, where her grades were sliding steeply. Richard complained that she challenged him at every turn: "With Jo, everything is an argument; everything I say or do is subject to her criticism."

As is the case for many married couples, the child's behavior affected the parents differently. Denise dismissed it as normal adolescent rebellion. Indeed, admitting little use for rules herself, Denise rather admired her daughter's "high spirits and independent thinking," whereas Richard abhorred the change. Valuing good manners and consideration, he was offended by Jo's "boorishness." Richard had always been the stricter of the two parents, but in the past little Jo, who did not disobey the rules he set, gave him no reason to discipline her. Now, however, she instigated his wrath. Denise was appalled by her husband's rages against their daughter. His inflexible standards of conduct, which she had tried to overlook since the start of their marriage, had not softened over the years but had solidified instead. In therapy Denise confided that during this past tumultuous year she had often wondered whether marrying Richard, whose personality was so different from her own, had not been an awful mistake. "How could I have deluded myself into believing we were compatible as a couple and as parents?" she asked.

Because Denise considered Richard's parental demands excessively harsh, she tried to offset them by becoming increasingly permissive. If Richard told Jo to be home by 8 o'clock on school nights, Denise told her to be home by 11; if Richard insisted that Jo pull up her grades to A's, Denise assured her that learning, not grades, was important. Not surprisingly, just as Richard's high parental standards provoked Denise to lower hers, Denise's laxness caused Richard to become more demanding. Pulling harder and harder against each other in this dangerous game of tug-of-war, Denise and Richard were tearing their marriage apart. Moreover, as parents they locked themselves into rigid roles: Richard became the ogre of the family, Denise the kindhearted, reasonable one to whom Jo turned more and more.

Only after we had been meeting for several weeks did Richard reveal how much the alliance between his wife and child wounded him and how it contributed to his irrational outbursts against Jo. For example, one time after reprimanding Jo at the dinner table for being ill-mannered, he noticed that Denise was smiling at her sympathetically. "It was a smile that simultaneously mocked, condemned, and betrayed me. Without any further provocation from Jo, I began to rant and rave at her; I screamed that she would never be allowed to have dinner with us again and, like a wild man, smashed her dinner plate against the wall. I lost all control. I let Jo have it, but I was more furious at Denise for making me feel like such a monster and such a fool."

Unwittingly, Jo had brought her parents dangerously close to dissolving their marriage, yet at the same time she forced Richard and Denise to take a hard look not only at each other but at themselves. On occasion newly married couples come to me to discuss the advantages and disadvantages of having children. I never promise that parenthood will bring them joy or a fulfilled old age (although it may very well), but I guarantee that it will present them with countless opportunities to grow and become better people. Jo provided her parents such opportunities.

Although Denise and Richard initially asked whether or not it was advisable to split up, I refused to make a judgment. As I explained to them, my therapeutic role was limited to helping them articulate their feelings and to helping them understand each other's world. Accomplishing these goals, they would be in the best position to decide their own fates. With this understanding, Denise and Richard participated in weekly therapy sessions. At the tenth session, they let me know that they wanted to try to make the marriage work.

By listening to one another, as they were forced to do in marriage counseling, rather than defending or "scoring points" against the other as they had gotten into the habit of doing, Denise and Richard rediscovered a basic fondness for one another. Of course, in a less fortunate instance marital therapy may have the opposite effect. In getting to know the other better, the spouse may discover that his or her partner is quite unlikeable or incapable of mature loving and intimacy, in which case it is usually best to dissolve the unhappy union. I am often touched as I observe my clients get to know each other because they are, perhaps for the first time, giving their marriage partners full attention, tuning them in rather than tuning them out. On occasion I ask clients to close their eyes so that they can focus on the nuances of their partner's voice and meaning. After such an exercise, one elderly man said that for the first time he heard the layers of sadness that his wife's cheerful demeanor ordinarily masked, and his wife in turn heard his fear and insecurity, which he usually covered with a tough veneer.

In the course of their therapy, Denise and Richard opened their hearts to share with one another their fears as well as their dreams. Often one would exclaim to the other, "But I had no idea!" or "I never knew you felt that way." As a supplement to their sessions with me, I urged the Konners to set up one or two weekly dates with each other, just as they had done during their courtship. Resistant to this idea at first, Denise and Richard eventually took to it with enthusiasm. Meeting for lunch at fancy restaurants; going on picnics; visiting museums, the zoo, and the botanical gardens, they began enjoying each other's company again. Mothers and fathers all too often forget that they are also wives and husbands; and wives and husbands often forget that marriage can be fun.

When the Konners began treatment, their family, like most other dysfunctional ones, was poorly arranged. Instead of the husband and wife standing close to one another with the child slightly to the side, Denise and Jo huddled together as Richard moved further and further away. An excluded spouse typically expresses any number of negative behaviors. For example, it is not uncommon for a husband bewildered by envy of his wife's exclusive relationship with their child to delude himself that his wife is involved with another man. Too embarrassed to admit envy of his own child, the husband displaces it from the child to the imagined lover. Although Richard did not develop a pathological jealousy, he did act in other negative ways. For example, instead of directly confronting his wife, he displaced his frustrations with her onto their daughter, whom he treated with excessive harshness. Moreover, humiliated by his loss of status at home, he tried to empower himself by acting the part of the tyrannical patriarch, which served only to increase his wife's disrespect and make him feel all the more foolish.

As we discovered through our therapeutic work, Denise's reasons for promoting the alliance with her daughter against her husband were twofold. On the one hand, in her role as homemaker Denise did not have much opportunity to test her mettle. Through her overidentification with the defiant Jo, Denise could fancy that she was the bold, spirited woman whom she had always wanted to become. Without being aware of it, Denise depended on Jo's escapades, which she subtly encouraged, to enliven her own uneventful middle age. Although she did not intend this, Denise was acting quite selfishly. As one of Oscar Wilde's characters points out in *The Importance of Being Earnest*, selfishness is not living as one wishes to live but asking others to live as one wishes to live. At the same time, in colluding with her daughter against Richard, Denise was at last expressing pent-up resentment that she had harbored for years. Although she had agreed to live the life of traditional homemaker and mother, secretly Denise blamed Richard for holding her back from realizing her potential. Like Lewis Carroll's Alice, who imbibed the potion that made her so big she could no longer squeeze into her house, Denise was intoxicated by the excitement of the times and wanted to burst out of her too-small life, but she did not know how to open the doors that would free her. Watching so many other women—including her own daughter—leave the hearth to create new opportunities for themselves, Denise became envious and filled with despair. How angry she was at Richard for having encouraged her to remain at home all these years and to content herself with meaningless part-time jobs as he elevated his own status in the world!

One time Denise dreamed that she was locked in a cell to which Richard held the key; she cried, "Please give me the key, Richard," but he ignored her because he was on his way to an important meeting. After waking from this dream, Denise could not shake off her bitter feelings. She wanted to make Richard feel small and unimportant, just as she felt. Argumentative and rude, only Jo had the courage to stand up to her father, to debunk his values, to make him feel ineffective. Through Jo's defiance of her father, Denise indirectly vented much stored-up rage against her husband.

For both Richard and Denise, Jo had become the convenient buffer that kept them apart. Instead of encountering each other, they used her to express their terrible despair, resentment, frustration, and pain. Yet, what Richard wanted above all else was a close, loving relationship with his wife, whose respect and acceptance he needed; his status in academia meant less than the love of the person most dear to him. And Denise wanted encouragement from her husband so that she could become strong, competent, and successful in the work world; she needed Richard to support her growth and change. (This support was, after all, the missing key from her dream.) Although their early married years had been compatible, it became clear to both of them that they needed to move on to higher, more mature ways of loving and caring for each other. As things now were, neither was satisfied.

George Bernard Shaw observed that every young girl marries believing that she will change her groom for the better, that every young man marries believing that his bride will never change, and that both are inevitably disappointed. A mature, fulfilling union between two people must be flexible and strong enough to contain their individual differences (even the annoying ones) and their changes (even the threatening ones). During the earlier years of their marriage, Denise and Richard managed to cover up their differences to maintain their peaceful, conflict-free little kingdom. Instead of dealing with their problems, they swept them under the rug. As Denise recalled, when uncomfortable issues came up, they would often jump into bed, make love, and forget about them. New lovers typically delight in and, even more, require the appearance of homogeneity, which they confuse with intimacy. As psychologist Louise Kaplan explained, all goes well with the lovers as long as they are as one, as long as "the exquisite sympathy" between them is not disturbed by some indications that there are serious differences of opinions, values, wishes, and desires. When an adolescent girl falls in love, she is likely to bubble over with joy as she contrives to find the ways she and her "soul mate" resemble one another. "You won't believe this," an infatuated client gushed, "but Tom and I discovered that the numbers on the very first houses that we lived in when we were babies are the same; Tom lived at 685 Juniper in Boulder, Colorado, and I lived at 685 West 204th Street in New York City. Can you believe that! Every time we are together, we realize how much we are alike."

Over time, Denise learned not only that Richard and she were temperamentally different but that she could not make him over in her softer image. Unlike frogs turned into fairy-tale princes, the demanding, high-strung Richard failed to transform himself into a lighthearted and easygoing fellow. Indeed, under the stressful conditions of parenting a rambunctious adolescent daughter, he became even more tense. Seeing with fully open eyes Richard's flaws, Denise finally learned to love him as he is, not as he might be.

As long as marriage partners insist on illusions of sameness, they will discount each other's needs. For example, Denise, who had a high tolerance for mess and chaos, had not taken seriously Richard's need for neatness. As she explained to me, "Because *I* was not bothered by unwashed dishes in the sink, I really didn't think *he* was, although, goodness knows, he told me often enough that messiness drove him crazy." In coming to recognize Richard's differences from her, Denise began to respect them. "Recently we had a dinner party. Instead of leaving the unwashed dishes in the sink overnight as I had always done, Richard and I took care of them as soon as the guests left. I knew that it was important for him to have the kitchen tidied up right then and there. Richard is a little compulsive, but that's okay—that's just how he is." Kindness and respect multiply. Richard, moved by his wife's increasing sensitivity toward him, was determined to pay more attention to her needs. He explained that despite the fact that Denise complained about his "girl watching," he had continued this habit. "I figured that what I was doing was pretty harmless, so whenever Denise told me that by looking at women I humiliated her, I paid no attention. I thought, 'I wouldn't mind if she noticed other men, so why should she mind if I admire pretty women?' Because I'm not possessive, I just discounted her possessive feelings. Now I know that my behavior really hurt Denise, and I don't want to hurt her."

Family therapist Carl Whitaker explained that real marriage does not begin until the unrealistic assumptions and expectations that one inevitably brings to a new marriage are dissolved, and that this cannot usually be done in less than ten years' time. One must relinquish the hope of creating the perfect partner before one can genuinely love the real one. Mature love, unlike early love, is tolerant of imperfection. It values human ordinariness, that mixture of strengths and shortcomings that is each of us. During a therapy session, I presented a poem by Dianne di Prima to Denise, which she later pinned to her bulletin board:

A Poem in Praise of My Husband [Taos]

I suppose it hasn't been easy living with me either,
with my piques, and ups and downs, my need for privacy
leo pride and weeping in bed when you're trying to sleep
and you, interrupting me in the middle of a thousand
*   poems*

did I call the insurance people? the time you stopped a
     poem
in the middle of our drive over the nebraska hills and
into colorado, odetta singing, the whole world
     singing in me
the triumph of our revolution in the air
me about to get that down, and you
you saying something about the carburetor
so that it all went away
but we cling to each other
as if each thought the other was a raft
and he adrift alone, as in this mud house
not big enough, the walls dusting down around us,
     a fine dust rain
counteracting the good, high air, and stuffing our nostrils
we hang our pictures of the several worlds;
new york collage, and san francisco posters,
set out our japanese dishes, chinese knives
hammer small indian marriage cloths into the adobe
we stumble through silence into each other's gut
blundering thru from one wrong place to the next
like kids who snuck out to play on a boat at night
and the boat slipped from its moorings, and
     they look at the stars
about which they know nothing, to find out
where they are going.[1]

Just as Denise learned that her husband's temperament is
fixed and that she cannot make him over, so Richard discovered that the "homebody" he had married was growing out
of her role, much as compliant little Jo was growing out of
hers. Both the women in his life were now moving ahead in
tandem and, as he admitted, he secretly had hoped that they
would stay in place. Richard was wary of the changes Denise
and Jo would demand, the unknown directions their lives
would now take, and the way these would affect him. His
boat was slipping from its moorings and oftentimes he felt

adrift, but going back to port was no solution. He had to learn that loving his growing, middle-aged wife was different from loving the younger woman he had married. Rather than protective care, she asked for an encouraging and enabling care to help her become the strong, capable woman of her dreams—to bring out the best in her. Having set out for other ports of call, she wanted her husband on her side as well as at her side.

By becoming loving partners, Denise and Richard were able to parent more appropriately. Together, they negotiated family rules and helped each other to enforce them. Jo herself, who early on had joined her parents for one therapy session, confessed that Denise's overpermissiveness was as confusing as Richard's inflexibility was infuriating. "Sometimes I wish I could mix my parents the way I mix food in a processer or the way artists mix paint on a palette. My father is too strict and my mother is too nice." In a dysfunctional way, Denise and Richard had established some kind of balance in their family by offsetting one another's style of parenting. Now they learned to modify their positions and, instead of polarizing, to move closer together. Two people of equal weight can balance a seesaw by sitting at its far ends, where there is a risk of falling off, or by moving toward its fulcrum, which seems much cozier.

In order to achieve a workable and unified set of family rules, Richard and Denise learned negotiating skills in therapy. At first, when their relationship was antagonistic, they required a formal structure for these negotiations; having a set procedure prevented their discussions from becoming emotionally heated and encouraged them to stay with their task. Later, as they began to trust that each had Jo's best interests at heart, they dropped the formalities and discussed parenting issues casually. Although their philosophies about raising children are not identical, Richard and Denise were able to devise family rules with which all three could live.

By setting reasonable but firm limits for Jo, Richard and Denise provided the safe ground that she, like any other adolescent, needs. Denise came to understand that her overpermissiveness would not in fact empower Jo; quite the contrary, it would weaken her. Every healthy adolescent will try to push her parents' limits. As she formulates her own values, a young girl necessarily challenges her parents' values, but she cannot afford to topple them. Pushing against her parents to test herself, the fortunate adolescent will discover that they do not give way to her pressure.

A Chinese martial art called "Pushing Hands" illustrates how, rather than an act of kindness or support, giving way may be destructive. In this form, the passive movements of giving way throw the opponent off balance. The opponent thrusts forward expecting to meet resistance but finds none, and so is made helpless by his or her own overture. Similarly, the adolescent who pushes against a yielding parent is likely to lose her balance and fall; she is undone by her own healthy energy. A young woman can become strong only by testing her strength against her parents' strength. She needs assurances that when she pushes against them, they will not cave in.

I am not suggesting that parents respond in an uncompromising way to their teenager's challenges. A strong family structure is flexible, not rigid. Although giving in to the adolescent's unreasonable demand is a sign of parental weakness, negotiating with her toward an acceptable compromise is a sign that the family is healthy, growing, and changing. Without relinquishing the appropriate task of guiding the youngster, the parents validate her perceptions and initiative by encouraging negotiations with her. In this way too the adolescent understands that her views command respect and consequently she feels worthy.

Just as an adolescent is hurt by violating the dignity of a parent, the parent humiliated suffers greatly also, as Denise came to understand. As her resentment against Richard waned and her affection grew, Denise could no longer bear to see Jo abuse him. Rather than ally with her daughter during these attacks, she took her husband's side. On a recent occasion, Jo shouted at Richard because he had inadvertently thrown out her homework, which she carelessly had left lying amid a pile of old newspapers. During her tirade, Jo looked toward Denise for the familiar sign of approval but was met instead by her rebuke: "You are never to treat your father with disrespect. Never. You offend us both when you do." At last Denise was willing to support her husband. By doing this, she taught their daughter what married love is all about. Loving married people do not allow their partners to be treated badly—not even by their own children. Instead, they stand by each other; they are good to one another: They are best friends.

I worked with the Konners for six months and then recommended that we terminate treatment. Through her adolescence, Jo will continue to test their limits by pushing, prodding, and provoking, but, no longer warring with one another, Denise and Richard will meet her challenges with a united front. They have learned to live their married life in the spirit of mutual kindness. As Richard once said, "Loving my wife is really quite simple. It means acting in ways that enhance her growth. It means building her up, not tearing her down. It means encouragement."

Jo is not yet aware that she is luckier than many of her peers. Unlike them, she will trust that some relationships do not end badly.

When my clients—adolescent daughters and middle-aged mothers—tell me that they no longer know what love is, I suggest that they conceive of it as a genuine, lasting friendship between a man and a woman. Unfortunately, in today's America, people tend to devalue friendship, thinking it too dull, just as they tend to overvalue romance, mistaking it for true love.

In his elegant tribute to human love, *We*, Robert A. Johnson compared friendship, which is the essence of human love, with romance. Married people who are committed friends know, care for, and are sexually attracted to each other as they are. They see their spouses as individuals and make individualized relationships with them. Romantic partners, on the other hand, necessarily lose their individual identities. In Johnson's words,

> They are Tristan and Iseult or Romeo and Juliet—actors in a collective play where the script is predetermined and the scenes are known beforehand. It is precisely because one has ceased to be oneself and has become a player in a universal drama, that one feels so intense, so out of the ordinary, and at first, so wonderful.[2]

But because romance does not allow its players to be themselves—ordinary human beings with quotidian needs and wants—but casts them as gods and goddesses, it always ends.

> People often say that they are "burned out" by a relationship. It is literally true. They are so exhausted by the sheer intensity of romantic love as we try to live it, by the ecstasies and battles, the partings and reconciliations, that there is finally nothing left—neither life force nor goodwill nor affection—with which to love and companion someone on a human level.[3]

Several of my middle-aged clients, some of whom have fallen from one doomed love affair into another, cannot settle into married life because it is necessarily ordinary. Stella, who recently began counseling, is confused and frightened but also tempted by her attraction to the handsome young instructor who has recently joined the university's chemistry department, where she is a senior professor. She does not think that she can resist his seductive ways, although she knows that giving in to them will end only in heartache. Stella does not want to jeopardize a marriage (her third) with a husband who is intelligent, kind, and loving, nor does she want to create havoc in her adolescent daughter's life (the young girl has already suffered through two of her mother's divorces.) At the same time, Stella wants a marriage that is romantic—and theirs is not. "What is wrong with me that I crave more?" she sobbed at our first meeting.

It is too easy to dismiss Stella as a shallow woman who will never be satisfied. Her desires for a mid-life romance are common to so many women that we must make the effort to understand rather than condemn them. We would be wrong to insist that Stella bury her intense longings, because they would necessarily emerge in some unhealthier form. Moreover, her feelings are not to be despised but, like all human feelings, to be treated tenderly and seriously. Stella—and so many other women who are similarly conflicted—must be helped to create a holding place for her passions and dreams, where they can be both treasured and safely contained.

Like Stella, most of us, no matter how sophisticated we become, yearn for a passionate love affair from time to time. We want to be swept up by a perfect lover in an ecstasy of mutual adoration. When our daughters fall in love, our own longings for romance only intensify. Her springtime carries us back to our own, awakening dreams of that time long past when, in the arms of a sweet first love, we too were celebrated:

> *Aye, there it is! It wakes to-night*
> *Sweet thoughts that will not die*
> *And feeling's fires flash as bright*
> *As in the years gone by!* . . .
> Emily Brontë, July 6, 1841

When I was just eighteen, my grandmother came upon me reading a love letter just received. With a kindly smile she said, "After you have read this letter many times over, put it safely away and keep it always—even if you stop liking this boy or he stops liking you." From time to time, when I feel dreary or time-worn, I retrieve the yellowed letter and, in daydream, relive my first love. Indeed, by deleting the painful memories and exaggerating the delightful ones, I am able to create an illusion of a perfect love that never really was. But after being with my fantastic, eternally-young lover for a spell, I am ready to return to my good, everyday life and to the real companionship of my husband. My grandmother taught me that fantasy and illusion, as long as they are not too insistent or confused with reality, can allow one some respite from the ordinary when it becomes *too* ordinary. She was a wonderful teacher because she lived what she taught.

As a little girl, I often accompanied her to the ballet. During a performance of *Cinderella*, I noticed that sometimes Grandma would close her eyes and take on a dreamy expression. I was quite certain that in her reverie she was transforming herself into the beautiful Cinderella floating in the arms of the handsome prince, and that only after the curtain came down on the final act would Grandma return to the tiny, plump, white-haired woman I knew. Because I, like other lucky children, was comfortable in my own fantasy worlds, I never thought it peculiar that my grandmother could, at will, become a fairy-tale princess and fall in love with a prince.

As a therapist, I try to pass on my grandmother's wise ways to my clients. I am trying to teach Stella that although her everyday relations are bound to be homey—as is simply the nature of things—her inner world can hold wonderful, *impossible* dreams. In her fantasy she can go off for a time with her handsome and perfect young lover to indulge her wildest longings. But if she tries to transform fantasy into reality by living out her romance, she will know much suffering, partly because she is sure to discover that her new lover is, like her husband, ordinary. In fact, extramarital affairs are more predictable than marriages; they follow a fixed script and almost always have a disappointing ending.

A friend, Fred Stein, who is an avid moviegoer, told me a charming story that points up the differences between romantic fantasy and reality. Attending a special showing of a silent movie, he found himself falling in love with its divine heroine, a woman more sensuously beautiful than one could imagine. To everyone's surprise, after the performance the organizer of the film festival announced that the celebrated actress was actually in the audience and had agreed to say a few words. Moving through the hushed crowd, the usher approached a bent-over, withered women of ninety, and led her to the podium.

Some women clients I have counseled are afraid of indulging their sexual and romantic fantasies. They try to suppress them because they believe that these daydreams are acts of infidelity or signs of impending infidelity, which they are definitely not. (I believe a great number of extramarital affairs would be prevented if husbands and wives gave freer rein to their fantasies.) Others consider fantasies a cowardly escape from reality, mistakenly believing that an experience is valid only if it is acted out. But as long as it does not encroach on reality, fantasy allows us to experience in a wonderful yet harmless way what would be destructive to live out. Our fantasy world is a safe repository for our most passionate desires, our most tender feelings, our most innocent dreams. It is also the breeding place of art, poetry, music, and dance, which are the divine expressions of the human soul. Like my grandmother, mothers who let their daughters know that daydreaming and fantasizing are healthy outlets and positive human capacities, do them a great service.

Myrna discovered that her unhappy relationship with a passionate but irresponsible young artist was, in one way, her attempt to bring color to her own life. Although she was not blind to his blatant defects of character, Myrna was deeply in love with him. When, without warning, he disappeared from their love nest, she fell into the blackest despair. Those friends who knew him told her that he typically abandoned his lovers and that she would be wise to forget all about him—he was really an unsavory chap. But, try as she did, Myrna could not release herself from his haunting presence. One night in the guise of a medieval page, he came to her in a dream and set a palette and artist's brush before her;

then he disappeared, just as he had done in reality. Soon after the dream, Myrna began painting again, an avocation she had abandoned years ago after the birth of her first child. Although Myrna no longer mourns for her lost lover and would not have him back in her real life, he lives quite happily in her inner life as a muse. Myrna's dream lover empowers her—her artwork is alive and full of passion.

"Perfect love" can flower only in fantasy or in the artistic expressions of fantasy. Women who insist on searching for lasting romance and lasting passion in the real world necessarily suffer and cause suffering. (Interestingly, in its original definition, the word *passion* means suffering.) Commonly, the memory of their youthful love affairs, embellished by time, is awakened by their adolescent daughters' infatuations and becomes the standard for the romance they crave. My client Stella, like many other middle-aged women who do not want to accept the ordinariness and limitations of human relationship, is tempted by a young man, who, like youth itself, promises endless possibility. But if Stella chooses to live out her romance, she will not only betray her husband but her adolescent daughter.

Instead of becoming a guide to her children, someone who can provide direction because she is more knowing, the mother who acts the part of love-struck adolescent reduces herself to a peer and dissolves the necessary differences between the generations. As they pass from one life stage to the next, parents indirectly assure their children that they in turn can make safe passages. Conversely, by refusing to move on, parents fail to lay paths for their children. True love, as D. H. Lawrence wrote, is not a goal but a traveling. The daughter of the mother who moves backward rather than forward in her love relationships will not know where to go herself.

Many women fall back into regressive love relationships because they cannot imagine the joys of mature ones, which may never have been modeled by their own parents. Today's middle-aged women typically remember the sad, entrapped marriages of their mothers—marriages that brought out the worst in them—and justifiably, they do not want to emulate these. Also, when they hear psychotherapists, like myself, talk about the ordinariness of human marriage, they may become discouraged. ("If that's what love is, I'll settle for infatuation," a young female client moaned.) In a world that idealizes bolder, better, bigger, the idea that ordinariness is good finds little favor. If today's mothers and daughters are to experience relationships that do not end badly, however, they must learn the principles of mature love and redeem the value of human ordinariness.

Robert A. Johnson uses the phrase "stirring-the-oatmeal" for human love. As he explains, stirring oatmeal is a humble, ordinary act that symbolizes a relatedness that is down-to-earth. To stir the oatmeal means to find the value, even the beauty, in the everyday tasks of life that married people perform—preparing meals, keeping house, going to work, living within a budget, caring for the children. "Like the rice hulling of the Zen monks, the spinning wheel of Gandhi, the tent making of Saint Paul, it represents the discovery of the sacred in the midst of the human and ordinary."[4] Married love is best expressed through small acts: a caring word when the other feels blue, a quiet conversation at the end of a busy day, an invitation to take a walk together, a little gift for no reason, a good laugh at a shared joke, an embrace.

As I talk to Stella, it occurs to me that much of her disenchantment with married life stems from her belief that it should be something more than it is—the "gusto" beer commercials talk of grabbing. She reminds me of a younger woman who tried desperately to love and be loved with extraordinary intensity every moment. On the fiftieth day of her marriage Monica sent her husband fifty long-stemmed roses; on his birthday she arranged a midnight ride in a hot-air balloon; on the anniversary of their first meeting she published a love sonnet in the local paper. At first the young man tried to match her generosity, but, not as ingenious as she was, he inevitably disappointed her by his uninspired gifts. In the end, her insistence on turning their marriage into an extravaganza became so oppressive that he left her. Human love and marriage are much less than their romanticized versions. At the same time, they are much more.

The day I most appreciated the wonder of love was not when, as a radiant bride of twenty, I stood in white lace under the marriage canopy beside my handsome young husband. It was the day, twenty years later, when I came home in tears from the periodontist's office, believing his warning that my unflossed teeth were about to fall out, and my husband took me in his arms and whispered that he would always love me with all his heart—even if I became toothless. Stirring the oatmeal together, year after year, has thickened our love, which in its early form, like every new love, was necessarily thin.

Years ago, during one of those homebound stretches with a sick child when there is time to do the small things usually left undone, I sorted through boxes of playbills, ticket stubs, letters, photos, and postcards that my husband and I had collected. Rather than filing these mementos in a scrapbook, I cut, arranged, and pasted pieces of them onto a huge primed plywood board to form a collage of sorts. Since its creation, my husband and I have added other memorabilia—a favorite recipe, a lost baby tooth (dropped by the tooth fairy as she flew out the children's bedroom window), a matchbox from a special restaurant, a notice for a job, a flower picked on a mountain walk, a button from a political campaign—so that hardly an inch of uncovered board is left. This memory board, which hangs in our hallway, reminds me each day how my husband and I have stirred the oatmeal together; it is a growing record of many small shared joys that have created a unity from two separate and quite ordinary human lives. We have never presented each other with dozens of long-stemmed roses, or taken a ride in a hot-air balloon, or published love sonnets, but we continue to stir the oatmeal that nourishes us. And it is now, in our middle age, that we are coming into the most fulfilled love of our lives.

In an earlier chapter, I recounted a dream in which mourning for the days of active mothering led to a deeper intimacy with my husband. The dream told me to rechannel some of the tremendous energy I had invested in my maternal caretaking functions toward my marriage partner and our relationship. With this in mind, I suggested that we go on a grand vacation to Europe, where we had lived for a year as a young married couple. So, on the night of December 31, 1986, Bruce and I dined in a restaurant on the Seine and held hands under the table—far from the kids, the house, the obligations, the everyday. The oatmeal that we have stirred over the years continues to nourish us day by day. Still, once in a while, it is lovely to wash it down with something out of the ordinary—a few sips of sparkling French champagne, for example.

As a young girl, I dreamed of falling into a great love. Then, as a young woman in the midst of toddlers' demands, overflowing laundry, crushing bills, and an over-stressed husband, I dismissed great love as the invention of Hollywood movie moguls and foolish poets. Now, as a middle-aged woman, on this Parisian New Year's night, I vindicated the sweet hopes of the innocent young girl I once was. I knew without a doubt that I had a great love—not one *fallen into*, however, but one *earned* through twenty-two years of living in an atmosphere of mutual kindness and respect.

In concluding this chapter, I offer an interpretation of one of our civilization's most celebrated love stories, the ancient Greek myth of Psyche and Eros. We are a culture with few models of good living. Unfortunately, the advertising industry, which has become our most popular teacher, has trivialized the meaning of human love by its successful efforts to sell romance. Marshall McLuhan once said that "the medium is the message," and the message of these advertisements, with their dazzling pace and skillful cutting, is easy and prolonged excitement. If we are to help our adolescent daughters (and ourselves) create fulfilling relationships, we must renew our faith in the possibilities of human love, not its sensationalized counterfeits. Although Psyche and Eros are gods, they nevertheless shed an earthly light on human relationship and have taught me that lasting love, like all great achievements, comes only through struggle.

In Apuleius's second-century version of the myth, we find a king, a queen, and their three daughters, the youngest and loveliest of whom is named Psyche, the Greek word for both soul and butterfly (or moth). Although the older sisters are married off when they come of age, to the great distress of her father, Psyche cannot find a suitable husband. Finally, at the command of an oracle, she is betrothed to Death himself. Shackled to a lonely crag, the frightened maiden waits for her groom. But most unexpectedly the love god Eros (who is also known by the names Cupid and Amor) rescues her from this grim fate and, without revealing his godly identity, takes her for his own bride. Carried away by a gentle west wind, Psyche is brought to a magnificent palace in a peaceful kingdom, where invisible servants attend to her every need and Eros, who is the sweetest and most tender of lovers, visits her nightly. In exchange for the care lavished on her, Eros asks only one thing of his young bride: She must never look at him or make inquiries about him. Should she break this vow, he will leave her immediately. Complying with her husband's wishes, Psyche lives contentedly in her idyllic castle.

But Psyche's two sisters, who visit her often, plant seeds of fear about her husband's identity, and she begins to doubt his integrity. When they suggest that Eros, who is such a lovely husband in the dark, is in reality a monstrous snake, Psyche can no longer tolerate her ignorance: She must have a full look at him. At her sisters' insistent urging, she devises a plan to discover his real form, which she now suspects is hideous, and to decapitate him. One night, armed with dagger and lamp—half expecting to find a vile reptile in her bridal bed—Psyche pulls the covers from Eros's sleeping body. In the light of her lamp, she beholds not a monster but a lovely boy-god. Shaken by the awareness of what she has done, Psyche inadvertently jostles the lamp and spills drops of burning oil on Eros, which painfully wake him from his love sleep. Humiliated at Psyche's exposure of him, the injured young god flees from her.

Before continuing with the plot, let me make some interpretations. Like all great literature, the myth of Psyche and Eros has layered meanings. At one level, for example, it teaches that romantic love cannot tolerate the light of full consciousness; romance is always dependent on illusion, magic, even deception. Psyche can delight in the condition of perfect love only as long as she is willing to stay in the dark. At the moment that she insists on looking with wide-open eyes at her perfect lover, he necessarily disappears: He awakens from *her* dream and flies off.

In part, Eros flees because he knows that this lovely romance and the accompanying illusion of his perfection could last only as long as Psyche was willing to be deceived. But his secretiveness has deeper meaning still. For fear of exposing himself to her, the young god cannot stand for his bride to look at him. He can be charming, obliging, and sexually attentive only as long as Psyche does not insist on making a real relationship with him, one in which she would see him as he is. When, against his wishes, she uncovers him, he flees, injured and humiliated.

At this early stage in their relationship, Eros does not have the capacity to be intimate, to share the meaning of his life with a wife. Most young couples, it seems to me, fail to achieve a real intimacy. Typically, young women are frustrated by their male lovers' withdrawal and lack of emotional commitment. They want to be close to their boyfriends or husbands who, just like Eros, flee from this closeness. For example, time and again new wives (and wives in marriages that have gotten stuck at an early stage) have complained to me how their husbands evade them, reading a newspaper, flipping on the TV, fidgeting with a gadget that needs fixing to avoid eye contact. Even more frustrating, new husbands are likely to turn moments of potential emotional intimacy into sexual encounters, which are less threatening to them because they can be less personal. Like Eros, they make love to their brides but do not share their secrets with them.

When, in the course of psychotherapy, I have asked these men why they shirk emotional closeness, they have often told me they are afraid that in truly knowing them, their wives will want to make them over. They are not confident that their wives can accept them for the men they are but will try to control them by "rehabilitating" them one way or another. Just as Eros evaporates into thin air, young husbands become evasive to avoid being dominated.

With her sisters' prodding but to her credit nevertheless, Psyche risks the delights of an illusory paradisiacal love for an honest one. She would rather confront a real snake than continue to live in a make-believe world with a deceptive lover. Like the moth after whom she is named, she too is drawn to the light. But before Psyche can be blessed with true love, she must undergo changes; like Eros, she is still too adolescent in her ways, too unformed, to be capable of true loving and of true intimacy. Just as the undifferentiated caterpillar must incubate in its dark chrysalis before it can emerge as a butterfly, for her metamorphosis from bride to wife, Psyche must make a long, painful inner journey, a soul search. Psyche, like her modern-day counterparts, must come to know herself before she can truly love another. She must become a complete, self-contained woman before Eros will trust her with his vulnerability; until then he must hide from her.

From my personal and clinical experience, I have learned that intimacy does not come quickly but evolves over many years; we must patiently work toward our rewards. As we realize our own lives—as we become ourselves—we no longer need to live through others. Women who are all they can be are not concerned with shaping their husbands. They are just too busy being themselves to have the time for rehabilitating others, whether daughters, sons, or spouses. Moreover, when husbands trust that their wives are not intent on making them over, they will not be afraid to allow a closeness; no longer on guard to defend their selfhood against intrusions, they are safe to become intimate. The paradox is that separateness—the claimed right to be oneself—is the necessary condition for togetherness.

Returning to the plot of the myth, we find Psyche in despair over her abandonment by Eros. Bereft, she first thinks she cannot live without her man and is ready to kill herself. All is not hopeless, however. The powerful love goddess, Aphrodite, who is Eros's mother, has the ability to reunite the newlyweds. (As a result of his broken romance, Eros has gone home to Mother!) Without a shred of compassion, Aphrodite berates her poor daughter-in-law for being stupid in love matters, but also tells her that if she can perform four tasks—all of which seem impossible to master— Eros will be returned to her.

Although Aphrodite appears to be a heartless and harsh mistress who jealously guards her son, she is actually the one who encourages, even demands, Psyche's evolution. As we will see, each of the tasks helps the young girl move into maturity. Again and again, myths and fairy tales remind us that growth must often be forced. Just as adolescent children unbalance their parents' world to create change (as was the case in the Konner family), so the most enabling mothers (and mothers-in-law) prod their daughters into womanhood. Solicitude and overprotection, those softer maternal aspects, must be replaced by maternal hardness at crucial times of the child's development.

Psyche's first task is to sort out a mountain of mixed seeds into separate, like piles; if she fails to do this before nightfall, she will be put to death. Of course, she is overwhelmed. Not knowing how and where to start, she sits still and waits. As she does, ants come to her aid and successfully help her to complete this task. Like Psyche, contemporary women must learn to sort things through, put them in order. The young woman whose internal life is chaotic is not yet ready for a marital partnership. First, she needs to quiet down—sit with herself as Psyche is forced to—and sort out her feelings, emotions, beliefs, values, wishes, and desires. She has to figure out who she is and what she wants to become before she can share her life with another.

The second task Aphrodite sets for her daughter-in-law is to collect the golden fleece of wild and aggressive rams. Again Psyche is crushed by the fear of failing; again she sits and waits. This time reeds whisper a solution. Instead of confronting the rams head-on, a strategy that could result in disaster, Psyche must wait for the evening, when the rams are sleeping, and then gather pieces of fleece brushed off by the brambles and low-hanging boughs where the rams roamed in the daytime. Following these directives, Psyche is once more successful.

In order to foster married love, mortal women need also to learn that aggressive confrontation is ill-advised. Women (and men) are wiser to find unaggressive ways to exert their wills. A study by Jeanette and Robert Lauer of three hundred long-lasting and happy marriages supports what the reeds teach Psyche. In the Lauers' words,

> Some marriage counselors stress the importance of expressing feelings with abandon—spouses should freely vent their anger with each other, letting out all stops short of physical violence. . . . But some social scientists argue that intense expressions of anger, resentment, and dislike tend to corrode the relationship and increase the likelihood of future aggression. . . . Happily married couples in our survey came down squarely on the side of those who emphasize the damaging effects of intensely expressed anger.[5]

Ramming against another, as Psyche learned and as the Lauers confirm, is self-defeating. Immature lovers are too impulsive, too needy to set aside their concerns; they demand instant gratification and, in the process, are likely to injure the other's feelings. When confrontations between married people are called for, they always require tact—and good timing. Psyche wisely waits until nightfall to accomplish her task. And a wise wife waits for the right time and circumstance to bring up delicate matters with a spouse, just as a wise husband does.

For her third task, Psyche must fill a crystal goblet with water from the Styx, the treacherous, fast-flowing River of Life, which is guarded by dangerous monsters. True to form, Psyche is at first immobilized by the enormity of her task and is required once again to wait patiently for a solution to come to her. This time she is saved by an eagle that fills the goblet. Flying high above, the eagle has a panoramic view of the Styx and, from this advantageous perspective, can see at which particular point the river is best approached.

From time to time, every marriage relationship is beset with problems that appear overwhelming. Psyche learns that she would only drown if she rushed headlong into the raging river. Similarly, married people must often back off, slow down, get a better perspective. Often marriage counselors are the eagles who, by virtue of their wider view, can help the troubled couple get a bigger picture of their situation, so that it can be approached at the most appropriate point. Finding a new perspective also means coming to see the other's world. This is what Richard and Denise Konner were able to do so well.

In his interpretation of the myth of Psyche and Eros, Robert A. Johnson points out the significance of the small vessel—the goblet—that Psyche uses to draw water from the River of Life:

There is a heresy abroad today which states if little is good, more is better. Advertisements tell us to "grab all the gusto we can" in life. This will not work. It means that one is never satisfied. Even while one is engaged in one rich experience, he is looking about for other possibilities. He is never content with anything because he is always searching for something bigger and better. . . . Our myth tells us that a little of quality, experienced in high consciousness, is sufficient for us.[6]

So it is with marriage. Before a young woman can nurture a lasting union, she must have the capacity to be satisfied with small experiences. A good marriage, like a goblet, is filled one drop at a time.

The fourth task that Aphrodite assigns Psyche is the most difficult and the most interesting. She must go down into the underworld, where Persephone reigns, and obtain for her mother-in-law a little cask of Persephone's own beauty ointment. A tower tells Psyche that she can make this underworld journey only by following these directions: She is to carry two coins in her mouth and two pieces of bread in her hand; she is to refuse to assist a lame donkey driver who will ask her to pick up his sticks; she is to refuse to grasp the hand of a drowning man who will plead for her help; and she is to refuse to assist the three women who weave the threads of fate. Instead, she must pay the ferryman with one of her coins so that he will take her across the Styx; then she must toss one of the pieces of bread to Cerberus, the three-headed dog who guards the entrance to Hades or hell, and while the three heads are arguing with one another over the bread, she must enter the underworld. There Psyche will find Persephone, who will give her the casket of beauty ointment. On her way back to earth, Psyche is directed to repeat the process.

Many theorists who study the psychological development of females regard Psyche's fourth task as the primary task of middle age. Psyche must curb her feminine inclination to nurture and care for the needy so that she can accomplish her goal. She must do what women find most difficult of all: She must say no. Even more, she must avoid the temptation to weave others' fates and instead concentrate on her own pursuits.

When a wife/mother gives up her caretaking role so that she can pursue her individual goals, she, like Psyche, must direct and focus her energies as never before. If she allows herself to become distracted by others' ongoing needs, she becomes too depleted, too scattered to be effective. As a family woman moves away from her familiar position of caring for her children and husband, one can expect all manner of trouble. In response to Denise's claim for a life of her own, Richard Konner became afraid—he felt his boat slipping from its moorings. A woman's mid-life transition, with her growing autonomy and new requirements for separateness, generates enormous tension in most marriages. I think it is possible for marriages to survive this crisis only if the woman has mastered Psyche's earlier tasks: sorting things through, finding unaggressive ways to exert will, and viewing the world from both her husband's perspective and her own.

When Psyche accomplishes her fourth task, she is transformed from an undifferentiated girl-bride into an autonomous, capable woman. By virtue of her difficult inner journey, she finds her soul: No more the humble moth, she becomes the full-winged butterfly.

If this were a conventional romance, the story of Psyche and Eros would end here with their joyous reunion. But it is not. The myth has deeper meaning still. Instead of giving Aphrodite the vial of beauty ointment, which Psyche worked so hard to procure, she decides to take some for herself. (Even mature women seem not to be able to turn away from the promise of more physical beauty. And for some—remember the tragic lives of anorexic and bulimic women—this may have lethal effects.) When Psyche opens the vial, she is overcome by a deadly sleep. Somehow Eros senses that his wife is in danger, and he flies to her, wipes the deadly sleep from her eyes, and takes her to Mount Olympus, where she is made a goddess. What this part of the myth teaches me is that even accomplished, capable, strong women require their husbands' help, just as capable, strong husbands require their wives' support. Moreover, it teaches me that in the best marriages, when, from time to time, husbands and wives act foolishly—as they are sure to do—they can count on each others' forgiveness. A good marriage, finally, is an alliance of kindness.

Let us briefly consider the evolution of Psyche and Eros's relationship. Nothing much comes of its romantic beginnings: As soon as Psyche wants intimacy with a real partner, Eros flees from her, and she is evicted from the magnificent castle that houses her. But after courageously struggling through hardships and accomplishing the tasks that push her into mature womanhood, Psyche *earns* her goddess status and, more important I think, the blessing of real love.

Fortunately, as Psyche develops so does Eros. Psyche was, in one way, correct to have envisioned Eros as a snake. As Jungian analyst Mario Jacoby writes, the spirit of the serpent reflects the drive toward change, autonomy, and creative masculinity. With the casting of its skin, which is dead, brittle, and obsolete, the snake throws off its shackles and transforms itself. Freeing himself from his mother's control and trusting his wife's wholeness, Eros becomes capable of marital intimacy. Now their union is complete and, not surprisingly, something splendid comes of it—Psyche and Eros have a daughter, whom they name Pleasure.

Once in a while, we mothers might remind our adolescent daughters (and ourselves) that just as May dissolves into June and the hawthorn blossom ripens into the berry, relationships between men and women can reach completion. We must teach our daughters not to be afraid of the crises that are a part of relationships but, if at all possible, to accept them as opportunities for new growth, which may bear unexpected Pleasure.

$\underline{7}$

Sorting Seeds:

Mothers as Single Women

THE STORY OF PSYCHE AND EROS IS IN ONE RE-
spect a moving and poetic celebration of married
love between men and women. It is also a metaphor
for feminine growth and development. Each of
Psyche's four famous tasks pushes her toward higher levels
of selfhood and greater competency so that she evolves from
a formless girl into a woman of character. This chapter will
concentrate on the first of Psyche's tasks and how it applies
to single mothers. That task, as we learned in the last chapter, is to sort into separate piles a mountainous jumble of
seeds and grains: corn, barley, millet, lentils, chick-peas,
poppies, and beans. With the help of ants (which represent
both the spirits of the underworld and a woman's own inner
or instinctive knowledge), Psyche succeeds in setting each
seed and each tiny grain in place. By differentiating and
separating the unlike kernels from one another, she transforms confusion into order. On the surface, Psyche's task
appears to be an external sorting of things; at a deeper level,
however, it represents an inward calling that requires the

painstaking sifting through of one's emotions, feelings, needs, wants, motives, and obligations. The act of creative sorting, moreover, is never accomplished once and for all, as the simplified form of the myth seems to imply. It is repeated each time a woman questions the value of her life—its assumptions and habitual arrangements—and wants to make changes.

"Strife," the Greek philosopher Heraclitus says, "is the father and king of all. Some it makes gods, others men; some slaves, and others free." No life is without strife; no marriage is without strife. If married couples have a reservoir of good will and fairness, they can turn strife to their advantage. They can use it not to build up grievances but to make themselves and each other more supple and responsive and adequate to the world around them. In that case, both husband and wife are made freer by it, as Heraclitus would say. Without that reservoir of good will and fairness, however, strife makes one or both partners slaves to helplessness, resentment, guilt, and bullying. If that happens, and if the situation is intractable, a woman, sorting through her needs, motives, and feelings, may also have to separate herself from her husband. Such separations, even from an unloved or disrespected husband, are difficult for most women and painfully difficult when dependent children are involved.

One of my clients, a forty-year-old mother of two adult sons and a daughter of fourteen, had suffered through twenty-three years of marriage with an alcoholic, volatile husband. Despite the marital misery she had known—his embarrassing binges, one-night stands with women he picked up in bars, endless excuses for and denials of his drinking problem, broken promises to be a better father and husband— Lynn stayed married to Frank but pondered her leaving. One night a dream came to her that not only prompted her first visit to me but guided her through the difficult process of ending her marriage. I am retelling a portion of Lynn's dream because, although it belongs to her, it may serve as a guide to other women who are sifting and sorting through their values and personal meanings.

Lynn dreamed that she was put in charge of a magnificent, many-colored glass egg. Not knowing any better, she placed the treasure in an old shopping bag, which she gave to her husband to carry. But the unsteady man tripped, fell, and let go of the bag. Horror-struck, she expected to find the glass egg broken beyond repair. But, to her relief, it had remained intact. Just as the membrane of an egg holds the cracked pieces of its shell together, something prevented the pieces of glass from falling apart. The segment of the dream ended as Lynn gently placed the broken but salvageable treasure into a jeweled safe and carried it away.

Lynn and I derived a double meaning from this dream. In one way, it showed how careless she had been with her own life, whose dream-symbol was the magnificent many-colored glass egg, by putting it in a shabby shopping bag in the hands of an unreliable and uncaring husband. But now, the dream indicated, Lynn was taking care of and responsibility for her life—in the dream, she put the glass egg in a jeweled safe, which she carried herself.

In another way, the dream seemed to suggest that shattering the glass was necessary. We felt that the egg was an important symbol: An egg, after all, signifies transformation and new life. Just as a chick breaks its shell in order to hatch, Lynn, by beginning to separate from her husband, was bursting through the container of her old, unsatisfying life in order to be reborn into a new world. Although her spirits had been broken by an unfaithful husband and a failed marriage, something in her remained intact and full of promise.

"*Je suis un autre*," the poet Rimbaud said. "I am an other." Beyond the self that our habits, routines, and fears make familiar to us is this mysterious "Other," with which we make contact in dreams, visions, and religious experiences. And this Other can point us in the right direction if we are attentive, as Lynn was. During our year of psychotherapy, Lynn often referred to her special dream and to the unconscious Other that had pointed her toward more responsible living. The Other had reminded the conscious Lynn that life, like a colorful glass egg, is full of light and possibility but also calls for a careful tending that must not be delegated to another. Just as important, Lynn's unconscious Other would not let the conscious Lynn forget that, like the cracked but intact egg, she is resilient. A divorce would not make her fall to pieces.

Today Lynn is a single, working mother. Her life is not easy. Like so many other single mothers (who are being called society's "new poor"), she is beset by financial difficulties. Moreover, although her marriage was miserable, Lynn misses having *a* husband; once in a while she even misses Frank. Despite all this, Lynn believes that she is better off for having left him and that her daughter, who lives with her but often visits with her father, is also better off.

Lynn's positive feelings seem to be the rule rather than the exception among middle-aged divorced women. Research by sociologists Grace Baruch and Rosalind Barnett and journalist Caryl Rivers, published under the title *Lifeprints*, strongly suggests that after they have passed through the crisis of divorce, most mid-life women look back upon it as a constructive experience, a push toward greater autonomy and competence. Similarly, Susan Rosewell-Jackson, who conducted intensive interviews with fifty Colorado women between the ages of thirty-five and forty-five, maintains that the divorced women in her sample demonstrated significantly higher levels of well-being and self-acceptance than the married women, especially those in first marriages. Rosewell-Jackson suggests that divorce and singleness force women to become more self-sufficient, which in turn promotes their self-esteem.

What I sometimes see in my clinical practice, however, is a tendency in women on the verge of making a good single life to sabotage themselves. It is as if the very experience of self-sufficiency creates too much discomfort. When this occurs, they may take the magnificent, fragile glass egg that is their precious life and thoughtlessly hand it over to someone else—most often to a man.

A vignette from my practice illustrates this tendency. About a year after her separation from an unkind, overly critical husband, Eloise—who is usually reserved and soft-spoken—burst into my office and exclaimed, "Dr. Bassoff, today I made an incredible discovery. I realized that I'm not a half of a zipper! I know this sounds strange, but let me explain. You see, when I was a little girl in elementary school I wrote a composition about what it means to be a happy person, and I came up with the metaphor of the two-sided zipper. I wrote that every woman was like half a zipper waiting to be matched up with the other half that would fit it perfectly and make it complete. Just like one side of a zipper is useless, I thought that without a man I'd be useless too. This is the reason I stayed with my husband so much longer than I should have. But it occurs to me that I'm happy and useful without a man. I'm doing well. My daughters are doing well. I'm a whole zipper all by myself."

Two weeks after Eloise shared this insight with me, she went on a vacation, where she met "a decent but terribly boring man," who was quite taken with her. In a sad little voice, she told me that she had accepted a date with him even though the idea of a relationship with a dull man filled her with dread. When I asked why she had agreed to see him, she explained that because he was a *nice* person, she didn't have the heart to refuse him and also that she felt a vague obligation to accommodate any man who sought her out and to be thankful that he wanted her. Eloise also confided that although her new self-sufficiency was gratifying, it made her uneasy for reasons she could not yet understand. An expert in nurturing others' lives, Eloise was still a novice in nurturing the one life over which she had control and for which she was responsible. Like so many other women, she was not yet able to turn away a vulnerable man, although accommodating him threatened her own well-being. The last and hardest task that Psyche is required to master requires that she reject the appeals for help from a lame donkey driver and that she refuse to give her hand to a drowning man. Even for a mythical princess, saying no to the needy is almost too difficult.

As we talked, Eloise and I also came to understand that it was not coincidental that just at the time she was delighting in her well-being as a single woman, she should accept a date with an undesirable man. It is a shortcoming of human reasoning to look for evidence that confirms what we think we know and to disregard evidence that goes against this knowledge. Eloise, like so many other women, learned that she could be happy and whole *only* in a relationship with a man. Therefore—not yet convinced that she was, in fact, like a whole zipper, complete in her self—she devalued her own experience of feeling happy without a man. And although her growing self-sufficiency pleased her, becoming an independent woman created an anxious feeling as well, much like the separation anxiety babies necessarily pass through as they break their symbiotic bonds to their mothers and become more differentiated beings.

Fortunately, despite her feelings of anxiety around separation, Eloise did eventually reject her suitor and begin to lay claim to her own full life. She is no longer apologetic for her single status but, on the contrary, delights in it: "I enjoy having my own place; I like fixing it up according to my tastes. I enjoy not being held accountable to a husband's timetable; anytime I want I can go out to a movie with friends and not worry about coming home to a grumbling man. And I love the feeling of accomplishment I get for doing it all on my own. After a demanding week, I can say, 'Eloise, you're a pretty terrific gal.' Things are really good for my little family—my two daughters and me. You know, even if a Prince Charming came along, I'd probably send him on his way." However, her near-regression reminds us that the well-being accompanying independence is not only hard to achieve but also hard to sustain.

Just as women can become healthier after a divorce, so

can their children. Researchers and mental health practitioners strongly suggest that children living with *consistently*
incompatible parents tend to suffer more psychological illness than do children of divorce. For example, professor of
psychiatry Arthur D. Sorosky claims that hostile parental
relationships are likely to turn adolescents into angry and
irritable people. Neurotic spousal arrangements, in which
the children are exploited as pawns, scapegoats, go-betweens,
and allies, may infect the youngsters with guilt. And devital-
ized couples, who have lost feelings for one another but
pretend to be friends, often create in their teenage children
emotionally flattened personalities. When the antagonistic
parents finally decide to divorce, an adolescent is likely to
feel considerable relief; now she can at last look forward to
some stability, clarity, and emotional honesty.

I am not suggesting that her parents' divorce is a happy
solution for an adolescent. Sorosky points out that a divorce
usually precipitates feelings of profound grief and guilt. Later
the bereft adolescent may feel resentful or even ashamed of
her parents' marital failure and, believing that all love relationships are doomed, is likely to approach potentially intimate attachments with apprehension and an expectation of
being abandoned. I am suggesting, however, that the child
of divorced parents who try to lead healthy individual lives is
better off than the child of an embattled, embittered married
pair. By trusting that her parents are responsible enough to
take good care of their own precious lives, the youngster can
let go the too-heavy burden of taking care of them. In
addition, mothers who insist on making the most of their
own lives teach their daughters that they can do the same.
Conversely, mothers who suggest that unremitting misery is
part of the female condition train their daughters to be
masochistic.

For a woman in a hopelessly unhappy marriage, her seed-
sorting task begins but does not end with the decision to
separate. The task of sorting—separating and differentiating—
ideally continues in her relationship with her adolescent

daughter, who is also in the process of sorting through her values and individual needs. We must remember that the unique stresses that divorce or the death of a parent generate for the adolescent do not supersede the normal conflicts that are part of adolescence. Adolescent girls growing up in single-mother families, like adolescent girls growing up in two-parent families, must be allowed to separate from their mothers—a separation that may be more difficult in the absence of the father/husband, who ideally acts as a buffer between the two females.

I would like to retell a dream that a girl of seventeen shared with her newly divorced mother, who in turn shared it with me. It addresses the separation struggles common to so many teenagers living in homes with single mothers. Laura dreamed that she and her mother, dressed in identical tweed suits, silk blouses, and leather pumps, were fashion models in a department store. (In real life, the mother was a partner in a prestigious law firm.) Laura became frantic when she noticed that her outfit was so large she looked ridiculous in it. In the midst of her panic, her boyfriend arrived, but, rather than coming for her, he moved seductively toward the older woman. Spitting and flailing, Laura screamed wildly at her mother: "Why don't you pick on someone your own size?"

At the time of the dream, Laura's mother, Priscilla, was beginning to go out on dates. Interestingly, a few days after the dream, both she and her daughter were waiting for their respective beaux when Laura "jokingly" suggested that sometime they might double date. A wise woman, Priscilla sensed that despite the girl's banter Laura resented her mother's dating and was in fact worried that they were competing against one another. (Laura's dream fragment—"Why don't you pick on someone your own size?"—suggested this to Priscilla.) Reestablishing the generational boundaries that had been temporarily blurred for Laura, Priscilla explained that double-dating was out of the question because she and her male companion, by virtue of their middle age, had little in common with Laura and her teenage boyfriend. "Remember, Laura," Priscilla emphasized, "I am your mother and not your girlfriend. Moreover, I expect you to be home from your date at the usual time, even though I will be out very late tonight."

A later dream fragment reflected Laura's relief that she and her mother had resumed appropriate roles. Now Laura dreamed that the two were in a high school where Priscilla was a teacher and Laura was her student. Adolescents need their mothers (whether married or single) to assume what psychologists term the *executive functions*. In plainer words, teenagers do best when their mothers are comfortably in charge.

Despite this fact, a single mother who does not feel she can turn to anyone else in the midst of her anguish may turn to her adolescent daughter as a confidante or companion and share everything from financial to work to love matters. Alone and adrift, she is tempted to draw her daughter in to her, and the daughter may be tempted to be drawn. When the mother lets this happen, she forgets that adolescence is the time when a daughter ideally loosens rather than tightens her family ties. She also forgets that as accommodating, responsible, intelligent, and articulate as her daughter may be, an adolescent is not ready to bear the weight of adult problems and adult decisions, nor to be privy to accounts of adult sex.

My mother-in-law once told me that when my husband was five, she had suggested that he prepare his own school lunches. Indignant, he insisted, "No, that's your job; I'm too little to do that." Similarly, when her newly divorced mother told one of my adolescent clients to take an active role in the design and construction of their vacation home, she responded appropriately by insisting that whereas schoolwork and a part-time job were her responsibilities, the decisions about the new house were her mother's. The dream Laura presented also made clear that she could not do her mother's work (symbolized by Mother's clothes, which did not fit

Laura) and thereby act as her partner. Not all adolescents are confident enough to make their needs known however. My daughter, for example, told me about a youngster in her high school class who was often truant because her mother persuaded her to skip school in order to take care of a baby brother and sister.

Difficult as circumstances are, the single mother needs to guard against the tendency to encourage her daughter's adulthood too early. I am *not* suggesting that the adolescent be spared taking on more household chores or finding a part-time job to help out. In fact, cooperation among family members is most desirable. I *am* suggesting that mothers must not forget the differences between mid-life and adolescence—and the activities appropriate to each. This is part of their seed-sorting task. For example, a dear friend of mine claims that her adolescents grew into such capable adults in great part because they had learned to pitch in during years of economic adversity following her divorce. Aware of the dangers of pushing them into a premature adulthood, however, she made sure that her children's after-school jobs still allowed them social lives and time to do their schoolwork.

Researchers who study family life concur that girls and their mothers are not meant to be best friends or partners. For example, in their scholarly article on single parents with young adolescents, psychologists David Glenwick and Joel Mowry insist that the maternal message, "We're in this together, kid," tends to create undue pressure for the adolescent, which may lead to myriad psychological problems. Drawing from my clinical experience, I would suggest that even the older adolescent is not emotionally steady enough to bear the weight of her mother's burdens.

Turning to fairy tales for explanations of healthy human development, child psychiatrist Bruno Bettelheim interprets Snow White's long deathlike sleep, which symbolizes adolescence, as the necessary period of gestation that prepares her for maturity. He points out that because a young girl has reached physical adulthood, we must not fool ourselves into believing that she is intellectually and emotionally mature. Such maturity proceeds slowly during the teenage and early adult years. As I explained in a previous chapter, Snow White's stepmother tried to turn the girl into a sexual woman before she was ready; similarly, single mothers who relate to their daughters as peers may force an undesirable precocious development. The immature mother of a fifteen-year-old girl I saw some months ago manipulated her into taking full charge of three younger siblings. The young girl dutifully carried out her mother's obligations and did not express resentment outwardly; her bulimic symptoms did the "talking" instead. By binging, she tried to take in the maternal nurture she still needed; by vomiting, she tried to spew the premature adulthood—the "poison apple"—that her mother had forced her to swallow. Finally, by becoming too physically ill to carry on, she rebelled against the inappropriate caretaking role imposed upon her.

Just as Psyche differentiates the various seeds into distinct groupings, mothers and daughters must separate their feelings and needs from one another's; they must be free to be different from one another, to be themselves. Human mergers are never healthy, and so Psyche's unassorted seeds are nothing but a mass of confusion.

One of the ways a single mother may inadvertently undermine a child's right to be separate from her is by confiding bitter feelings about her former husband. In doing this, she forgets that although she is no longer her husband's wife, the young girl is still her father's daughter. Certainly, a woman wronged by an ex-husband does well to acknowledge and express her anger at him, either directly with him or in discussion with sympathetic friends or a therapist. But she should realize that her anger is not her daughter's and that she must not muddle the young girl's emotions with her own. If she does, she undermines the girl's right to her opinions and reactions. When a daughter says (as she is likely to), "Mother, please stop talking badly about Dad," she is, in addition to expressing her filial loyalty, trying to sort out her own feelings about him from those of her mother.

One of the most generous ways a single mother can separate her needs from those of her daughter is by recognizing the girl's special attachment to her father. Celeste's story is a beautiful example of this. When, at fifteen, her daughter first suggested that she would like to live with her father and his second family in another state, Celeste was adamantly opposed. As she confided, "I had a full-fledged tantrum when Grace brought this up. I shouted her down with reason after reason why this was a terrible idea and even called her a selfish brat. Then, after my outburst, I wept uncontrollably and fell into a depression. I had been slowly preparing myself for her eventual leave-taking and had anticipated that our separation would occur after she graduated from high school—when kids normally go off to college. But Grace wanted to *rip* herself from me now . . . and *I* still needed her. For twelve years, it had been just the two of us. I thought that I could not face losing her permanently. Her wish to leave me *forever* for her father broke my heart."

Through couple therapy with her daughter, Celeste came to appreciate Grace's wish to strengthen her ties to her father and to her stepfamily. Growing up in a single-parent home, Grace missed knowing a more traditional arrangement, the kind that her father now headed: mother, father, children, even basset hound. Before it was too late for her, Grace wanted this experience to balance the (good) family experience she had had in her mother's home. In addition, Grace and Celeste's extremely close relationship made it difficult for the young girl to grow separate from her mother. Although she did not articulate this, Grace no doubt realized that her physical leave-taking would facilitate her necessary emotional one. Celeste, who had divorced because she needed to "be my own person," knew in her heart that her greatest gift to her daughter was to encourage her to be her own person too. Now her daughter was ready to accept this gift. On Mother's Day (what better day!), Celeste gave Grace her blessings to move to her father's home, and the girl left her mother by the summer's end.

Understandably, it took Celeste several months more to adjust fully to her daughter's leave-taking, for which she had so little emotional preparation. As theorist Bernice Neugarten points out, critical events that occur off schedule (like Grace's early departure) are more difficult to adjust to than those that happen on time (like a child's move away from home after her high school graduation).[1] Nevertheless, with the support of loving friends and a sympathetic therapist, Celeste has worked through her grief and is enjoying a full single life.

As Celeste and her ex-husband demonstrate, incompatible spouses, like incompatible seeds, often have a chance to thrive once they are planted in separate ground. I have known insufferable couples who, after divorcing and taking new responsibility for their individual development, evolved into the wonderful people they were meant to be. What is more, separate from one another, they also became far better parents. Grace (and other girls like her) is fortunate to have been spared the tension of living with mutually antagonistic parents. Instead, she is now free to move from one flourishing parental "field" (her mother's vital, nontraditional home) to the other (her father's cozy nuclear arrangement).

Just as women ideally differentiate their needs, feelings, and desires from their ex-husbands' and their daughters', adolescent daughters ideally respect their mothers' separateness. For example, a mother who does not interfere in the relationship between her former husband and their adolescent daughter is justified in insisting that the girl not share stories about him (or about his new girlfriend!) if these are painful or uncomfortable to hear. Some single mothers who have little trouble honoring their daughters' needs for separateness are reluctant to claim similar rights. While they tenderly close their daughters' doors, they leave their own wide open. Mother-daughter separation, however, is a mutual process. Adolescent girls are called on to sort seeds into separate piles as well.

Renee's and Rhoda's relationship is an example of failed separation between mother and daughter. When Renee, who had been divorced for seven years, began to date, her daughter was especially threatened; nineteen-year-old Rhoda, a young woman who seemed to have little purpose or direction, was unwilling to break the exclusive tie with her mother, who catered to her needs. Strident, loud, and rude, she succeeded in making her mother's new companions feel very uncomfortable. Moreover, she would convince Renee that each of the men she dated was a "real loser." Not surprisingly, Renee's relationships inevitably fizzled after one or two meetings. (In my imagination I envisaged Rhoda as the sorceress who hides Rapunzel in an inaccessible tower and then viciously pounces on the prince who dares to steal her away.)

Instead of insisting that her daughter behave with civility, Renee shrugged off her rudeness as something the young woman could not help. In therapy, however, Renee came to understand why she allowed Rhoda's tyranny. Renee recalled that a severe depression during the two years before her divorce prevented her from caring for Rhoda when she was a vulnerable young girl. Although seven years had passed since the breakup, she still could not shake off her guilt; she was convinced that the divorce and the years of emotional instability that preceded it had damaged Rhoda. By indulging her teenage daughter's demands for an exclusive mother-daughter relationship, she was trying to compensate for past maternal deprivations. (She may even have encouraged Rhoda's aggressive anger. When we feel guilty, we are likely to provoke the subject of our guilt to punish us.) At the same time, Renee's masochism ensured that she would not lay claim to the full social life she wanted but did not think she deserved. By virtue of her misguided maternal love, Renee only held herself and her daughter back: Renee failed to cultivate desired relationships with men, and Rhoda was locked into the unappealing role of saboteur and brat.

All too commonly, divorced women attribute their children's personal difficulties to the broken marriage and try to undo the perceived harm by overindulging them, blaming themselves, or both. It is true that divorce (like any number of other disruptive, unplanned events) may negatively affect a child, but neither spoiling nor paying penance can do any good. Rather, mother and daughter are helped if they articulate the past hurt, apologize for past wrongdoings, mourn for what is lost, and then move on. Usually, an empathic outsider can facilitate this process. Mother and daughter cannot be each other's psychotherapist; "getting into each other's heads" will only frustrate their necessary separation from one another. Renee, despite the possibility that she had failed her daughter in certain ways, had a personal responsibility to take good care of the precious "glass egg" in her charge—her life. Renee also had a maternal responsibility to encourage Rhoda to do the same, whereas indulging Rhoda's infantile demands reinforced her inappropriate dependency. As it was, bound to one another by virtue of their regressed mother-daughter relationship, Renee and Rhoda were also held back as individuals.

In her moving prose, Tillie Olsen describes the need to let go of maternal guilt, from which Renee and so many other single mothers suffer. *I Stand Here Ironing* is her short story of a single mother whose harsh living conditions affected her daughter's emotional health. Fully aware of the adolescent girl's psychological impairment, this mother is nevertheless able to extricate herself from the bondage of guilt and her daughter from the bondage of helplessness. As she stands ironing, she says to herself (and to all mothers burdened with the knowledge that their children have missed having a good family life):

Let her be. So all that is in her will not bloom—but in how many does it? There is still enough to live by. Only help her to know—to make it so there is cause for her to know—that she is more than this dress on the ironing board, helpless before the iron.[2]

For single mothers, just as for Psyche, the task of sorting—identifying needs, wants, and obligations; separating from incompatible spouses and from their children—is bound to generate anxiety. In fact, upon Aphrodite's command to sort the welter of seeds, Psyche has a major anxiety attack, wherein she collapses and is even driven to thoughts of suicide. In addition to the psychological sorting that is required of them, single mothers are typically confronted by a growing mountain of financial responsibilities that they must somehow sort through. For women hampered by greatly diminished monetary resources—as most divorced mothers are—creating economic order for themselves and their children may seem like an impossible task. I cannot recall even one case in which I counseled a single mother in whom anxiety was absent.

Anxiety is a most uncomfortable, at times painful, state characterized by any of a host of physical symptoms: fatigue, agitation, insomnia, headaches, sweating, tingling, trembling, racing heart, banging heart, "missed" heartbeats, palpitations, choking or suffocating, gastrointestinal disorders, and even visual aberrations. At an emotional level, anxiety is a diffuse, pervasive feeling of dread that makes one feel unsure and helpless. As philosopher and psychiatrist Rollo May pointed out, in anxiety our "core" or "essence" is threatened; we feel that we are coming apart. Similarly, Sigmund Freud likened anxiety to a cosmic experience because it invades our whole subjective universe.

Because anxiety is such an unpleasant experience, it is quite natural that its sufferers try to defend against it. Normal anxiety, however, becomes pathological if these defenses are fixed and maladaptive. Consistently denying that any personal problems exist, behaving compulsively, anesthetizing oneself with drugs and alcohol, and working frenetically but joylessly are just a few examples of such unhealthy defensiveness. Although in the short run armoring oneself against anxiety wards off pain, this strategy is costly in the long run, because anxiety is a necessary condition for creative growth. Every writer beginning a new chapter, every painter facing an untouched canvas, every scientist confronting an unsolved problem *and every single mother restructuring her family life experiences anxiety*. Anxiety is the painful labor of internal reorganization that gives birth to new solutions; without it, there is no change, no creativity. Hence, the philosopher Soren Kierkegaard wrote: "He therefore who has learned rightly to be anxious has learned the most important thing."

Rollo May conceptualized anxiety as a "cleavage" between expectations and reality. The creative work of anxiety involves building a bridge between the two. For the mothers of adolescents, the creative work of anxiety often means reconciling their secret expectation that they will always be intimately involved in their daughters' lives and the reality that their daughters are growing apart from them. For single mothers without love partners to cling to, such separation anxiety may be especially intense and lead to depression: an awful feeling of abandonment and all aloneness. Moreover, in our culture expectations of the "good life" include being married, raising carefree children, and enjoying material comforts—expectations that contradict the realities of single mothers. These mothers may then ask themselves: "Is there something wrong with my life? Is there something wrong with me?" One of the psychological tasks of a single mother is to change her conception of the good life and of the good mother so that it is more congruent with her true conditions. This often involves learning that self-worth, security, and happiness do not depend on having a husband or an unchanging, intimate relationship with the growing daughter, and that an adolescent's well-being does not depend on a two-parent home.

Working through anxieties is no less important than working through loss, both of which are normal experiences of parenthood. Unfortunately, most of us are taught to flee in terror from our darker moods instead of letting them in and exploring them. Because medical practitioners, like the rest of us, have learned to fear suffering, they may prescribe antidepressants or sedatives too easily and try to pull their patients out of depression or anxiety prematurely. Because too few modern sources teach us natural ways to experience anxiety, it is a good idea to turn to our ancient teachers who welcome rather than shun even the darkest human emotions. Just as the goddess Demeter teaches us how to confront depression, our friend Psyche can teach us how to move gracefully through anxiety.

Although Psyche becomes terribly anxious when Aphrodite imposes her seemingly impossible tasks, she does not reach for a Valium or drink a glass or two of wine or take a six-mile run. Instead, Psyche learns to *stay with* her anxiety. She becomes very still, directs her energy inward, and waits for solutions to come to her. And they do.

From the last chapter, readers may recall that at one point an eagle provides Psyche with the solution to one of her tasks. This eagle, with its panoramic vision, symbolizes the healthy perspective we all need to make realistic assessments of difficult situations. In a state of anxiety, we often become alarmed and panic; we flail and thrash about in our desperate efforts to find relief but find ourselves all the more submerged in our troubles so that we are drowning. The better solution is to flow with our anxiety. In Joseph Conrad's words: "To the destructive element submit yourself, and . . . make the deep, deep sea keep you up." In this way we also release the eagle, whose keen eye and panoramic vision become ours.

As the author of *Hope and Help for Your Nerves*, Dr. Claire Weekes, explains,

> If our education had included training to bear unpleasantness and to let the first shock pass until we could think more calmly, many an unbearable situation would become manageable, and many a nervous illness avoided. . . . There is a proverb expressing this. It says, "Trouble is a tunnel through which we pass and not a brick wall against which we must break our head."[3]

When I counsel women who are in the midst of crisis, as is usually the case for new single mothers, I teach them Psyche's ancient ways. Confident that they can find solutions to their problems, I instruct them to find a quiet private place with a comfortable chair and to sit with their anxiety, allowing it to unfold as it will. As they attend to their inner voices, bodily sensations, and images that arise from the subconscious, their panic inevitably subsides so that they no longer feel so overwhelmed. At this point they begin to acquire the necessary perspective to consider ways of addressing their difficulties. Sometimes it is possible to find solutions to problems in one sitting; most often, however, many sittings over long periods of time are required to move through anxiety toward constructive resolution. Single mothers must not become too impatient with themselves, because they are not likely to find quick or easy answers for their difficulties.

Rebecca, a widow and the mother of a teenage son and daughter, provides one example of healthy adaptation to an anxiety-ridden situation. Within the span of a few weeks, many serious problems confronted her family. Her daughter was injured in a car accident, her son was suspended from school after the vice principal found him drinking in the boys' bathroom, and her position as a high school music teacher was threatened by planned layoffs in her school district. With this burden of sorrow and no one to lift it from her shoulders, Rebecca became depressed and anxious. Although she managed to get through her days, her nights, which she spent tossing and turning in bed, were particularly dreadful. During one of these sleepless nights, she crept from her bed onto the overstuffed easy chair that had been her husband's favorite and wept for hours. Then, quite exhausted from her fit of crying, she sat very, very still. Slowly a calmness, which she had not experienced in weeks, came over her. Now, at last, she was able to look at her problems without panicking; she could begin to sort things through. And now, for the first time, her problems didn't seem so terrible. In fact, suddenly her whole situation seemed *almost funny*.

In Rebecca's words, "My family was in such bad shape that the only thing left to do was laugh about our miseries. I had an image of the three of us—my daughter on crutches, my son swilling down a bottle of Gallo, and me looking like a bag lady—begging on the streets as we gustily sang "Oh, We Don't Have a Barrel of Money." I thought to myself that we probably were a bit raggedy and funny, but I also knew we'd somehow make it; as the lyrics go, we'd travel along, sing our song, side by side. After my 'revelation,' I started singing, so loudly in fact, that I woke up the kids, who then joined me. At four o'clock in the morning, the three of us laughed and sang in jubilation."

Rebecca's anxiety gave birth to laughter. As Sigmund Freud suggested, "Humor is a means of obtaining pleasure in spite of the distressing effects that interfere with it." Similarly, theorist George Vaillant, who has carried on Anna Freud's study of defense mechanisms, described humor as one of the mature human defenses that promote healthy adaptation to life. By renewing her sense of humor (the sense of humor that had faded since her husband's illness and consequent death), Rebecca could also begin to cope with the problems at hand. In fact, before morning she came up with a plan to give private music lessons, just in case her job did fall through, and to consult with a psychologist at an alcohol treatment center about her son's problems.

A wonderful mythological character named Baubo who visits the despairing Demeter at the Laughless Rock. As Baubo jokingly lifts up her skirt to expose herself, she also lifts Demeter's spirits. The Jungian writer Nor Hall writes that in telling funny stories and making obscene gestures, Baubo gives birth to laughter, specifically "belly laughs." Single mothers who are overwhelmed by life's demands do well to invite her into their hearts from time to time, as Rebecca was able to do.

For Rebecca, anxiety transformed itself into a heightened

sense of humor, but other women channel anxiety in different ways. Marsha suffered from severe anxiety after she learned that her eighteen-year-old daughter was a lesbian. She ruminated about the causes of her daughter's sexual orientation to the point of making herself physically ill. Unable to come up with a definitive explanation (just like those who deal with this phenomenon professionally), Marsha would instead end up blaming herself, her divorce, and her ways of mothering for "damaging my child." I suggested that instead of obsessively analyzing her daughter and their relationship, she might rather "sit" quietly with her anxious feelings to see where they would lead her.

During one of these sittings, which took place in our therapy session, Marsha experienced her anxiety as the voice of her mother screaming: "Marsha, you can't do anything right. Look, you managed to ruin your marriage and, worse still, you've messed up your daughter—turned her into a pervert!" Quaking, Marsha conjured up the image of her critical mother and, for the first time, challenged her. She heard her own voice, at first small and trembling, say, "No, Mother, I've raised a fine young woman and, to my credit, I've done this all on my own." Then it became stronger and more insistent: "Now I want to tell you something else. I will not let you belittle my child or me ever again!" In her mind's eye, the image of the disparaging mother suddenly dissolved into the image of her daughter—a lovely young woman. At a later meeting, Marsha told me: "As I am letting go of my need for my mother's approval, which I could never get anyway, I am also beginning to relax with my daughter. I say to myself, 'So what that she is gay . . . so what.' "

When I was a graduate student, a mentor, Carol Schneider, told me that she had come up with a wonderful therapy for anxious, perfectionistic clients called "the so-what therapy." As she half-jokingly explained, thinking and saying "So what!" transforms problems from mountains into molehills. In Marsha's case, it did even more: For Marsha, her daughter's homosexuality was no longer a problem.

When it is not rigidly defended against but bravely allowed instead, anxiety is a prelude to some kind of inner change and growth—an expansion of the self. Rebecca's revived sense of humor and Marsha's newly discovered ability to "let go" are two of many possible examples of such healthy adaptation.

Just like their parents, children of marriages that end through divorce or the untimely death of a parent are likely to experience considerable anxiety as they reorganize their disrupted lives. In the wake of this crisis, the ground underfoot does suddenly give way and, for a time, everything is shaken up, as thirteen-year-old Betsy's dream vividly portrays.

In her dream Betsy was sitting at the dinner table with her mother and little brother when suddenly the house began to shake violently. As they raced toward the picture window in the living room expecting to look out on the familiar grassy suburban landscape, they saw, instead, raging white water all around, which was sweeping their little house out to sea. In a panic, Betsy's mother screamed at her, "Take the helm and steer the boat." But Betsy cried, "I can't, I'm not twenty-one yet," to which her mother answered, "But, dear, neither am I."

As her dream so poignantly told her, Betsy, not yet twenty-one, was not mature enough to steer her family out of danger. Her mother, however, *was* over twenty-one. No matter how directionless and out-of-control Hannah's depression made her appear after the breakup of the marriage, it was her maternal task to lead the family and to assure her daughter of this fact. During a shared therapy session, Hannah did just this when she said, "Betsy, your father's decision to leave me is a terrible blow. Because of it, I'm depressed and anxious now, and I have a right to be. We all have a right to be very, very upset. *You* have a right to your fears and nightmares. But I can promise you that I won't let you or your brother down. It may take a little while for me to get my bearings, but I won't let you down. . . . *I* know

you can count on me, and I want *you* to know this too."
Over time, with the help of supportive psychotherapy and
with her mother's continuing assurances, Betsy became less
overwhelmed. She gained confidence that she could move
through her anxiety, just as her mother seemed to be doing,
and she learned that it was acceptable to be an ordinary
thirteen-year-old.

Let us remember that anxiety (as long as it does not
become incapacitating) is a sign of psychological growth for
an adolescent girl just as it is for a grown woman. It is a
normal response to a trauma, such as the loss of a parent
through divorce or death, and a prelude to internal reorganization. At the same time that mothers need to intervene (as
Hannah did) to ensure that their adolescent daughters are not
overwhelmed with unmanageable psychological tasks, they
must not pull them out of normal anxieties prematurely.

The value of anxiety is affirmed through a little-known
story by the Brothers Grimm called *The Fairy Tale of One
Who Went Forth to Learn Fear*. In it the hero, who recognizes his lack of fear as a human deficiency, takes it upon
himself to learn how to "shudder" and thus is able to find
satisfaction in life. In the same vein, Claire Weekes ad-
vises: "A certain amount of suffering is good for us, particularly when young. We should not be sheltered too much.
The experience you gain from your present suffering could
be your staff in years to come."[4]

When my children are in an anxious state (and I sense that
their problems are manageable ones), I let them know that
inner turmoil is a kind of growing pain and that even their
worst feelings will not harm them. I also let them know that
although I am there for them, I have confidence that they
will work through their turmoil in their own special ways.
Then I leave them to their own sorting. A wise little twelve-
year-old was in part responsible for my growing comfort with
my children's normal depressions and anxieties. A month
after her father died of a heart attack, she told me that her
relatives prevented her from being too upset. "They are

always trying to cheer me up, but I get the feeling this cheering up is making me worse. I wish they'd just let me and my mother be crazy for as long as we have to."

Single mothers—and all other mothers who bravely pass through their own anxieties in order to create new and better lives for themselves—have the perfect opportunity to teach their daughters to do the same. Changing Kierkegaard's wise words ever so slightly, let us say that *she* who teaches her daughter to be anxious rightly, teaches her the most important thing.

Some adolescents, however, react to the crisis of divorce or the death of a parent in unhealthy ways; they do not know how to be anxious rightly. Rather than adapting to their new situation over time (and it does take considerable time to make this adjustment), they continue to be incapacitated by their anxiety. For example, as her safe little world is suddenly swept off to sea, a youngster may, in her efforts to regain a sense of control and to ward off further "catastrophe," fall into a pattern of excessive vigilance. To borrow my friend Judah Levine's description, the anxious girl must carry an umbrella even on a cloudless day, but still she is not protected because the anticipated storm might blow away the umbrella, so that soon she will need to carry two umbrellas, which are also not sufficient to guarantee her well-being because they too can be blown away.

I know one young girl who, two years after the death of her father, rarely ventures from her home. By staying in the house, she entertains the illusion of protecting herself and her depressed mother from further trauma, but her anxiety, which nevertheless breaks through, reminds her that they are still not safe. Not unexpectedly, her reclusiveness is also frustrating a desirable psychological separation from her mother and depriving this adolescent of the adventures that are part of growing up.

Another maladaptive reaction of the adolescent who experiences parental loss may be to feel fatalistic. Her logic is that bad things must happen and there is nothing to do but resign herself to this fact. For example, some of my older adolescent clients think that their love relationships are doomed to end as painfully as their parents' marriages have ended. They anticipate the "inevitable" heartache and thereby bring it on themselves. Sabotaging their relationships allows them some control, whereas simply waiting for the expected breakup reinforces feelings of helplessness. One young man told me that he couldn't conceive of a good relationship. Because of his parents' bitter one and nasty divorce, the very idea of two people loving each other forever was beyond his wildest imagination. For this reason, he entered every new relationship with a cold heart and, at the first sign of a girlfriend's dissatisfaction with anything he said or did, abandoned her.

Mothers can help heal their wounded children by re-empowering them, encouraging them to feel effective rather than impotent. Like the girl in Tillie Olsen's short story, they can know that they are not limp dresses, "helpless before the iron." Moreover, they can learn healthy forms of self-control, unlike the unhealthy ones represented by eating disorders. I have observed wise single mothers help their daughters retake control of their own lives in all sorts of constructive ways. For example, Peggy knew that her small income and meager child support payments would eventually force her and her daughter, Mary, out of their upper-middle-class neighborhood. Realizing that her daughter was still reeling from the unexpected divorce and would not adapt well to another sudden change, Peggy did everything she could to prepare the young girl. She let her know exactly when the move would occur and invited Mary to accompany the real estate agent who would show them houses in less expensive neighborhoods. Peggy also assured her daughter that her preferences for neighborhood and house would weigh heavily in Peggy's decision. As a result, Mary felt more in control and more effective; she did not have to wait in dread for another unpredictable storm but could forcast future changes with reasonable accuracy.

Another woman, Freya, whose husband was killed in a plane crash, moved her family to the town where her in-laws live. As she explained to me, "My mother-in-law and father-in-law are both robust people in their sixties and have enjoyed forty years of marriage together. I wanted my children to have them as models and to see that it is possible for couples to live good, long, full, healthy lives with one another. I really want my kids to know that, by and large, they can be in charge of their lives just the way their grandparents are and, despite their father's terrible plane crash, have faith that the sky won't fall in on them."

To conclude this chapter, I would like to return briefly to the myth of Psyche and Eros, where Psyche's reward for accomplishing the nearly impossible tasks that her mother-in-law, Aphrodite, imposes is a loving reunion with a lost husband and the birth of a daughter named Pleasure. In our modern-day usage, we associate "pleasure" with leisure and sensual delights, but as Mario Jacoby notes, the ancient Greeks considered it somewhat differently. For them virtue, as well as happiness, is a part of pleasure. Accordingly, a person is rewarded with pleasure only if she becomes conscious of her values and personal meanings. In this view, pleasure is akin to our modern concept of inner development and self-realization; it is the fruit of psychological struggle and maturation.

The single mother who conscientiously sorts her seeds despite the anxiety that such sorting generates is pregnant with Pleasure.

8

Beyond Dr. Seuss:

Adoptive Mothers

WHEN MY CHILDREN WERE LITTLE, I LOVED to read them a story by Dr. Seuss called *Horton Hatches the Egg.* Horton is a very dear elephant who comes to the aid of a flighty, flaky bird named Mayzie by agreeing to sit on the egg in her nest (no mean feat for an elephant) so that she might take a short vacation in Palm Beach. Horton does not yet know that fun-loving Mayzie will decide not to return to her egg-sitting duties, but this turns out to be the case. Caring and "faithful one hundred percent," Horton lovingly tends the abandoned nest left in his charge despite all sorts of obstacles, including his becoming an object of derision in the animal world. And when, after many months, the egg in the nest hatches, instead of a baby bird, a baby *elephant*-bird with ears, a tail, and a trunk just like Horton's bursts from the shell. The last drawing in this picture book depicts the proud Horton with his adopted baby, surrounded by their admiring animal friends, looking pleased as can be because they belong to each other "one hundred percent."

At this happy ending, my children always clapped their hands, and I always became teary-eyed; in Dr. Seuss's delightful storybook world, caring and faithfulness are duly rewarded.

I suspect that every parent of a baby wants to believe what Dr. Seuss implies: When baby grows up, she will reward her generous caregiver with love, happiness, and perhaps even gratitude. As many adoptive parents come to know, however, Dr. Seuss does not tell the whole story. For a mother and her adopted daughter, the normal conflicts around separation tend to be especially intense and the years of the girl's adolescence are often fraught with problems. If a psychotherapist were to write a sequel to Horton's story, one version might read something like this:

Horton is determined to be the finest parent in the world to Elephant-Bird. In fact, he becomes a "Super Mom." More than the other mothers in the jungle, he indulges his little one by providing her with the best of everything. The other mothers are casual about their children, but Horton, who suffered through so many trials and tribulations to hatch Elephant-Bird, does not ever take their relationship for granted. Indeed, he gives up his own pleasures to accommodate Elephant-Bird's every wish, watching over her with a vigilant eye to make sure that she will grow up to be fulfilled and responsible; and, indeed, she is a delightful child.

Sometimes, however, Horton worries that his little charge may have inherited some of the undesirable characteristics of her birth mother, lazy Mayzie. So, whenever Elephant-Bird is daydreaming or lolling around, Horton gets uptight and insists that she do something productive. But even when Elephant-Bird complies, uncomfortable feelings nag at Horton that she is taking after Mayzie. Because Horton, for reasons he can't pinpoint, has never felt completely at ease among the ordinary mothers, he sometimes thinks that it would be helpful to share his concerns with other special mothers like him who have adopted children, but he is too embarrassed to seek them out. So he puts lazy Mayzie out of his mind and pretends that everything is just fine; since Elephant-Bird doesn't bring her up either, Horton begins to believe that Mayzie is not really important to their lives—and this is a great relief to him. Despite the slight discomfort regarding Mayzie and the usual annoyances of parenting, Horton loves being a mother; he is the Demeter of the jungle. For twelve years, mother and daughter live in peace and harmony.

However, on Elephant-Bird's thirteenth birthday, things begin to change. Elephant-Bird develops wings—just like Mayzie's—and, against Horton's wishes, flies far from the savanna that is her home whenever she has the whim. In addition, she turns away from the well-adjusted elephants who were her childhood friends to keep company with a flock of rowdy birds. At home, Elephant-Bird is sullen much of the time and refuses to comply with Horton's house rules. When Horton beseeches her to change her disagreeable ways, Elephant-Bird rudely flaps her wings and caws. One day, a note from the junior high school principal arrives in the mail, which informs Horton that Elephant-Bird, once an excellent student, is failing her courses. Gentle Horton is now at the end of his wits. With flapping ears, he angrily demands that Elephant-Bird provide some good explanations for her unacceptable behavior, to which she screeches, "I don't have to do anything you say. YOU'RE NOT MY MOTHER!"

Horton is stunned by his daughter's cruel words. Choking back tears, he backs away from Elephant-Bird. "What has gone wrong between us? How have I failed as a mother?" he asks himself. Full of despair, Horton lowers his big body to the ground and weeps; he is frustrated and miserable one hundred percent.

My extension of Horton's tale brings us to the subject of this chapter: adoption and how it affects mothers and adolescent daughters. Curiously, there is little published information that addresses this subject, so that a great many adoptive mothers are unprepared should their well-adjusted children do less well as adolescents. "Why didn't someone forewarn me?" is a common refrain. If their adolescents temporarily turn against them, as is quite often the case, these women may ask themselves Horton's question, "How have I failed as a mother?" Horton's self-blaming question is, however, the wrong one, one that leads nowhere.

The more meaningful questions are: "How is the relationship between a mother and her adopted child special and different from the one between a mother and her biological child?" "Why is the adopted daughter's adolescence often a difficult time?" "What can be done to promote the healthy adjustment of both mother and daughter?" In order to answer these questions, we must first understand the conflicts that underlie the early attachment and ensuing relationship between an adoptive mother and her adopted child. Specifically, we must understand the personal losses that each brings to their shared life. Let us begin by exploring the world of the adopted child.

Whether she is a few days or a few years old, the adopted child begins her relationship with her adopted mother because she has lost the one with her birth mother. Even in those cases when a baby is adopted soon after birth, she has lost the woman who carried her for nine months. Science is not yet sophisticated enough to explain the impact of disrupting the bond between an infant and the woman who conceived her and in whose womb she grew. What happens in the dark prenatal world and how it affects us later on are still mysteries. But we must not make the mistake of underestimating the anguish—its intensity and duration—of the child's loss of the prenatal mother just because the child does not have the words to express it. As the poet May Sarton writes, ". . . there are griefs so still/None knows how deep they lie. . . ."[1]

Also, just because scientists cannot yet measure it, we must not discount the influence that the prenatal mother might have on her baby. Marilyn, the adoptive mother of a sweet-natured adolescent, said that she was convinced her daughter had been blessed by a loving birth mother, who instilled in her a sense of innate goodness; Andrea, the kind and devoted adoptive mother of a self-despising adolescent who had made several suicide attempts, told me she could not help but believe that the girl's rejecting birth mother, an unwed teen who had hated being pregnant and the fetus she carried, had emotionally poisoned the child while still in the womb.

For most children, the adolescent years entail difficult separations from their mothers. For many adopted children, the normal separation from the adoptive mother is also likely to stir memories of the unmourned, vaguely felt separation from the birth mother, and as these memories are stirred, some young women may experience feelings of great rage. Whether for the best or the worst of reasons, the original mother probably relinquished her child when she was a helpless infant, and the adolescent now asks herself, "How could my birth mother have left me?" "How could she care so little for me that she would turn me over to a stranger?" "Is it because I am defective in mind or body or spirit that she abandoned me?"

Rage expresses itself in countless ways—indirect as well as direct, against others as well as against oneself. Through acts of rudeness and defiance, the adolescent daughter may displace rage against her first mother onto her adoptive parents, against whom she may hurl false accusations: "You never loved me!" "You're glad that I'm unhappy!" "I know you think I'm dumb and ugly—I know you *hate* me!" Or she may turn rage against herself through such self-destructive behaviors as doing poorly in school, abusing drugs and alcohol, behaving promiscuously, lying and stealing, sabotaging her successes. She may tell herself, "I am unloved because I am dumb, ugly, and bad: What does it matter if I hurt myself or let others hurt me? I don't matter." Furthermore, if she believes her birth mother abandoned her because she is a damaged child, she is likely to expect that someday her adoptive parents will do the same. Rather than wait in dread for the inevitable rejection, she may try to bring it about herself (and thereby gain some sense of control) through provocative acting out. For example, when an adoptive couple whom I had been counseling decided to place their drug-abusing daughter in a residential school for troubled adolescents, she said to them, with part bitterness and part relief, "I always knew it would come to this."

To complicate matters, the adopted girl's feelings of indignation regarding her relinquishment may be entangled with benign feelings for the lost mother—curiosity and romanticized fantasies and tender longings. Indeed, her adolescent quest for a personal identity may move her to search for the original mother, who holds the key to their shared heritage. Moreover, at the same time that she idealizes her birth mother, she may devalue her adoptive mother by thinking or even saying to her: "My *real* mother wouldn't treat me this way." "My *real* mother wouldn't make my life miserable, the way you do." "My *real* mother is a hundred times better than you."

In the Boston Museum of Fine Arts, there is a stunning painting by Paul Gauguin titled *Where Do We Come From? What Are We? Where Are We Going?*, which portrays the human longing for self-knowledge. The central figure in this painting gives visual form to what I imagine the intense longing of many adopted girls must be: Gauguin's Tahitian Eve, standing among clusters of reclining young women, stretches her arms high over her head to pluck the fruit of a tropical Tree of Knowledge, while the others relax and chat among themselves. Unlike her nonadopted friends, who can take for granted their own genetic and cultural identities, the adopted young woman must reach and strain for hers. And just as Eve creates all sorts of trouble by plucking the forbidden fruit, so can she.

To take some examples, a colleague of mine who treats many adopted adolescents described one young client, the adopted daughter of two highly educated and well-to-do parents, who turned away from her social class to socialize instead with a group of drunken, drug-addicted transients.

The young girl believed she could find her own true identity as well as the spirit of her birth mother, who had been a poor, homeless girl, among this group of ne'er-do-wells. (Perhaps Elephant-Bird chose her rowdy new friends for a similar reason.) Another of my colleague's young clients channeled her longing for her lost mother into an obsession with a movie star, who was the same age as the birth mother and may have resembled her physically. Bedecked with magazine clippings and memorabilia, the young girl's room was turned into a shrine honoring the movie goddess, where the young girl spent excessive amounts of time daydreaming about her. Indeed, for a while she was so absorbed by her fantasies that she lost touch with the real world of peers, family, and school. The most self-destructive expression of the search for the lost mother that I have observed involved two orphaned teenage sisters whom I was treating. In what I interpreted as a desperate effort to reunite with their dead mother, the girls devised a sinister plan, which was fortunately intercepted, to commit suicide together.

I do not want to suggest that the adopted adolescent's search for and wish to make a connection to her birth mother is necessarily a sign of mental sickness. Most often, in fact, it is a healthy striving. In her pioneer study into the life histories of adults adopted as children, *Adopted Children: How They Grow Up*, Alexina M. McWhinnie emphasizes that although adopted people identify their adoptive parents as their true parents, they want very much to know about their biological parents. In particular, they want information that portrays their biological parents in a favorable light and that does not imply that they were rejected by them. All too frequently, however, adopted children censor their interest in the birth parents so as not to hurt the feelings of the adoptive parents by making them jealous or insecure.

The importance of a positive attachment between a child and her first mother is tenderly told in the fairy tale "Cinderella." The Brothers Grimm version begins, "The wife of a rich man fell ill, and when she felt that she was nearing her end she called her only daughter to her bedside and said, 'Dear child, continue devout and good. Then God will always help you, and I will look down upon you from heaven and watch over you.' " When she is old enough, Cinderella plants a twig from a hazlenut tree on the mother's grave. Nurtured by her frequent visits and watered by her tears, the hazlenut twig grows into a tree with magical powers that enhance the young girl. Showering her with silver and gold, the mother-tree transforms the shabby little girl into a dazzling young woman worthy of a prince's love.

The growing tree symbolizes the internalized Good Mother of the child's infancy who watches over her. All children, adopted or not, want to know that the birth mother loves and values them. Without the maternal affirmation of their innate goodness, they are likely to feel unworthy or even defective (as drab as a Cinderella in rags).

Like Cinderella's stepsisters, who are greedy for jewels, pearls, and fine clothes, girls who feel unlovable may wish to possess expensive things, which they experience as extensions of themselves and proof that they are dear and valuable too. I knew one adoptive girl who was badly affected when she learned that through private dealings babies are sold by the birth mother and bought by the adoptive parents. The idea that she may have been traded for money made Hilary feel not like a priceless human being but like a commodity with a price tag. As compensation for her feelings of intrinsic inferiority, she became very materialistic. But like Cinderella's stepsisters who, despite their finery, are rejected by the prince, Hilary, despite her designer labels, continued to believe she was unlovable.

Just as the fairy tale "Cinderella" celebrates the communion between the child and the spiritual birth mother, Wim Wender's movie, *Paris, Texas* focuses on a reunion between a child and the mother who gave him away. On the surface, his story is the realization of an adoptive mother's nightmarish fantasy: A vagabond, himself lost and without an identity, abducts his biological son from the home of loving middle-class adoptive parents in order to reunite him with his mother, who is a "hostess" in an Eros center that caters to men's sexual fantasies. At a deeper level, however, Wender's film addresses the human need to know who one is, to know from whom one comes, and to be allowed to return to one's maternal source. It is to experience familiarity rather than strangeness, belonging rather than alienation—to experience Paris, France, not Paris, Texas.

This movie brings to mind the experience of a middle-aged client whom I saw many years ago. Although Cassandra enjoyed a warm relationship with her adoptive parents, she was intent on identifying her birth parents and, despite many frustrations with bureaucrats, finally secured a copy of her original birth certificate. As Cassandra explained, just by seeing the names of her first mother and father on this commonplace document she felt special, not in the sense of being odd or different or better, but in the sense of being a *somebody* with her own personal history. As is so often the case for adopted people, Cassandra had little desire to meet her birth parents; affirming their existence was enough to affirm her own.

Whereas, like Cassandra, many individuals discover themselves through rediscovering their birth parents, others accomplish this through strengthening their ties with their acquired ancestry. Nora, a twenty-year-old client, spent a restless and agitated adolescence in and out of psychiatric institutions. Gentile by birth, she had been adopted when she was three by a Jewish couple with two children of their own. In the Jewish tradition, one's birth mother determines one's religion. Therefore, strictly speaking, Nora was not a Jew, a fact that haunted her and, I thought, reinforced her feelings of alienation from herself, from her adoptive family and from their world, with which she wanted to identify. During the course of our therapy, Nora became passionately involved with a sect of orthodox Jews and, despite a learning disability, was intent on mastering the Hebrew language and Jewish law so that she might become a "legitimate Member of the Tribe." Upon her formal conversion to Judaism, Nora took the Hebrew name Nashamah, the word for "soul," because, as she explained to me, she had at last found hers.

I have also observed that some daughters who have been cut off from their birth mothers are particularly drawn to the natural world, to "Mother Nature." The Brothers Grimm tell us that "Cinderella went to the [mother's] grave three times every day. She wept and prayed there, and every time she went a little white bird came and perched upon the tree. And when she uttered a wish, the little bird threw down to her what she had wished for."[2] It is as if the mother spirit lives in this gentle dove and the other small birds that come to Cinderella whenever she is overwhelmed. Other girls who have lost the first mother—and the blissful state of wholeness she symbolizes—may, like Cinderella, rediscover her in their friendships with animals. Through caring for (feeding, holding, stroking) these living creatures, they are themselves nurtured. The relationship with animals, because it is basic, simple, and unconditionally loving (like the original mother love), can foster the healing of old wounds. An unfortunate client, who as a girl had been shunted between foster homes, told me that the only times she feels good are when she is in the company of her dog or when she is backpacking in the high country and is one with nature.

The adopted daughter's oftentimes desperate search for identity surely affects her adoptive mother, especially when it involves a spiritual reunion with the birth mother. Just as the adolescent girl may have internalized rage toward the woman who relinquished her, the adoptive mother may harbor hostile feelings of her own. For example, she is likely to ask herself, "How could this woman have abandoned her child?" and "Why should my daughter—whom I have cared for all these years—want this irresponsible person back in her life?" (Readers will recall that gentle Horton himself does not have kind thoughts about birth mother Mayzie. In fact, her potential influence is so disturbing to him that he chooses to put her out of his mind altogether.)

But just as the adopted girl's adolescence provides an opportunity for her to reconcile feelings regarding the birth mother, it may also be a time for the adoptive mother to come to better terms with the woman who bore their child. As Sarton writes, "It is the incomplete/The unfulfilled, the torn/That haunts our nights and days/And keeps us hunger born."[3] When adoptive mothers make a real peace with the birth mother—that shadowy "other woman"—a new inner peace becomes possible.

However, acknowledging the significance of the relationship between the daughter and her birth mother can be threatening. Several adoptive mothers have told me that, although they try to suppress such feelings, they have always worried that their daughters would one day love their birth mothers more than them. During her adolescence, the daughter's normal distancing from Mother may exacerbate these fears. Moreover, since adopted children, because of the early abandonment by the birth mother, tend to harbor more rage than their nonadopted counterparts, they may act especially rejecting toward the adoptive mother, the target of their rage, reinforcing her expectation that she will lose the girl's love altogether. (Elephant-Bird's cutting words to Horton, "I don't have to do anything you say. YOU'RE NOT MY MOTHER!" is the blow for which many adoptive mothers wait in dread.)

It was Sigmund Freud who first identified the tendency for prepubertal children to invent fantasies about their beginnings. In their daydreams they often imagine that their true mothers and fathers, unlike the plain folks who call themselves their parents, are noble, grand, beautiful, rich, benevolent, and famous; and that one day they will be returned to these magnificent people and lay rightful claim to their own *aristocratic* heritage. At this time, they will be relieved of their drab daily existence and the terribly ordinary mother and father who impose it on them.

The psychological purpose of this universal fantasy is to help free the child from the parents from whom she must inevitably separate. It is, after all, easier to leave parents who are perceived as flawed than it would be to leave the perfect, all-knowing parents of one's early childhood; devaluing the real parents by inventing other and better parents eases the anxiety that separation from them necessarily entails. What is a fantasy game for children living with their natural parents, however, is a real condition for the adopted child, who most likely has two sets of living parents. And although many biological mothers can take in stride their adolescents' devaluation of them because they sense it is a normal part of growing up, adoptive mothers may be highly threatened by it. They may sense that they are not in competition with an imaginary idealized version of themselves but with a real woman—the feared "other woman."

One of my most touching clinical experiences has been with Colleen, who relinquished her baby born out of wedlock. Although Colleen loved the father of her child dearly, she knew that he was not responsible or emotionally stable enough to parent, and she felt very strongly that the birthright of every child is two caretaking parents. Moreover, she understood that as sole provider, she would not have the opportunity to stay at home with the baby, whom she would have to place in day-care centers, a condition she could not accept. In her third trimester of pregnancy, Colleen decided to relinquish the baby to a stable married couple able to give him their full attention and love. Not surprisingly, she grieves deeply for the child she so lovingly and selflessly gave away, but she is reconciled to this.

What is still impossible for her to accept is the adoptive parents' utter rejection of her special meaning to the child, evidenced by their cold response to her suggestion that when he is older she will send him a letter describing his birth parents and explaining their reasons for relinquishing him. She senses that they are thwarting such written contact out of fear that they might then lose his filial loyalty. Colleen is haunted by her own fear that the little boy will never know about his birth mother and birth father and about their love for him, and that in not knowing he will suffer unnecessarily. And, as therapist, I am frustrated that the adoptive parents have not been helped more by the social workers who coordinated the adoption to understand the importance of allowing a spiritual tie between their son and his birth parents.

In certain unfortunate cases, the adoptive mother may not only discount the importance of the birth mother but may actively demean her. Because her adopted daughter is likely to have been born out of wedlock, the adoptive mother may, for example, categorize the birth mother as promiscuous and immoral. For example, in McWhinnie's study, one of the adoptive mothers reported that her daughter's illegitimate birth was an indication of the birth parents' "weak wills" and that it was her maternal duty "to see that she [the adopted daughter] not go the same way."[4]

There are dangers in devaluing the birth mother. First, the adoptive mother may convey to her daughter the idea that the birth mother was defective, and this can only encourage the girl to feel defective herself, the product of damaged stock. Second, the adoptive mother may in fact come to believe that the girl is a bad seed, prone to be the "shameless hussy" her biological mother presumably was. Her dire expectation may then lead her to discourage or belittle the maturing girl's sexuality. (Similarly, we saw how anxious our friend Horton became when he thought Elephant-Bird was assuming Mayzie's lazy ways and how he forbade his daughter's quite normal tendencies to loll and daydream.) Furthermore, expectations are often self-fulfilling; the adolescent girl, aware that her mother expects her to become promiscuous, may fulfill that expectation—in despair or in defiance. As a pregnant adopted teenager told me, "My mother accused me of having sex with my boyfriend even when I wasn't. When I finally gave in to him, it was like giving in to her too—doing what she had expected of me all along."

Of course, there are destructive birth mothers—those who

emotionally or physically abused their children. In these instances, the adoptive mother's hostility toward the birth mother is natural. Nevertheless, she will be wise not to display her righteous anger in front of the child, who may not be ready to accept the fact that her first mother could not love her, but to vent her understandable rage in the presence of a sympathetic friend or counselor. There are other situations where the adoptive mother may be concerned that a birth mother's physical, emotional, or cognitive defects have been passed on to the child. Again, a knowledgeable counselor who is able to weed out irrational fears from rational ones might help the worried mother find a better perspective.

What may prevent some adoptive mothers from developing a benign attitude toward the birth mother is the very fact of her fertility. For adoptive women unable to birth children themselves, assumptions that the other woman became pregnant easily (and thoughtlessly!) may trigger feelings of outrage against her. Although these adoptive mothers may suppress such responses during the daughter's early years, they may be aroused during her adolescence. The nubile teenage daughter, who symbolizes the promise of fertile womanhood (just as her birth mother symbolizes its realization), may remind the adoptive mother of her biological inadequacy.

Perhaps no one articulates the desperation and envy of the barren woman more openly than the biblical Rachel: "When Rachel saw that she bore Jacob no children, she envied her sister; and she said to Jacob, 'Give me children, or I shall die!' Jacob's anger was kindled against Rachel, and he said, 'Am I in the place of God, who has withheld from you the fruit of the womb?' "[5] (Gen. 30:1–2). I suspect that many women who want but cannot bear children will feel at one time or another what Jacob bluntly puts into words: For some unknown, but no doubt terrible reason, God is punishing her by depriving her of the fruits of womanhood.

Marion, an adoptive mother, told a colleague of mine that

she has always felt like Hester in Nathaniel Hawthorne's *The Scarlet Letter*. The letter A she wears, however, does not stand for "Adulteress" but for "Adoptive mother" and, according to her, announces to all the world that she is biologically deficient as a woman. Like those who assume the guilt of original sin, Marion perceives her infertility as a sign of badness. When a woman suffers from such feelings of inadequacy, she may very well turn them outward, against the birth mother endowed with life-giving powers and even against the adopted adolescent girl who, most likely, will one day bear children of her own.

The adoptive mother's task is to understand infertility as an ordinary human physical limitation rather than as a "sign" of inferiority, badness, or lack of femininity. Moreover, it requires that she discriminate between the physical act of bearing a child and the emotional capacity to mother. Some adoptive mothers muddle the two. They believe that because they were unable to bring about pregnancy or birth, they are not *real* mothers. (As we saw in Horton's case, he became a "Super Mom" as if to prove he was worthy of his child by being more Mother than the biological mothers. Moreover, his discomfort among these mothers may have derived from his feelings of inferiority.)

Psychotherapist Sue Weatherley, who has headed the adolescent and family unit at Boulder's Mental Health Center for many years, tells me that when she treats troubled adopted adolescents and their overwhelmed mothers, her therapeutic work often includes reminding these discouraged women that they are—and have always been—good mothers. They must come to understand that their inability to bear children and their adolescents' present emotional difficulties are not caused by a lack of motherliness on their parts. As Weatherley says, "So often these women are terrific mothers—caring, conscientious, devoted. But because their kids are having severe problems, they think of themselves as failures. They berate themselves unduly for problems they haven't caused. They think something is wrong with them as mothers."

When a woman is confident of her own adequacy as a mother, she is much more likely to develop a benign relationship with the birth mother. Insecurity breeds mean-spiritedness; self-acceptance breeds generosity and goodwill. The following vignettes illustrate the ways two adoptive mothers—one who is a friend of mine, the other a colleague—encouraged their daughters to form positive attachments to their birth mothers.

From the time her daughter was little, Rosalind told her stories about the courageous fifteen-year-old girl who, despite social pressures, lovingly carried her baby within her womb for nine months and then unselfishly gave her over to parents who had the means to care for her. Rosalind's daughter grew up believing in the goodness of her biological mother, which enhanced her own self-perceptions. Interestingly, Rosalind confided that, unbeknownst to her daughter, she was actually given very little personal information about the child's birth mother but thought it was in everybody's best interest to assume that she was a wonderful person.

Jeanette, who adopted an abandoned Vietnamese baby, created a scrapbook with colored photos of Vietnam and of beautiful Vietnamese women who may have resembled the unidentified birth mother of her daughter. For the young girl, this scrapbook—a tribute to the unknown birth mother from the adoptive mother—was always a prized possession, one that she proudly displayed to her schoolmates for show-and-tell. Well aware of the importance of her daughter's Vietnamese parentage, Jeanette has promised her a trip to her homeland as a high school graduation present. Although Jeanette realizes that she cannot present her daughter with a ready-made identity, she is determined to facilitate, rather than discourage, the girl's search for it. Also, unlike well-intentioned but misdirected adoptive mothers who minimize or even ignore their children's racial or cultural differences, Jeanette celebrates her daughter's. For example, she has always encouraged her daughter to meet other Vietnamese youngsters and their families, with whom she might feel a special kind of communion, a special familiarity and coziness.

In addition to accepting herself and the birth mother, the adoptive mother who has not borne a child is required to make a final peace with another: the baby who was not born to her, the dream child who never materialized.

In a sense, all mothers of adolescents are in mourning for the little child who has abandoned them. By separating from their mothers, adolescents lay claim to their own identities, interests, purposes . . . and souls. No longer the babies who molded their bodies to the contours of Mother's holding arms or the little ones who willingly conformed to Mother's standards or the school-age girls who idealized Mother's very being, they now insist on their differences from her; and she, in turn, must mourn this separation and let go. In the case of biological parentage, however, this process is made easier by the fact that the daughter is likely to resemble the mother in many ways—physically, intellectually, temperamentally, and artistically. Their shared genetic heritage ensures a continuity between them, however much the daughter may assert her differences.

As the adopted adolescent girl matures, however, differences between her and the adoptive mother may be more marked than with the biological pair; mother and daughter may find that they are more unlike than alike. Consequently, the adoptive mother cannot indulge in the narcissistic delight of having her daughter take after her. For this reason, she may once again secretly long for her *own* child—the flesh of her flesh who would have immortalized her.

The adoptive mother without any children of her own is deprived of a certain kind of maternal joy. I recall, for example, how my mother and I delighted when my own daughter suddenly showed interest and considerable talent in drawing. "There is no doubt about it. Leah has *inherited* your artistic talents!" my mother chimed as I swelled with pride. And I admit to feeling a sweet pleasure each time my husband exclaims that at a quick glance he cannot tell my

daughter and me apart. The adoptive mother who sometimes longs for the experience of having a biological child
who resembles her is not betraying her adopted daughter
nor demonstrating a lesser love for her; rather, she is expressing a normal, perfectly understandable yearning for
something missed.

Though I would not advocate that the adoptive mother
parade this yearning before her daughter, I would not advocate that she deny it either. Censored feelings tend to express themselves anyway—often unbecomingly. The adoptive
mother who is forthright enough to admit some sadness at
having missed birthing a child inevitably adjusts to her loss;
she works through her grief. Moreover, by admitting to her
own disappointments, the adoptive mother becomes more
sympathetic to her daughter's—what one adopted young
woman described as "the great sadness of never knowing the
comfort of seeing in my mother's face an older version of my
own." The adoptive mother who is less open may find that
she is angry, often at her adopted daughter, without direct
cause; her masked sadness disguises itself as hostility or irrita-
bility or contempt.

In Edward Albee's *Who's Afraid of Virginia Woolf?* we
see the brutal effects of incomplete grieving. Here the pro-
tagonists, the childless couple Martha and George, have
invented an imaginary child who is central to their lives:

As Martha says, "And as he grew . . . and as he grew . . .
oh! so wise! . . . he walked evenly between us . . . a hand
out to each of us for what we could offer by way of
support, affection, teaching, even love . . . and these hands,
still, to hold us off a bit, for mutual protection . . . to
protect himself . . . and *us*."[6]

This invented dream child—"Beautiful; wise; perfect"—is
meant to make them whole and to deny their raw grief for
the real baby never born to them. Despite their shared
fantasy, however, their equally shared and unexpressed grief

transforms itself into a bitter protracted hatred, which they direct against themselves and each other. In the end, as a gesture of murderous spite against his wife, George has the imaginary son "killed" in a car accident. Whereas in one way the beautiful boy was the promise of their salvation, in another way he was the jailer who imprisoned them in their barren fantasy world. As George with uncharacteristic tenderness says to Martha, it was time for him to die. And without the child standing between them—"protecting" Martha and George from each other and from the truth—Albee hints that they may have a chance to become whole together.

For some couples, rather than compensation for a biological child, the adopted child takes on more significance than a child born to them possibly could: she is their mission. In their offspring, parents look for and soon find the ordinary and familiar: the little one might have Grandma's gray eyes, Mom's bow-shaped mouth, Grandpa's funny ears, Uncle's hot temper, and Dad's poor eyesight. An unrelated adopted child, however, is mysterious, and for this reason one may see in her any and all possibilities. She arrives—for many adoptive parents quite suddenly—in her lovely wrappings of bunting and booties like an angel dropped from heaven. Unlike biological children, who as often as not are unplanned, the adopted child is always wanted, sometimes desperately so.

It is her *over*-specialness to her new parents that, paradoxically, may lead to feelings of unworthiness on her part: an uneasy sense that who she is will never match what she is expected to be, and that however she tries she cannot possibly repay her adoptive parents for giving her so much. But feelings of indebtedness eventually lead to feelings of hostility. It is a human tendency to resent the people to whom we are always owing gratitude. I treated one couple who saw themselves as superior human beings for adopting a hard-to-place child and who expected to be rewarded through her gratitude and achievements for their humanitarian efforts. As

one might expect, the child paid them back not with gratitude but with rebukes. I knew another adoptive couple who
expected that through their adoring love and sacrifices to
provide the finest medical care, the finest furnishings, the
finest clothing, the finest cultural opportunities, and the
finest schooling, their adopted daughter would grow up to
be the queen she was meant (or more accurately, *they* meant
her) to be. Because this child grew up to be quite ordinary
and, in fact, demonstrated less than average intellectual
ability, her parents felt betrayed by her.

Like George and Martha, every couple must let go their
imaginary child—the dream child—in order to live honestly.
Such mourning is always painful, but when it is completed,
adoptive parents may attach themselves to a real child—one
who, like each of us, is limited and flawed but real—instead
of a dream child, required to be an idealized reflection of
them.

At a recent meeting of adoptive mothers, I listened to a
woman describe the tragically destructive path her adolescent daughter had taken. Despite the love and kindness of
this woman and her husband, the young girl never developed the capacity to feel for others—she was incomplete. It
was only after many years of failed attempts to find effective
treatment for her that the parents came to understood that
nothing would "fix" this emotionally disabled child. But coming to terms with their daughter's severe and permanent
defect allowed the couple to find an inner peace and to know
the deepest kind of parental love: At last, these exceptional
people were able to accept the real daughter, a suffering,
impaired human being, and let go the dream daughter, the
hoped-for healthy, happy child.

Before further describing the ways troubled adoptive children affect their parents' lives, I would like to make my own
biases known. Because I am a psychologist, I tend to see
people who are in crisis; by and large, the adoptive mothers
and adopted daughters who come to me—and my colleagues—

are beset with problems. But my focus on the emotional difficulties of adopted children and adoptive mothers is not intended to imply their inevitability. I am sure that there are many families with adopted children that traverse a more or less smooth path. Nevertheless, because every adoption is the result of the lost relationship between the child and her first mother, I believe that serious emotional problems are more common among families with adopted children than they are among biological families.

Sue Weatherley tells me that when adoptive parents of deeply troubled teenagers come to her for counseling, they are usually very tired emotionally, both as marriage partners and as parents. Before seeking professional help, most parents have already tried countless unsuccessful ways to calm their angry children, thus depleting their parental resources. They may now feel hopelessly discouraged. Many, exhausted by their adopted children's provocations, may be planning to send them away to boarding schools or foster homes, or, where there are severe psychological problems, to residential psychiatric institutions, thereby realizing the adoptees' prophecy that they will be abandoned a second time.

Not surprisingly, in their frustration and guilt these overwrought parents may lash out against each other. Through therapy they often learn ways to redirect their energy and turn lovingly toward, not blamingly against, one another; it is only when they are reunited that they may be able to help their distressed child effectively. Indeed, McWhinnie's study convincingly shows that the adjustment of adopted children is strongly related to their parents' marital satisfaction. Weatherley suggests that participating in ongoing support groups composed only of adoptive parents may help distressed couples deal with their special strains and tensions. In fact, she suggests that, as a preventative intervention, it may be a good idea for adoptive parents and their children to take part in such support groups even before family problems arise. At the recent meeting of adoptive mothers that I attended, I asked what would have helped them through

their difficult times. One woman replied that simply knowing that her daughters' severe problems were in part attrib-
utable to their adoption and not to bad parenting might have
eased her considerable suffering and that of her husband: "I
needed someone to tell us that we were not bad or crazy
parents. Because of our daughters' problems, we felt so
horribly inadequate as human beings." (Readers may recall
that Horton himself sensed that sharing his ongoing concerns
with other adoptive parents would be comforting.)

Even when the adolescent daughter does not act out, she
may trigger explosive issues in the family. One of the major
events of a girl's adolescence, of course, is her sexual transformation from child to young woman. Melinda helped me
understand how her own marriage was threatened by her
fourteen-year-old adopted daughter's emerging sexuality. As
she explained, "One morning as I was sitting across from my
husband and daughter over our Sunday breakfast, I became
keenly aware that Amelia was no longer a kid. Seemingly
overnight she had become a ripe, round, lusciously sensual
young woman. In fact, her breasts had become fuller than
mine, and I was jealous! Picking away at the pink grapefruit
in front of me, I was noticing that my husband was also
noticing her new voluptuous beauty, and all at once I felt
sick to my stomach. I had to leave the table because I was
overcome with envious rage toward her and sudden mistrust
toward him. I thought to myself, 'David must be thinking
that Amelia is more woman than me,' and for this I hated
them both."

To one degree or another, every woman fears that her
daughter's developing sexuality is surpassing her own and
that, for this reason, the young girl will now be favored by
the father/husband. Moving away from her mother emotionally and toward her father, the normal directions of adolescent females, the young girl is likely to exacerbate these
fears. Bruno Bettelheim points out that the early versions of
the "Snow White" fairy tale make explicit the oedipal
entanglements common during the daughter's adolescence. In

one of these versions, a count and countess (the parent symbols) who are driving along in their coach encounter the lovely Snow White (the nubile adolescent daughter) and enjoin her to ride with them. (They make the mistake so many parents make and seat her *between* them.) The count's admiration of the maiden so enrages the countess that she figures out a way to be rid of the girl. Upon the countess's request, Snow White descends from the coach to gather a bunch of roses and, as she does, the countess orders the coachman to drive away with great speed.

Normally, the relationship between the father and the adolescent girl is not sexualized because the incest taboo between them is so strong. Most mothers, then, can rest assured that their daughters are not serious competitors for the father/husband. In the cases where the daughter is not a blood relative of the father, however, the incest taboo is weaker—or the mother/wife may fantasize that it is. For example, as Melinda saw Amelia physically mature, she temporarily lost her protective maternal feelings and experienced the child as an unwelcome intruder, the sexy "other woman," who was intent on stealing away the husband. At the same time, she began to suspect that her husband would fall prey to the attractive young girl.

Melinda was eventually able to understand the reasons for her fears. Indeed, Amelia's sexual development awakened painful memories: "Once again I was dealing with the nightmarish experience of my infertility. In dreams and fantasies, the humiliating examinations by gynecologists, the medical tests, the anxiety-laden waits for results, the inevitable monthly disappointments, and the envy toward my pregnant friends came back to me. I felt as unfeminine and sexually undesirable now as I did then. In a way, I suppose I thought Amelia had become more woman than me, and I projected these feelings onto David, who in reality is very satisfied with me as his wife."

With a great store of goodwill and mutual kindness, Melinda and David could openly discuss the ways their daughter's sexuality had threatened their marriage. Assuring Melinda of his continuing sexual commitment to her alone, David helped her to regain self-confidence and to let go maternal envy. In turn, Melinda was able to support Amelia's and David's increasingly close relationship; fatherly David—like all appropriate parents—was not seductive with his child and, unlike less fortunate girls, Amelia did not have to pay the awful price of losing her father's affection for her new womanliness.

Up until now, I have dwelled on the effects of a woman's infertility on the adoptive and marital relationship. Of course, many adoptions come about even if her infertility is not an issue. Many couples with biological children also adopt children, and it is not uncommon for women thought to be infertile to bear children after having adopted one. Moreover, there are other cases in which adoption is a result of the husband's rather than the wife's inability to conceive.

When a wife first learns that her husband is unable to produce children, she is likely to feel a mixture of angry resentment *and* tender protectiveness toward him. Attuned to his feelings of inadequacy and humiliation, she will probably try to bury her own great disappointment under a cover of sympathy. If the couple consequently adopts a child, she may believe that the husband's impotency is no longer a problem. The tumultuous years of her adopted child's adolescence can, however, stir up her past grievance against him. For example, if their adopted adolescent daughter is troubled, the wife may unconsciously blame the husband for preventing her from bringing forth her own "perfect" child and forcing this "flawed" one on her. Oftentimes and mistakenly, the aggrieved wife may resist articulating or even acknowledging her resentments—after all, she knows that her husband did not intentionally deprive her of bearing children. But unexposed wounds do not heal well. In Sarton's words, "There are old griefs so proud/They never speak a word;/They never can be mended./And these nourish the will/And keep it iron-hard."[7]

For troubled adoptive families, healing involves self-acceptance on every side. The adoptive adolescent must learn that she is a valuable, inherently good human being, not a "damaged product" discarded by the original mother. Adoptive parents must learn to value themselves as well, which includes making peace with the fact of their own or their partner's infertility. Realizing the inordinately difficult task of raising adopted children, they do well to develop reasonable self-expectations—learning, for example, to be satisfied at being "good-enough" rather than perfect parents and learning to allow their children their necessary struggles for identity and toward reconnection with the birth mother. As husband and wife, they do well to cultivate a spirit of mutual kindness and, in Mother Teresa's words, "to cling to one another" in the face of trouble.

In concluding this chapter on adoptive mothering, I will briefly return to Horton and Elephant-Bird. Earlier, I wrote that Dr. Seuss's charming rendition does not tell the full story about adoption. Still, Dr. Seuss, being the wonderfully perceptive and sensitive person that he is, tells us what is most important. In his drawing of baby Elephant-Bird, we see a little creature with a trunk and tail just like Horton's. This portrayal correctly implies that the adoptive parent can pass on parts of herself to her child. During years of loving, caring and sacrificing for, worrying about, and delighting in her daughter, the adoptive mother creates an irrevocable bond with her daughter; the adoptive mother is the *real* mother and the adopted daughter her *real* child. But Dr. Seuss also paints little red wings on Elephant-Bird. To me this means that all children (adopted or not), like Elephant-Bird, must one day fly away from mother.

Mother's ongoing parental task is to ensure that her child's wings become strong and healthy enough to carry her off. All things being equal, leaving the nest is more difficult for the adopted child than for her nonadopted counterpart. Probably wrenched away from the first mother when she was a helpless, dependent babe or a small child, she may not feel comfortable about separating from her second mother even when it is time. Consequently, her attempts at separation may be especially clumsy and disruptive. Being unsure of herself, she may, in fact, alternate between grandiose gestures of departure and clinging infantile behaviors so that sometimes she appears very independent and other times most immature. But despite such wavering, Mother must not discourage her daughter's necessary flight and search for identity by clipping her wings.

When all is said and done, all mothers—adoptive as well as biological—have the same parenting task, which is to let go of rather than to hold on to their adolescent children, and perhaps the adoptive mother is better prepared to master this task. She recognizes from the beginning of her maternity what other mothers must struggle to learn over the years: that her child is not an extension or replication of herself. Because they do not share a genetic or cultural history, the adoptive mother and her adopted daughter are forced to see more clearly their differences and to respect each other for them.

Jeanette, the adoptive mother whom I discussed earlier, made this especially clear to me: "My older daughter, who is not adopted, looks like me, talks like me, and is good at the things I'm good at. Sometimes I do her the disservice of assuming she is a replication of me. I take her successes and failures very seriously, as if they belonged to me, not to her. My adopted Vietnamese daughter, on the other hand, reminds me constantly of our differences and moves me to love her for *herself,* not as an extension of myself."

A poem by Kahlil Gibran expresses Jeanette's feelings about her younger daughter and implies a love untainted by narcissistic motives—a love all of us mothers might strive toward:

Your children are not your children.
They are sons and daughters of Life's longing for itself.
They come through you but not from you.
And though they are with you yet they belong not to you.

*　　*　　*

You may strive to be like them, but seek not to make
them like you.

For life goes not backward nor tarries with yesterday.

You are the bows from which your children as living
arrows are sent forth.

The archer sees the mark upon the path of the infinite,

And He bends you with His might that His arrows may go
swift and far.

Let your bending in the archer's hand be for gladness.

For even as He loves the arrows that flies, so He loves
also the bow that is stable.[8]

9

Goldilocks' Dilemma:

Stepmothers

ALMOST EVERY LITTLE GIRL GROWS UP HOPING to be a mother someday. But has there ever been one who dreamed of becoming a stepmother? Stepmothers, after all, personify wickedness: the scheming wife who cajoles her weak husband to abandon Hansel and Gretel in a forest inhabited by hungry animals and an evil witch; the vain, materialistic mother who indulges her own daughters' greed but condemns poor Cinderella to rags and ashes; the envious queen who coldheartedly arranges to have the fair and innocent Snow White killed. What most little (and not so little) girls ignore, however, is that stepmothers are also millions of ordinary, well-meaning women struggling to be fair and effective caretakers.

An emerging literature on remarriage is telling us that stepmothers (more than stepfathers) are having a difficult time with their stepchildren, and that stepmothers of adolescent children are having the most difficult time of all. The common distress associated with this role has even led two Canadian clinicians to give it a name: the "Cinderella's Stepmother Syndrome." Katalin Morrison and Airdrie Thompson-Guppy suggest that the stresses induced by the stepmother's precarious position in the remarried family and the negative attitudes that most people have about such families create a syndrome marked by feelings of low self-esteem, anxiety, hostility, guilt, and sadness.

To explore the causes, consequences, and solutions of the Cinderella's Stepmother Syndrome, I will focus on the personal stories of a middle-aged couple, Roger and Lee Hancock, who came for assistance because of increasing tension in their marriage of two years which was precipitated by the strained relationship between Lee and Jill, her twelve-year-old stepdaughter. Although the circumstances of each family are unique, it is my sense that the Hancocks' concerns are shared by so many others that they are worth recounting.

Roger, who is a banker, is a large, red-cheeked man with flashing blue eyes, a booming voice, and a full laugh. Lee, a concert pianist, seemed small and shy next to him, a delicate mountain flower hidden from view by a great tree. In fact, during our first meeting she hardly said a word, leaving it up to her husband to explain their situation.

According to Roger, since his daughter joined the household one year ago, he had become disenchanted with his marriage and with family life in general. Although Lee, who is childless, had seemed enthusiastic about the prospect of mothering Jill, Roger saw her turn cold and harsh within a few months after the girl moved in with them. Moreover, he was convinced that Lee's unfriendly manner provoked Jill's withdrawal from and hostility toward her. Because each came to him with grievances against the other, he found himself in the ungratifying position of family mediator, pulled in two opposing directions.

What disturbed Roger most, however, was the fact that Lee, who could be warm and loving with him, was "failing his daughter," a girl who, he was sure, needed maternal nurture. With all his heart, he had hoped that the three could become a "real family"—the kind of close-knit and warm family he and Jill missed having with his alcoholic first wife—but his dream seemed to be collapsing. Furthermore, because he got along so well with his daughter, he could not understand the reasons for Lee's coldness toward her. Sometimes he wondered whether Lee simply lacked the maternal capacity to love a child and to parent effectively. Other times he suspected that Lee was intentionally harassing his daughter. For example, Jill had complained to him that when he was out of town for a week, Lee would not permit her to go out with friends but insisted she remain at home. What he construed as Lee's unreasonable restrictions prompted him to take over all parenting responsibilities, but this only added to his resentment against Lee and his disenchantment with their marriage. Could I, he asked at the conclusion of our session, teach his wife parenting skills? Could I find out *what was wrong with her as a mother?*

Before working with the Hancocks as a couple, I suggested that Lee have individual sessions with me. I wanted to hear her story, believing that Roger's dominating and critical style inhibited her expressiveness. Reluctantly, she agreed. Our first hour together was awkward. Dodging my questions and averting contact with my eyes, Lee stayed out of reach; in fact, she often reminded me of the tender edelweiss that grows high in the Swiss Alps and is inaccessible to all but the most persevering mountain climbers.

In time, however, Lee began to trust my assurances that I did not think badly of her, and she was willing to open up. She explained that she had looked forward to caring for Jill and to loving this child in a way that Jill's "emotionally crippled, alcoholic mother" never could. In fact, for the month before Jill's arrival, Lee had indulged in wonderfully sweet fantasies, envisioning going on shopping sprees with Jill, having heart-to-heart talks about boys and hairstyles and fashions, and even teaching her how to play the piano. One of her favorite fantasies was imagining the two of them at the grand piano playing classical duets. From their first meeting, however, things between Lee and Jill went poorly.

"When Jill got off the plane, she walked past me without a word of acknowledgment and fell into Roger's waiting embrace as if they were lovers, not father and daughter. On the way to the baggage claim, the two of them walked arm in arm, chatting happily, as I trudged five feet behind, weighted down with her overstuffed carryall. Then, on the drive home, Jill jumped into the front seat next to her father, and I was left sitting in the back with her luggage for company.

"At first I tried to talk myself out of the disturbing idea that Jill is competing against me for Roger, but the thoughts that Jill wants to break up our marriage persist. For example, she constantly criticizes me in front of Roger—how I cook, how I keep house—as if she is determined to cast me in a bad light before his eyes. When I suggest to him that his daughter is wedging herself between us, he accuses me of pathological jealousy. Dr. Bassoff, am I crazy? Or is Roger oblivious to his daughter's scheming?

"It is true that I am hostile toward Jill now, but during our first months together, I tried especially hard to think well of her. I dismissed the incident at the airport; I looked the other way when Jill flirted with Roger and discounted me, as she so often does. I tried to like Jill. I tried to *love* her—as a new mother should love a child. I bought her pretty things, filled the refrigerator with the mini-pizzas and yogurts and Hansen's sodas she loves. I introduced her to my friends as 'my daughter' and invited her to call me 'Mom.' I did everything I could in warmth and kindness to make up to her what her real mother failed to provide. But she continued to treat me with disdain. She never allowed me to get close to her physically or emotionally; we have not had a single hug. When I complain to Roger about her arrogance and coldness, he only turns away, accusing *me* of being cold, and turns more toward her. They are always on the same side, while I am more and more on the outside."

At a later individual session, Lee elaborated her self-doubts. "Roger thinks that because I have never had a child of my own, I do not know how to relate to Jill, and I suspect that he has a point. I am doing something or not doing something that from the start has turned her against me. As time passes, her hostility toward me only grows, and I become more insecure about parenting. I want Roger to make all the rules and carry out the discipline because I am afraid of making mistakes with her. Anyway, Jill never minds what I say, so even if I had more confidence it would be futile to try to take a parental role with her. For the most part, she comes and goes as she pleases and doesn't lift a finger to help out in the house.

"Still, Roger thinks that I am particularly harsh with Jill—I think he sees me as a horrible fairy-tale stepmother. He seems to believe that when I made Jill stay home during his business trip, I was being wicked to her. The truth is that I was terrified that something awful would happen to her—a car accident or kidnapping—while he was gone, and that he would blame me for being a bad mother. I kept Jill at home to keep her safe, but I dare not share this with him. He would think I'm out of my mind. I'm afraid of Roger's disapproval. I'm afraid of losing him . . . I wonder if I haven't already lost him."

I should like to stop at this juncture and explore Roger's, Lee's, and Jill's troubled relationships. By identifying certain faulty expectations that the couple held, we can understand why things went so badly for them and consider ways of restructuring their family life.

What struck me as I listened to the Hancocks was their assumption that Lee could and should *love* Jill the way a mother loves her child and that this love had to be achieved *instantaneously*. The literature on remarried families suggests that Roger's and Lee's expectations of instant mother-child love are common; yet, the truth is that the loving relationship between a woman and her adolescent daughter culminates a history of togetherness—nine prenatal months of oneness, a labor and delivery followed by years of holding, feeding, cuddling, sheltering, clothing, fretting, teaching, conversing, laughing, scolding, sacrificing, and letting go. How can a woman who hardly knows an adolescent girl—as was Lee's case with Jill—expect to love her as a mother loves her own?

Babies elicit what developmental psychologists call the "cute response": their smallness, softness, funny gestures, and sweet cooing noises invariably enchant adults, who easily fall in love with them. Gum-chewing, loud, and raucous teenagers, with their moody temperaments and infuriating pretenses, definitely do not inspire the cute response from adults. I remember when a friend who had just had a frustrating confrontation with her seventeen-year-old about curfews, sighed and said to me, "Only a mother could love her!" Yet Roger and Lee fully expected that Lee would automatically love the unfriendly adolescent girl who stepped off the plane into their world.

Along with their expectation that Lee love Jill was the Hancocks' expectation that Lee also replace Jill's natural mother, whom they dubbed as worthless. The couple seemed unaware that Jill did not want a replacement for her mother, and that this woman, though she is alcoholic, remained important to her. In part, Jill rejected Lee's maternal offerings—heart-to-heart chats and mother-daughter shopping excursions—for the very fact that they were *maternal*. She would reject any woman who threatened to usurp her own mother's position.

In a paper on stepmothering, Margaret Draughon described three roles that a stepmother may assume: She can try to become the child's "only" or "primary mother" by psychologically supplanting the biological mother, which is what Lee was trying to do. (A more famous substitute mother, Anne Sullivan, decided to foster Helen Keller's complete dependence on her by taking the girl away from her mother.) She can become the "other mother" to the child so that the child has two mothers at the same time; or she can become the child's adult friend and not assume the role of mother at all.

As Draughon pointed out, although a child depends on a mother for her psychological survival, she experiences a friend as less essential—someone with whom she can be close or someone with whom she can enjoy a more casual relationship. We can assume that when a mother is living, her child is likely to experience her as the primary source of love and warmth; ". . . the likelihood is good that the child will not consciously want a new mother . . . and will reject any attempts by a 'stranger' to replace his 'mother.'"[1]

Jill's rejection of Lee *as mother* reminds me of another young woman's rejecting response to her stepmother. At a luncheon celebrating her brother's graduation from college, Angela was seated next to her father's new wife. In the middle of their warm and animated conversation, Angela abruptly excused herself, explaining that the sunlight shining through the window behind them was giving her a migraine headache, and moved quickly to the other end of the table, where her own mother was sitting. Needless to say, the light near her mother was just right, and the girl's headache subsided as suddenly as it had started.

Emily and John Visher, who have done extensive research on stepparenting, point out that the prefix "step" comes from the old English "steop," meaning bereaved or orphaned. The term *stepmother* came into use when it was almost always the death of the wife/mother, rather than divorce, that led to remarriage with a new wife for the surviving husband and a new mother for his children. A mother's death, *after it is fully mourned*, allows the child, especially the young child, to attach to a new maternal figure, who will not be experienced as a competitor. However, the child of divorce (and the overwhelming majority of today's stepchildren are children of divorce) is not likely to replace her living mother with a new one or grant this "stranger" the status of "other mother" without feeling disloyal. Yet Lee and Roger expected Jill to do just this. Because she did not, Roger suspected there was something wrong with his wife.

To my mind, the term *stepmother* is a misleading descriptive term; it directs the new wife of a divorced man to become a mother for his "orphaned" children. Unfortunately, until some clever word maker comes up with a better term than *stepmother*, we are resigned to use it and will be hurt by its implications. Perhaps some readers will think that I am a stickler for detail and am exaggerating the ways terms themselves structure our experiences. Allow me to digress briefly with an anecdote that illustrates how awkward it was in my own family not to have accurate names for relatives. When I was growing up, my maternal grandmother lived with my parents and me. My father, who was not a boorish man by any means, would get Grandmother's attention by *grunting*; in our twenty years of living under the same roof, he could not bring himself to call her "Mother" or "Mom," because, as he told me, "It's just not right—she's not my mother." Because he considered calling her by her first name, Grete, too informal and calling her by her last name, Mrs. Frank, too formal, he resorted to clearing his throat as his form of salutation. My father's seemingly peculiar habit was, however, his way of honoring the title Mother, and the one woman in his life who deserved it. Had a clever word maker devised a suitable way of addressing one's mother-in-law, my father's and grandmother's interactions might have been less strained. Similarly, a clever word maker with a substitute for "stepmother" would do many people a service.

Let me leave the issue of terminology and return to the related problem of finding a proper role for stepmothers. Although many women might agree that *mothering* an adolescent stepdaughter is impossible, they might also wonder about the feasibility of befriending her. How does a friendship between a teenager and a mature woman "look"? Do the competitive feelings among stepmother, (step)daughter, and natural mother preclude goodwill among them? If not, how can such mutual kindness be fostered? If a stepmother becomes a friend to her stepdaughter, does she relinquish her authority over her?

An acquaintance of mine provides one example of a rewarding stepmother-stepdaughter relationship: As she got to know seventeen-year-old Tina, Gloria promised that she would never presume to become her other mother but that maybe, over time, the two could become friends—not "girlfriends" who are privy to each other's secrets, but rather *across-two-generations friends* who are mutually caring. This wise woman made sure to speak respectfully of Tina's mother, so that the growing stepmother-stepdaughter relationship did not compete with the deeper and more attached mother-daughter one.

Had Lee been encouraged from the start to develop such a friendship with Jill, instead of a maternal love-at-first sight, both would have been spared much suffering. As it was, to defend against the tyranny of Lee's pretended motherly affection, Jill acted cold and rejecting. At the same time, Lee suspected that she was somehow flawed as a woman because Jill did not accept her as a mother.

Far from being negligible, the role of adult friend is full of wonderful possibilities. In sharing her wisdom and interests, an adult friend can enlarge and enrich a young girl's life. (As counselor and adult friend to many adolescents, I am often made aware of my influence on their lives. Moreover, my young clients energize my world through their fresh enthusiasms, so that we are all the better for our association.)

A sixteen-year-old client, who spends weekends and vacations with her mother and Chloe (her mother's live-in lover), told me that it is with Chloe that she has been able to share her ignorance, fears, and early feelings of shame about her mother's new lesbian life-style. "I couldn't say certain things to my mother because I thought they would hurt her too much. Chloe, on the other hand, can listen to me without feeling guilty or crying or making me feel guilty. She is really drawing me out. Because of her I am also understanding things that my friends, who don't have a homosexual parent, can't possibly understand. Chloe is teaching me that all loving is wonderful, that it doesn't really matter if it's between men and women or if it's between women and women; it's just the love part that counts. She's helping me to become a more tolerant, open person. I don't know if Chloe will remain with Mother much longer—she's restless and always wanting to move on—but I'm really glad she's passing through our lives."

Although my own daughter and I are deeply attached to one another, she keeps me out of her world for the most part; after all, at this time in her life her psychological task is to separate from me. She has, however, invited a few very special women in to be her guides, and because they are enriching her life, I am ever grateful to them. One incident stands out in particular. On the afternoon that I arrived too early to pick Leah up from her acting class, I watched unobserved as her teacher, Melody Page (a woman my age), confidently guided my inexperienced daughter through a tender kissing scene with a young, similarly inexperienced actor.

The natural distance between Melody and Leah—expert and apprentice—paradoxically allowed a kind of sharing that is not possible between mother and daughter, who, during the girl's adolescence, must guard against being overly close. Whenever I have initiated discussions about love and sex, Leah has shut them down. But with Melody, she seemed perfectly at ease and unembarrassed practicing her new and lovely womanly powers. The very fact that Melody is not Leah's mother allowed her a certain freedom and spontaneity that I do not have with my daughter.

With her usual eloquence, Anne Morrow Lindbergh describes a kind of relationship to which stepmother and stepdaughter might aspire:

A good relationship has a pattern like a dance and is built on some of the same rules. The partners do not need to hold on tightly. . . . To touch heavily would be to arrest the pattern and freeze the moment, to check the endlessly changing beauty of its unfolding. There is no place here for the possessive clutch, the clinging arm, the heavy hand; only the barest touch in passing. Now arm in arm, now face to face, now back to back—it does not matter which.[2]

Just as dancers cannot move freely on a cramped stage, a stepmother and her stepdaughter require ample space around their relationship so that it may grow and take its unique form. But this does not mean that their relationship should be without any structure or hierarchy. Some stepmothers who try to befriend their stepdaughters incorrectly assume that the two can be equals. I think that it is vital for a stepmother to realize that although she does not have the emotional privileges of the girl's natural mother, she is, together with her husband, the head of the household. It is in the older woman, not in the adolescent, that authority is vested. The across-two-generations friendship of stepmother and stepdaughter does not suggest a peership; to expand Lindbergh's metaphor, we might say that to dance together with grace, both partners must know the steps and sometimes one must take the lead.

Roger unwittingly was doing Lee a disservice by stripping her of all rights to set limits for Jill. And Lee reinforced her own feelings of incompetence by relinquishing all authority to him. Surely, it is a mistake for a stepparent to take on the role of disciplinarian (the adolescent child is likely to resent deeply the stepparent who "takes over" the household by setting and enforcing new rules and becoming her taskmaster). But it is also a mistake for the stepparent to allow discourtesies or abusive behaviors against herself. Striking a balance is a tricky feat, one that requires a husband's compassion (both for the daughter who resents being told what to do by an "outsider" and for the new wife who is trying to find a legitimate role in the family). I have encountered several stepmothers who are frustrated because they are divested of any authority with their husbands' teenage children. Reluctant to antagonize the children for fear this will incur the disapproval of their husbands, these women are forever walking on eggshells. Even when these teenagers exploit them through direct acts of rudeness or defiance, they are afraid to assert themselves.

I suspect part of the reason that many stepmothers do not claim their rightful authority, which may involve setting limits, making demands, and sometimes confronting angrily, is their worry that if they do they are doomed to become wicked stepmothers. We should not underestimate the persuasive powers of the fairy tales that have created that invidious, intractable stereotype of the mean stepmother. Psychologist Michel Radomisli writes,

> Decent women, upon becoming stepmothers, begin to doubt their own decency, excoriate themselves mercilessly for the slightest sign of impatience or anger, are prevented by their constant self-vigilance from enjoying the new relationship with their stepchildren, and cannot assert their rightful adult roles because they are so afraid of justifying the dreadful expectations of all concerned.[3]

Because their husbands are not immune to cultural stereotypes, they may exacerbate the situation by anticipating that the lovely women they married will sooner or later transform themselves into wicked stepmothers. To protect their hapless children against their treachery, these men may discourage their wives from making even reasonable demands on them, which is what Roger was doing.

It would be both arrogant and absurd of me to suggest that developing a friendship, one that combines comradeship and authority, with one's adolescent charge is an easy matter. Even the woman who maintains a respectful distance and does not presume to become a replacement or second mother is unlikely to receive a warm "welcome to the family" from her adolescent stepdaughter.

I do not think, for example, that Jill's initial coldness toward Lee was unusual. Unfortunately, both Roger and Lee expected an easy relationship between stepdaughter and stepmother to develop quickly. A stepmother, however, threatens her stepdaughter in ways that an unrelated adult friend does not. At least during the early stage of their relationship, the girl will perceive her father's new wife as an intruder and spoiler rather than as a potential friend. Just as mountain dwellers know that it can take centuries for the fragile flowers of the tundra to form and bloom, stepmothers are wise to wait patiently, sometimes for years, for their stepdaughters to open up to them.

A short anecdote illustrates the anger an adolescent is likely to feel about her father's new lover or wife. Many years ago (when divorces and remarriages were still shocking community events) a colleague told me how dismayed he had been when his thirteen-year-old daughter shunned his paramour. According to him, the girl refused to say a single word to his woman friend, although the latter went out of her way to be hospitable. "Why should I be nice to her," the girl tearfully shouted after she and her father were alone, "when she has taken you away from Mother and me? I will always hate her because she is my family dream breaker."

Although Lee did not break up Roger's family (the two began to date after he had separated), Jill still saw her as the woman who had replaced her father's true wife and who was the obstacle to her parents' reunion. The doctors Visher contend that even after remarriage children often cling to the fantasy that their natural parents will reunite. In an effort to make this fantasy come true, they may unconsciously or consciously try to split up the new couple. Lee's perceptions that Jill was trying to come between Roger and herself were probably quite accurate. At least part of Jill wanted to take her father away from Lee, "return" him to his first wife, and hence restore the original nuclear unit.

Yet, if Jill had succeeded in breaking up her father's new marriage, she would have suffered a Pyrrhic victory. What Jill, like every other young adolescent, needed (and I believe she knew this) was a stable family environment. Whereas

Jill's biological mother, because of her untreated alcoholism and related emotional problems, could not carry the burden of single parenting, Roger and Lee could provide Jill with a strong home base. It was not in Jill's best interest to split them up, because had she been able to do so, her life could only become more chaotic. For Jill's sake as well as their own, Roger and Lee needed to affirm the strength and permanence of their marriage instead of pulling against each other, as they were doing.

Suzanne Pope, a family therapist, once told me about a visit to the San Diego Zoo, where she spent an hour observing a family of gorillas. Every time mother and father gorilla became amorous, baby gorilla would swoop down from a nearby tree to land squarely in between them. Frustrating as the situation was, the adult pair did not give up on each other but repeatedly pushed baby away and returned to their twosome.

Human couples, such as the Hancocks, do well to follow the gorillas' lead and protect their own twosomes. With my prodding, Roger eventually took it upon himself to make clear to his daughter that his place was next to his wife, and that he would not tolerate Jill's maneuvers to drive them apart. At the same time, he learned to reassure Jill that hearts are very spacious and that, as his daughter, she always would have a special and sacred spot in his. Finding time for just the two of them—a dinner together, a walk in the woods—was Roger's way to realize this sentiment.

An adolescent stepdaughter typically fears that her new stepmother will steal father away, just as she stole husband away from mother. Unfortunately, out of their own insecurities, some stepmothers do prevent daughters and fathers from becoming closer. One of the most generous gifts a stepmother can give to both husband and stepchild is her full approval of their relationship—separate from her. As Anne Morrow Lindbergh writes, "We all wish to be loved alone. . . . The one and only moments are justified. The return to them, even if temporarily, is valid."[4] What daughters must accept, of course, is that they cannot have their fathers to themselves continuously or permanently, only for special moments.

Gloria, the stepmother whom I so admire, told me that it was she who first initiated father-daughter outings by convincing her husband that they were important for the whole family. At first, Leonard felt awkward with his teenage daughter and did not quite know what to do when they were together. Gloria was the one who suggested movies, restaurants with just the right ambience, and special community events that both would enjoy. Over time, Tina and Leonard learned to take great pleasure spending time just with each other. Gloria believes that she was able to win Tina's trust in part because the young woman did not have to compete against her for Father's attentions.

We must not forget that just as stepdaughters are threatened by their stepmothers, so stepmothers are threatened by their stepdaughters. In his eagerness to have a loving family, Roger did not anticipate that Lee would feel rivalrous toward Jill. He did not anticipate that his new wife would resent giving up her exclusive arrangement with him to make room for his daughter.

The tensions between newcomer and settled family members are vividly portrayed in the familiar and deceptively simple folk tale "Goldilocks and the Three Bears." Although this old tale does not present solutions, it does illustrate the problems that confront many modern stepfamilies. Bruno Bettelheim points out that the original source of "Goldilocks" is probably an ancient Scottish tale in which a she-fox intrudes on three bears, who devour her. In a later rendering of the story, the intruder helps herself to milk and rests in the chairs and beds of the bears, who severely punish her for her transgressions. "Trespassers Beware!" is the cautionary message of the tale. The bears—who symbolize the established family group (and in our case are akin to Lee and Roger)—do not tolerate a stranger's (Jill's, the stepchild's) disruptions.

In the version of "Goldilocks" with which most of us have grown up, we observe that before the girl's intrusion, the bears' household is orderly, and each has a distinct position in it that is symbolized by the bears' separate and unlike chairs, beds, and dishes of cereal. Goldilocks inadvertently brings chaos to this order by eating the porridge off their plates, breaking Baby Bear's chair, and undoing the neatly made beds.

Similarly, the sudden arrival of an adolescent stepchild disorganizes the family system—whether this is a two-people family, such as Roger's and Lee's was, or one with other (step)children. Merely the clutter (scattered clothes, books, papers, candy wrappers, towels, makeup, sneakers, emptied soda cans, unwashed dishes) and noise (stereos blaring, phone calls night and day, moody outbursts) that seem to follow every teenager is sure to throw a household into turmoil.

Bettelheim suggests that because Goldilocks first chooses Papa Bear's dish to eat from, his chair to sit on, and his bed to lie in, she reveals her wishes to relate to him most. As he notes, "It is hard to come closer to the girl's oedipal wishes than by suggesting that Goldilocks tries to share bed and board with a father figure."[5] Not only does Goldilocks undo the bears' tidy domestic haven, but she implicitly threatens the exclusive relationship between Mother and Father Bear (just as Jill tried to come between Lee and Roger)—and this is cause for alarm!

In the "Goldilocks" tale, the bears oust the attractive girl (the she-fox of the earlier tale) from their dwelling so that she is no longer a threat to their unity. Lee, however, could not be so brazen: Her "Goldilocks" was here to stay.

During our early interviews, Lee emphasized her wish to love Jill. It took considerable time before she made peace with the (natural and normal) feelings of hostility she harbored toward this "outsider." Because Lee could not at first accept her hostile feelings, she disguised them. Her terrible fears that something catastrophic—a car wreck or kidnapping—would happen to the girl during her father's absence were, in part, Lee's unconscious and censored wishes to have harm befall the girl. In the various versions of "Goldilocks," Bettelheim tells us that the Bears devour her, throw her into a fire or out the window, drown her, or drop her from a church steeple. (In our watered-down modern version, we let her disappear into the woods.) What the Bears carry out, Lee could do only in her imagination. Even so, the idea of being violently angry at the girl was so abhorrent to Lee that she had to hide such feelings from herself and others under a cloak of maternal solicitude and overprotection (keeping Jill at home, safe and sound).

As we proceeded in our therapy, Lee acknowledged her hostility and came to see it as something that is normal and natural and, when not acted out, quite harmless. Talking about our inner demons—jealousy, anger, vengeance—brings them out into the open so that they can be understood and tamed. In our imaginations, however, they loom so large and so fearsome that they tyrannize us. After many individual sessions and with Lee's approval, Roger rejoined us in therapy. It was important for him to become less afraid of his wife's angry side too; he had turned away from her when she brought up her jealousy because he mistakenly believed that by validating her darker feelings he was promoting them.

For Lee's part, it was important to recognize that Jill was not as dangerously seductive or scheming as once imagined. After all, Jill's own self-interest depended on the stability of her father's new marriage. Indeed, if Jill were to steal Father away from his present wife, one wonders what she would do with him! Goldilocks herself discovers that appropriating Father's porridge, chair, and bed does not suit her. Bettelheim reminds us that sexual intimacies with one's parent, just like Father's porridge, are always too hot and badly burn the child; and, like Father's too-hard chair and too-high bed, are uncomfortable and out of reach for her.

Through our continuing discussion and to Roger's delight, Lee began to empathize with Jill—to understand what it is like to join a new family. (From my own experience, I have found that it is nearly impossible to sustain hostile feelings toward a person with whom one empathizes.) Actually, their situations were so similar that it was not difficult for Lee to see Jill in a more compassionate light. Just as Lee sometimes feared that she was an outsider in Roger's world (the woman in the backseat), Jill was similarly unsure of her rightful place in the Hancock family. *Both women at times were Goldilocks struggling to belong.*

As the popular tale goes, things do not turn out well for Goldilocks—for the girl either comes to a violent end or disappears back into the woods. Modern-day stepchildren and their stepparents are pressed to find happier solutions to their dilemmas than poor Goldilocks and the frustrated bears did. Remarried families need not be hostile growing environments for adolescents or their caretakers; they may even provide certain advantages that conventional nuclear families lack.

My friend Alice Levine likens families to water. Water can be contained in any number of holders—a drinking glass, a tank, a concrete pool, or by formations like jetties, sloping banks, rock, or sandy ocean beds. Similarly, a family can have various forms. It might be housed under one roof or more, have one, two or several adult heads, be tightly bound or loosely associated. Roger's original conceptualization of family, however, tended to be limited. He saw it only as the cohesive group of father, mother, and child. When Roger said he wanted to have a "real" family, he was imagining only this traditional one. Moreover, he failed to realize that his twelve-year-old daughter no longer needed the togetherness that may have benefited her when she was younger. Through our discussions in therapy and through contacts with other remarried fathers, Roger eventually developed less rigid ideas of what a good family can be like.

But Roger's early prejudice against the newer forms of family appears to be widespread. I am reminded of a story that a friend shared about a bat mitzvah she recently attended. As is customary at this rite of passage, the adolescent who is being initiated into adulthood presents a short speech in which she pays tribute to those dear to her. In this young woman's case, she concluded her address by saying, "Above all, I would like to honor and thank my wonderful parents—all four of them," at which point the members of the Conservative congregation laughed nervously. As my friend explained, their laughter was not malicious; rather, it was the kind of laughter one hears in a child who thinks, but is not quite sure, that you are pulling her leg. Like Roger, this assembly of decent-enough people was not sure if it could take seriously a family with four parents: Was such a family normal?

Roger first assumed that the nuclear family not only is more normal or real than his less conventional remarried one but that it is superior. And like Cinderella's stepsisters, who squeeze their feet into a shoe that is too small, Roger tried to cast his daughter and new wife into a traditional mother-child mold, which did not fit them. Remarried families are, of course, real and, we may discover, in certain ways perhaps more adaptive than tightly knit nuclear families.

Certainly, adolescent children have the best chance of thriving if their families are stable, but the overly close relationships that often characterize traditional and single-parent families may work against the adolescent. Adolescence is a time of leaving the parental nest, which is now too small and too safe. The adolescent with not one but two families has the opportunity to move from one parental territory to the other and thereby enlarge her experience of the world. Leaving Mother's home to live in or visit Father's allows a teenage girl to disentangle from her. The second parental home becomes a stepping stone between the overly protected maternal haven and the still forbidding world at large. Moreover, the stepmother, because she is less invested in the adolescent's success than is her mother, can offer a relationship that is neither prodding nor clutching; she can be the adult friend every girl who is coming of age needs.

When I was a teenager growing up on New York's upper West Side, I had a friend who lived between his remarried parents' apartments on 157th Street and 181st Street and spent more or less equal time with each family. In those days of "Father Knows Best" and "Leave it to Beaver" families, Larry's style of living was somewhat of a rarity. Instead of carrying ballpoint pens in his jacket pocket, Larry carried a toothbrush. At sixteen, he was enormously self-sufficient and (I thought) marvelously sophisticated. What is more, he seemed happy and at ease in the world. He explained that the four adults in his life did not pull at him but allowed him to turn to them as he needed. One time Larry described his unconventional households as "refueling stations" and my traditional one as a "nuclear fortress."

Historians of human adolescence tell us that in some cultures children at puberty were "placed out"—sent to live away from their parents—and suggest that such placing out, more than a way of ensuring the young person's vocational or educational development, may have been a way to separate the generations at a time when there might otherwise have been unbearable tension between them.[6] Excessive squabbling between mothers and their adolescent children, which is so typical in modern households, may be a sign that the two generations can no longer live in harmony under one roof, that they have outgrown each other, and that they had best be separated.

Stable remarried families provide the adolescents with two homes to move between. As my friend Larry used to tell me, when he felt stifled in one household, he just packed his overnight bag, took a short subway ride, and settled in with the other family for a spell. Although at the time, neither of us considered how his comings and goings affected his parents and stepparents, I can imagine now that they also derived some benefits from such a flexible arrangement. An exhausted acquaintance once said that what every mother with adolescents needs is a "kibbutz somewhere in Kansas," where the kids are sent from time to time so that their mothers can have some peace and quiet. Larry's second parental home (not a kibbutz in the plains but an apartment at the foot of the George Washington Bridge) provided such a function: there he could safely go when relationships in the first parental home became too tense.

In the Hancocks' case, Roger, Lee, Jill, and Jill's mother eventually agreed that it would be important for Jill to visit her mother often. As it turned out, not only did the mother and daughter benefit from their short stays with each other, but, when Jill was away, Lee and Roger could enjoy the "one and only" moments that every couple deserve. As Lee told me toward the end of our course of therapy, "It's getting easier to like Jill's mom. After all, she is always nice about having her daughter visit with her, even going out of her way to accommodate our time schedules; and each time Jill goes off for a few days, Roger and I can enjoy a kind of intimacy that is not possible when she is around."

As Jesse Bernard demonstrates in her book *The Future of Motherhood,* our society has structured motherhood in most maladaptive ways. In their lonely nuclear nests, today's harried, overworked, understimulated, full-time mothers all too often vent their frustrations on their children and succumb to clinical depressions themselves. How much better off were their mothers, grandmothers, and great-grandmothers who lived in extended families with extra arms to hug a needy child and extra ears to listen to her complaints! I recall the sadness of a friend of mine—a traditional mother— who, overwhelmed by the emotional demands of her large family and the tediousness of managing a big house single-handedly, would sigh, "Tell me, is this a life?"

Now I wonder if our new forms of family—these remarried, reconstituted, blended, stepfamilies with their several adult caretakers and numerous (step)children (what one researcher calls a Cecil B. deMille production with a cast of thousands)—are not a reincarnation of the extended family. Might not these new families provide a way of lifting the too-heavy burden of child-rearing from the shoulders of one set of parents or a single parent by dispersing it among several adults? Is it too Pollyannaish to hope that stepmother and real mother (and stepfather and real father) can join to provide the adolescent family members the support and guidance they need?

Sad to say, I have not known many stepfamilies that have achieved a high level of cooperation and goodwill. Lee's early devaluation of Jill's mother exemplifies the antagonism that all too often characterizes the relationship between stepparent and biological parent. But I recall one especially nice exception to this disturbing pattern, which I hope can serve as a model of healthy relationships for others. A few months ago, Ruth, a fifty-year-old client of mine, shared this story:

I must say that after my divorce and my ex-husband's remarriage, I was—for years—jealous of his new wife. Although the thought that she could make him happy and I had not filled me with despair, I was more upset by the idea that my little daughter, Emily, might come to prefer her over me. From what Emily told me about her visits to her father's home, Sheila was very kind, very nurturing.

Of course, I rarely saw Sheila, but there was one family function—my former parents-in-law's fortieth anniversary luncheon—where we were thrown together. Even though Emily had come with me, she insisted on visiting with her father and Sheila, and, of course, I did not deter her. At one point, I noticed Sheila bending down tenderly to tie Emily's shoelace, which had come undone. As insignificant as that act might seem to others, it stabbed me like a terrible knife wound. I could not stand to have Sheila tend my daughter. That night I cried myself to sleep.

I don't quite understand how my hatred for Sheila dissolved, but in time it did. Perhaps over the years I simply got used to the fact that she is in Emily's life and worried less that Emily would love her more than she loves me. In any case, Sheila no longer threatened me, and our relationship became rather cordial.

Four months ago, on her sixteenth birthday, Emily was in a car accident. For days, we did not know if she would live or die. My ex-husband was so devastated and hysterical that he made our crisis worse. I could not bear for him to be around the hospital because *he* seemed to need comforting and could not give Emily the steady assurances she needed.

It was Sheila who came through for Emily—and for me. It was she who relieved me from the round-the-clock vigil at Emily's bedside. It is she who is calmly helping me see Emily through her long rehabilitation. It is she who offers to drive Emily to her daily appointments with the physical therapist so that I can do other things.

Needless to say, I have come to like Sheila very much. Because of our shared love for Emily, we are tied to each other. I think there should be a name for the relationship between a mother and a stepmother. But there isn't. No name, not even a word that validates our mutual attachment.

I agree with Ruth. Without a name for the healthy bondedness that is possible, we are left to believe that there is either nothing between mother and stepmother or that their relationship is one of pure rivalry.

Ruth's and Sheila's friendship reminds me of a short story, "The Double Pins," by the French writer Guy deMaupassant, in which a bon vivant enjoys the pleasure of keeping two mistresses. By alternating the days he is with each woman, he is able to keep one from finding out about the other. On one of her visits, however, the older mistress notices a particular black-headed pin, obviously belonging to a lady, in her lover's quarters. Without a word to him, she substitutes for this pin one of her own, which the younger mistress soon discovers. Before long the two women, by cross-hatching one pin with another, devise a communication. Being somewhat bolder, the older mistress eventually leaves her address for the younger one, and the two women set up an appointment. As the clever reader might suspect, the unfortunate man-about-town loses the affections of both mistresses, but the two women become intimate friends!

The possibilities for warm and supportive relationships among mother and stepmother have not yet been realized. Sadly, women have traditionally been pitted against each other as competitors for the attentions of men and children. No wonder then that the stereotype of the wicked fairy-tale stepmother has become an acceptable outlet for female-against-female aggression. Still, as more and more women find themselves in the role of stepmother or are forced to share the care of their sons and daughters with their exhusbands' new wives, they are faced with choices: They can remain strangers to each other; they can feed a jealous competition, which is what most of us expect of them; or they can become friends. Similarly, stepmothers and stepdaughters, on the whole, have not realized the possibilities for congenial mutual relationships. Still, there are some success stories to be told, and perhaps over time there will be many more.

At the last session with the Hancocks, I asked Lee if, along with all the problems, Jill had also brought her some joy, and she answered in the following way: "Before Jill arrived, I had so many fantasies about the way we would be together as mother and child. I really hoped, for instance, that Jill would let me teach her how to play the piano and that we could ultimately share a love for music. Jill and I will probably never play Mozart's Sonata in F for Four Hands, and maybe I'm a little disappointed. On the other hand, the other night Jill came up to me while I was practicing and asked if I could teach her to play a simple song. She didn't want to take up the piano in a serious way, but she wanted to be able to play just one tune. We ended up by doing a rousing rendition of 'Heart 'n Soul'—not exactly Mozart, but so what? We had an awful lot of fun. Yes, I would say that Jill is bringing me some joy . . . and in ways I never would have guessed."

Stepmothers are not doomed to envious, coldhearted relationships with their stepdaughters, as our fairy tales would have us believe. Instead, like Lee and Jill, with patience and determination they can learn to make light music together.

10

Letting Go:
Mother to Mother to Daughter

CARL GUSTAV JUNG WROTE THAT "EVERY MOTHER contains her daughter in herself and every daughter her mother, and that every woman extends backwards into her mother and forward into her daughter." In order to realize the full possibilities of her individual life, however, the middle-aged mother must not only separate from her adolescent daughter, she must also complete her separation from her aging mother. It is, after all, only as mothers and daughters *grow* apart, that each becomes a full woman.

Despite this fact, many mid-life women are reluctant or even afraid to loosen ties to their mothers. The girl-child in them clings to the illusion that Mother is endowed with absolute powers to know and protect and that only as long as they please her and conform to her standards will she be available to them. For these reasons, they may consider even appropriate acts of filial denial or disagreement potentially catastrophic. As my client Tanya put it, "If I dare say

'No' to my elderly mother, who is a very cranky and demanding lady, I am convinced that either she or I will die!"

Tanya's response is not unusual. Many other female clients have told me that going against Mother's wishes or criticizing her feels somehow dangerous—like a terrible violation for which they deserve to be punished. For example, after telling her mother that instead of coming to her house for Christmas this year, she would be celebrating the holiday with her husband's side of the family, Carol came down with a week-long migraine. And following an angry encounter in which she accused her mother of consistently undermining her, Natalie started to fantasize about suicide. Both these adult daughters seemed to be punishing themselves for having taken a stand against their mothers.

Well aware of the emotional toll of confrontation, not all women are willing to address unpleasant issues with their mothers. For some, the fear that Mother will become insulted enough to withdraw her love permanently may block any honest encounters. Clients have told me that they would rather endure Mother's manipulations or outrageous demands than tangle with her and make her angry at them.

For women who perceive their mothers as weak or frail, the fear that a conflict will emotionally destroy the older woman may deter them from taking a necessary stand against her. For example, after Natalie's angry encounter, she confided, "If I criticize my mother in any way, she just distances herself from me, much the way a wounded animal retreats from its attacker. When I say something that offends my mother I feel like a criminal—a murderer. It's just not worth it for me to tell her things that she doesn't want to hear, because I feel so guilty afterwards."

For all these daughters, the dreaded outcome is the loss of mother love. As the poet Adrienne Rich writes, "There is no indifference or cruelty we can tolerate less than the indifference or cruelty of our mothers";[1] and as Tanya puts it, "Although intellectually I know I have the right to do things that my mother might not agree with—after all, I am forty-four—some vague but pervasive feeling does not allow me to displease her. I still do as she says—or at least I pretend to her that I do."

Tanya, Carol, and Natalie—who have all successfully combined career with motherhood—impress me as insightful, bright, and disciplined human beings. Their difficulties as daughters remind me that even high-functioning women who have no trouble asserting themselves in the work world can have a hard time affirming their independence and separateness from Mother.

Although the term *separation* (along with its sister concept *individuation*) has become popular in the literature on child and adult development, its meanings are not obvious. Surely, separation does not imply the lack of strong relationship. Paradoxically, in fact, the mother and daughter who are appropriately separate seem to relate more lovingly than the overly dependent pair, for only when one is not constantly threatened by the other's control is it safe to become generous and open in relationship.

In my practice and personal life, I have observed several of these mutually enhancing relationships between autonomous mothers and daughters. Those who move toward separation develop what I visualize as a *side-by-side* relationship—with ample space in between—whereas those who do not separate are trapped *one inside the other*. In a side-by-side relationship, mother and daughter may be close but neither is encumbered. Each is free to move ahead without having to carry, pull, or push the other; each is free to navigate her life in her own chosen way and can tolerate conflicts between them. In a one-inside-the-other relationship, however, daughters and mothers crowd each other. Neither can change positions, stretch, or grow without irritating the other. Several clients have even described such entrapments as "devourings." As Carol said, "Sometimes I feel as if my mother is eating me alive; I am consumed by her."

Later I will turn to examples of healthy separations between grown women and their elderly mothers, but first I would like to explore some forms that failed mother-daughter separations take. Aurelia Plath, for example, described the fusion with her poet daughter as follows: "Between Sylvia and me existed—as between my own mother and me—a sort of psychic osmosis, which at times was very wonderful and comforting; at other times an unwelcome invasion of privacy."[2] In one of the last letters to Aurelia, Sylvia protested against the pain shared too freely between them, "The horror of what you saw and what I saw you see last summer is between us and I cannot face you again until I have a new life."[3] The joining of these two women is reminiscent of the unity of mother and embryo, who osmotically transmit their experiences of the world to one another. One can only speculate that the new life that Sylvia hinted at but that her suicide cut off might have been a more separate one—mother and daughter side by side rather than one inside the other.

Sometimes adult women replicate the unity with their mothers in relationships with their own children. As my client Carol explains, "There is a tradition of such closeness in my family. My mother expects me to share everything about myself and the family with her. If I don't call her several times a week, she is upset; if we cannot spend every holiday together, she is beside herself. But even though I resent terribly how she clings to me, I sometimes find that I cling to my own daughter. When Carla does not write me frequent letters from college, I think to myself that she is not a good daughter. And when she talks about not returning home after graduation but moving to Los Angeles or Chicago or some other large city, I have a sense of terrible loss. I want to tell her 'No, you must come back to me.' "

Researcher Susan Rosewell-Jackson's findings suggest that Carol's repetition of her mother's holding patterns is common. She points out that the middle-aged women in her study who as young adults failed to untie themselves from their mothers' apron strings tended not to let go of their own adolescent daughters and that the grandmothers of these middle-aged women had also not been able to separate from their daughters. Each generation held on tightly to the next much like the unfortunate characters who are stuck to one another in the fairy tale "The Golden Goose."

The yearning for fusion between mother and daughter can be played out less directly. For example, in adult sexual relationships one or both partners may simulate the original, primitive union of mother and child by having the lover serve as substitute mother. Urging her lover to provide sensually maternal functions such as holding, caressing, and nuzzling *in lieu of* genital sex, a woman can recreate the feelings she once knew in mother's enfolding arms. One particular clinical case comes to mind: A former client, Peter, explained that his thirty-five-year-old wife had made him feel brutish whenever he wanted to have genital sex with her and that, in order not to offend her anymore, he had agreed to limit physical intimacy to cuddling and kissing. Feeling increasingly unsatisfied and used in his five-year marriage, he eventually initiated divorce proceedings against her.

Certainly, healthy love relationships do allow the partners to offer and accept a certain amount of maternal loving; each of the lovers feels safe to abandon the responsibilities of being adult from time to time to become babyish or childish with the other. It is when the need for maternal loving crowds out more mature forms of relatedness or when one partner insists on always being the child (or the parent), however, that we can anticipate problems.

I have no way of knowing how common it is for mature women to prefer acts of maternal loving to acts of sex, but I have observed this tendency among a number of my younger women clients. For example, I have treated several teenagers who became pregnant only because they were assured of receiving the hugs and caresses they so desperately wanted by *giving in* to sexual intercourse; starved for maternal love, they *suffered* sex to be cuddled. Tragically, some later looked to their babies for maternal loving—nurturing, unconditional acceptance, positive reinforcement—and became disappointed or angry when these little ones did not give them what they craved but were needy themselves.

Although a regressive sexual liaison simulates the nirvana experienced in our oneness with Mother or provides for the first time the blissful mother-child unity that inadequately mothered women may long for, it also *reduces* a grown woman to the dependent and egoistical role of child. For some women such a liaison may be a stepping stone on the path toward a less dependent, more reciprocal relationship. But those who remain trapped in an unseparated relationship never come to know the joys of mature love.

Mature loving, whether between a mother and her daughter or two adult lovers, entails mutual awareness and respect and awe of the others' *otherness*. Immature loving, conversely, is simply using the partner for one's own pleasure, much the way the self-centered baby uses its mother's body for comfort and nourishment. I am quite sure that Peter felt used for this reason. Women (and men for that matter) who insist on being indulged and babied are generally left behind (as Peter's wife was) by the adults who sooner or later come to feel exploited by them.

Eva, a character in Toni Morrison's novel *Sula*, addresses the impossibility of recapturing the comfort, the security, and the ecstasy of merger with Mother that rightly belongs only to the infant or small child. Morrison portrays Eva as a kind of mother goddess who ferociously protects the lives of the children in her care. Despite her maternal generosity, however, she is not willing to tolerate her son, who because of his drug habit has regressed to an infantile state. Just as Mother Nature herself turns her back, often with unabashed cruelty, on those living creatures that are not fit to survive, Eva takes it into her own hands to kill the childish man who refuses to separate from her and grow up:

> He gave me such a time. Such a time. Look like he didn't even want to be born. But he come on out. Boys is hard to bear. You wouldn't know that but they is. It was

such a carryin' on to get him born and to keep him alive.
Just to keep his little heart beating and his little old lungs
cleared and look like when he came back from that war he
wanted to git back in. After all that carryin' on, just gettin'
him out and keepin' him alive, he wanted to crawl back in
my womb and well . . . I ain't got the room no more even
if he could do it. There wasn't space for him in my womb.
And he was crawlin' back. Being helpless and thinking
baby thoughts and dreaming baby dreams and messing up
his pants again and smiling all the time. I had room
enough in my heart, but not in my womb, not no more. I
birthed him once. I couldn't do it again. He was growed, a
big old thing. Godhavemercy, I couldn't birth him twice. . . .
a big man can't be a baby all wrapped up inside his
mamma no more; he suffocate. I done everything I could
to make him leave me and go on and live and be a man
but he wouldn't and I had to keep him out so I just
thought of a way he could die like a man not all scrunched
up inside my womb, but like a man.[4]

A protracted unseparated mother love not only suffocates
the grown child but—as both Aurelia Plath and Eva tell
us—saps the vitality of the mother as well: The older woman
is consumed by the adult child just as the adult child is
consumed by her. In order for a woman to realize the
possibilities of her late years, she must gradually free herself
from the needs of her children. "I certainly don't want to
insult my daughter," a seventy-six-year-old acquaintance confided, "but I am no longer willing to contend with her
problems: her financial ups and downs, the struggles with
her children and husband. It is all too much for me now. I
love her as always, but it is my time not to be entangled in
her life."
    The aging mother in relationship to her middle-aged daugh-
ter and the middle-aged daughter in relationship to her
adolescent child have parallel tasks: Each must combine the
right amount of maternal nurture with the right amount of

maternal distance. In my practice, I typically see mothers who err on the side of too much nurturing. But, on occasion, I have counseled women who, sometimes in their determination not to repeat the overly close ties they had with their mothers, are too removed from their own adolescent daughters. They do not respond to their daughters' appropriate cries for motherly support and motherly warmth but push them into a premature independence. These girls then feel abandoned and lost and are likely to seek maternal love from the wrong people—boyfriends, for example, or, worse still, the babies they bring into the world.

The art of motherhood, for the elderly mother as well as for the middle-aged one, requires finding that delicate balance between involvement with and disengagement from one's children, between holding and letting go. Similarly, one of the important tasks for the middle-aged daughter is to find that balance between closeness and separation from her mother.

The devitalizing effects of a failed separation, where there is too much involvement between a middle-aged woman and her mother, are revealed in a short story called "The Way of Peace" by a little-known American author, Alice Brown, who wrote at the turn of the century. The story opens two weeks after the mother's death, as Lucy Ann, the middle-aged daughter, sits alone with her grief in the house they shared. Rather than mourn the loss and complete the separation from mother, Lucy Ann sets out to reincarnate her by taking on the appearance and persona of the dead woman. Standing before a mirror, she begins to transform herself into the mother's image:

There she let down her thick gray hair, parted it carefully on the sides, and cut off lock after lock about her face. She looked a caricature of her sober self. But she was well used to curling hair like this, drawing its crisp silver into shining rings; and she stood patiently before the glass and coaxed her own locks into just such fashion as had framed the older face. It was done, and Lucy Ann looked at herself with a smile all suffused by love and longing. She was not herself anymore; she had gone back a generation, and chosen a warmer niche. . . . The change suggested a more faithful portraiture, and she went up into the spare room and looked through the closet where her mother's clothing had been hanging so long, untouched. Selecting a purple thibet, with a little white sprig, she slipped off her own dress, and stepped into it . . . She had resurrected the creature she loved; this was an enduring portrait, perpetuating, in her own life, another life as well.[5]

Through her regression, Lucy Ann succeeds in warding off the loneliness that a mother's death forces the orphaned adult child to face. By assuring herself of an eternal maternal presence, she assures herself of a certain peace and security. However, this same symbiotic union guarantees that Lucy Ann will never be vital, which seems to be the price of human merger: "She did not seem to herself altogether alive, nor was her mother dead. They had been fused by some wonderful alchemy; and instead of being worlds apart, they were at one."[6]

In contrast to Lucy Ann, a young girl named Nel, who is a character in Toni Morrison's *Sula*, expresses the joy of selfhood that separation from one's mother allows.

She got out of bed and lit the lamp to look in the mirror. There was her face, plain brown eyes, three braids and the nose her mother hated. She looked a long time and suddenly a shiver ran through her. "I'm me," she whispered. "Me," Nel didn't know quite what she meant, but on the other hand she knew exactly what she meant. "I'm me. I'm not their daughter. I'm not Nel. I'm me. Me." Each time she said the word *me* there was a gathering in her like power, like joy, like fear.[7]

When the young girl looks in the mirror, she wants to see her *self*; when Lucy Ann does the same, she is satisfied to see her mother.

Often one of the tasks of middle-age is to adjust to the death of one's parent or parents. In the healthiest adjustments, the adult child internalizes certain positive aspects of the deceased parent, which she can later draw on. When I am overwhelmed, for example, I often have "conversations" with my deceased father and grandmother. Remembering their loving advice, I am able to imagine how they would guide me through my present hardship. But at the same time, the orphaned adult child must be free to reject undesirable aspects of the parent. As researchers Miriam and Sidney Moss point out, personal growth requires a *selective* integration of the parents' values and way of life. Separation (before or after a parent's death) means that one can *choose* to emulate certain characteristics of the parent and disidentify from others. For example, I choose to assume my father's patient manner when I help my children with their homework, but I choose not to impose his perfectionistic standards of neatness on them.

It is because of a successful separation from our own parents that we are able to parent our adolescent children in a conscious way. The unseparated middle-aged daughter may find herself behaving just like her mother did—even when such behavior is destructive. Although she may have hated her mother's shrillness, she herself shouts at her daughter. Although she may have cringed at her mother's intrusiveness, she herself invades her daughter's privacy. The unseparated woman is, like Lucy Ann, fused to her mother not by a "wonderful" alchemy but by a primitive one that precludes autonomous behavior.

Not so long ago, my husband pointed out that I was repeating with our adolescent daughter the very behaviors I resented in my mother during my teenage years. Like my mother, I made far too many inquiries about my daughter's self-care: "Now what did you eat for lunch today?" "Are you sure you're getting enough sleep?" "Are you dressed warmly enough?" What I am just beginning to understand is that by repeating my mother's patterns, I was trying to hold on to her, to ensure a continuousness between us. Like Lucy Ann, I am wary of becoming too separate from my mother, and to prevent this I incorporated her behaviors, even those that offended me. In fact, whenever I nagged my daughter the way that my mother used to nag me, I would hear her voice coming through my mouth! Having been made conscious of my repetitive tendencies by my perceptive husband, I am first learning to choose the ways I want to be like and be unlike my mother as a parent.

Rather than fearing too much separateness from Mother, some women may be afraid of too much closeness with her. *Matrophobia,* a term coined by poet Lynn Sukenick, is the anxiety of the unseparated daughter (who in reality is strongly influenced by her mother) that, unless on her guard, she will *become* her mother and thereby lose the right to an individual life. Instead of enjoying her resemblances to Mother—or her daughter's resemblances to Grandmother—she despises them and vehemently denies them: "I am *nothing* like my mother. I take after my father one hundred per cent." Like me, the woman suffering from matrophobia must learn that she can decide what her inheritance from Mother shall be and shall not be.

Although the death of a parent is usually a sorrowful event for a middle-aged daughter, in the best cases its effect will be to promote growth. During their lifetimes, as the Moss's note, parents act as buffers between the child and death itself, since, in the normal scheme of things, the older generation dies before the younger one does. As long as the parents are alive, the grown daughter feels shielded. Without this buffer, however, she can no longer deny her mortality but must cope with the concept of finitude. In the process of making peace with the inevitability of her own death, the middle-aged parent also becomes able to soothe her own child's fears and act as a necessary guide. Several years before she died, when I was in my early teens, my grandmother told me that when her time came she wouldn't be afraid, and I believed her. Her courage made me feel more comfortable about the idea of death; in fact, it still does.

Paradoxically, it is the knowledge of our imminent death—that we are the next in line—that moves us to treasure our aliveness and realize our beautiful possibilities. Lulled by the illusion that she could retreat in time and resurrect the mother of her past, Lucy Ann misses the opportunity to come to grips with the reality that time inches forward, that at any moment death might cut off her life, and that she must therefore make the most of the present.

I have treated a few women who, like Lucy Ann, had resisted growth and change. Over-attachments to their mothers (or to compliant daughters or doting husbands who filled the role of Mother) seemed to shield them from both life's responsibilities and possibilities. Although they acted as tyrants among family members, for dependency always fosters hostility, they remained rather timid and childlike outside the home. Indeed, like young coquettes, they would sometimes flaunt their girlish incompetence as if it were a "cute" virtue. With the help of therapy these incongruously innocent and naive middle-aged women gradually relinquished their infantilizing attachments, became more independent, and were at last born into the world.

Connie, for example, had led a sheltered, pampered life. As an adult, she learned to navigate the world by her charm and good looks, and, like Blanche in *A Streetcar Named Desire*, to depend on the kindness of strangers. More than this, she depended on the care of her eldest daughter. From the time she was a little girl, Lois believed that she could not turn to her mother but that her mother should always be able to turn to her. The unfortunate role reversal forced Lois into a premature adulthood and, sadly, eventually alienated her from Connie, whose helplessness and almost constant demands for attention became unbearable. It was only after Lois informed her mother that, at least for a time, she would have nothing more to do with her that Connie was forced to begin to grow up and take responsibility for her own life; at sixty, she could no longer depend on the "kindness" of others.

Much like Connie, pretty Allison had been a "doll baby" first to her indulgent parents and then to her rich, solicitous husband. As a middle-aged woman, however, she was embarrassed by her failure to have made something of herself and by her years of parasitic living. Realizing it was "now or never," Allison for the first time refused her husband's overly generous "pocket money," rejected her mother's suggestion that she was being a "foolish girl" to change her life, and took a job as a waitress. Coming to a therapy session straight from work, she sighed, "I am exhausted, but for the first time in my life I've earned the right to be tired. You know, I'm damn proud of my swollen feet!"

What I find curious and sad is that well-meaning people (like Allison's mother and husband) often discourage women from outgrowing their childishness. In the summer of 1987, my husband and I attended the Telluride Film Festival, where a new low-budget comedy, *I Hear the Mermaids Singing*, was shown. The protagonist, a character in her early thirties, who describes herself as "organizationally impaired" and who seems to take great delight in her childish, incompetent ways, captured the hearts of many in the audience who responded to her deficiencies (for example, although she is a "gal Friday" she cannot type) as though they are endearing, cute feminine characteristics. The appreciative moviegoers were even sympathetic to her for "inadvertently" flinging a cup of scalding tea at her ultrasophisticated, successful lady boss, no doubt because they shared the cultural belief that such a woman deserves to be humbled. Infatuated with the image of the ever-sweet, ever-pleasing, unambitious, unaccomplished female, as are so many American men and women, they failed to recognize the hostile tendencies or passive aggressiveness that underly dependent characteristics and the tragedy of being an eternal girl. (Mermaids may sing for and charm others, but they are half-formed women and, recognizing this about themselves, are certain to become envious of those who are more complete.)

To be sure, women who eventually claim their independence may antagonize or even alienate those who would keep them in subordinate positions. For example, as long as his wife was totally dependent on him, Allison's husband could delude himself into believing that he was a good, strong, generous husband, and as long as Allison was child-like and helpless, her mother could see herself, by contrast, as competent. When the self-appointed caretakers perceive that their charge wants to free herself, they may hold on to her even more tightly. But by not claiming her independence and by not breaking away from her caretakers, the dependent woman remains a stunted human being. As Stanford professor of psychiatry Irvin D. Yalom summarizes, "Not to separate means not to grow up."

Separation is never painless, however. The awareness of one's independence and individuality generates not only feelings of personal power and joy but feelings of dread and isolation. As Connie explained, "After Lois severed our relationship, I felt terrified. It was like being cast off from the planet, like floating in space without any ground. For months, I didn't think I could survive on my own. I thought I would disintegrate."

In preparation for this chapter, I combed the literature in search of fictional middle-aged heroines who could guide our own growth in relationships. Unfortunately, as feminist critic Carolyn Heilbrun points out, few writers have been interested in creating middle-aged characters of any substance. They, like the general public, seem convinced that after her youth has faded, a woman has no story to tell, so that the woman's plot line does not go beyond some early romantic adventures, marriage, and birthing children. Fortunately, my husband, who is a literary scholar, pointed me in the direction of Virginia Woolf's work.

In *To the Lighthouse*, Woolf follows Lily Briscoe through her early and middle adult years and describes her changing relationship to the maternal Mrs. Ramsay. What one comes to understand through Lily's story is that separation from the mother figure is a necessary condition not only for selfhood but for artistic creation.

As long as she remains under the beautiful Mrs. Ramsay's influence, Lily is unable to paint, to sustain even a "miserable remnant of her vision." Instead, she is trapped in a one-inside-the-other relationship; she can see the world only through the eyes of the other: "What did the hedge mean to her, what did the garden mean to her, what did it mean to her when a wave broke?"[8] Mrs. Ramsey's death eventually allows Lily's necessary separation from her. Slowly, without devaluing the deceased woman, Lily comes to recognize that the object of her idealization was, in truth, an ordinary human being, flawed in certain ways. In recognizing Mrs. Ramsay's failures of understanding and her short-sightedness (knowingly, Woolf portrays the idealized Mrs. Ramsay as myopic), Lily begins to trust her own clear-sightedness. Becoming confident of her perceptions, her vision no longer overshadowed by the older woman's conventional view of things, Lily learns to see what she *herself* sees.

Toward the end of the novel, Lily, now forty-four, returns to the Ramsays' residence and once again takes up her brush to the unfinished painting she could never get quite right during Mrs. Ramsay's lifetime.

> There it was—her picture. Yes, with all its greens and blues, its lines running up and across, its attempt at something. It would be hung in the attics, she thought; it would be destroyed. But what did it matter? . . . With a sudden intensity, as if she saw it clear for a second, she drew a line there, in the centre. It was done; it was finished. Yes, she thought, laying down her brush in extreme fatigue, I have had my vision.[9]

Lily Briscoe's wonderful triumph is dimmed somewhat by the fact that she could differentiate from and humanize Mrs. Ramsay only after her death. Because of this, she missed cultivating a warm, accepting, perhaps even loving relationship with the older woman.

In *Lifeprints*, researchers Grace Baruch, Rosalind Barnett, and Caryl Rivers present the heartening finding that by middle adulthood most daughters seem to have an objective and mature view of their mothers. "These adult women view their mothers not the way children see them—through a magnifying glass as giants—but as people with whom they can, and have, come to terms."[10] It is only when grown women transform the all-giving, all-taking archetypal Mother into her human reality that reciprocal relationship becomes possible. The *angst* and anger that often characterize interactions between younger daughters and mothers (or older daughters and mothers enmeshed in a regressive relationship) abate as these daughters come to expect their mothers to behave as the imperfect, limited, ordinary people they are. Only after a woman takes in stride Mother's failures of understanding, empathy, and availability, instead of responding to these shortcomings with childish indignation and disappointment, is she ready to become her adult friend.

Also, as the middle-aged daughter develops reasonable expectations of her aging mother, she will be able to develop reasonable self-expectations in relationship to her adolescent daughter. No longer berating herself for being an imperfect mother, she will be satisfied simply to be good enough. Seeing oneself as an ordinary mother instead of insisting on being an extraordinary one is a wonderful relief. When my daughter recently accused me of treating her like a little kid—and, in this instance, she was quite right—I was able to say, "Look, I've never had a teenage daughter before. So we are just going to have to resign ourselves to the fact that I'll make plenty of mistakes trying to parent you! But you might take some consolation from the fact that since this is your first time being a teenager, we'll be tolerant of your mistakes too."

One of the marks of a mature relationship occurs when the daughter no longer sees her mother as a goddess, monster, or fool, but rather as a human being. Some of my middle-aged clients who have developed mutually rewarding relationships with their aging mothers describe their new "friends" in the following ways:

"My mother has always had a hard time expressing tender feelings. She just doesn't know how to be affectionate with me, or, for that matter, with my sisters. But she has a straight-forward, no-nonsense way about her that I've come to admire; I trust her and like being with her."

"My mother is a terribly overbearing woman who happens to have a terrific sense of humor and a foolproof knack for cheering me up."

"We don't agree on many things, but we care about and love each other. Is there any more to say?"

Developmental psychologists, gerontologists, and researchers all seem to agree that successful separation depends on the adult daughter's realistic appraisal of Mother—what Baruch and her associates call the "process of shrinkage" from giantess to normal-sized woman. What they often neglect, however, is the daughter's parallel process of reducing her self-expectations in relation to mother. Ideally, she will come to understand that as a limited, ordinary human being she cannot play the role of perfect, all-giving, all-loving daughter. From my personal and clinical experience, I find that of the important tasks—realistic appraisal of the mother's role and realistic appraisal of one's role as a daughter—the latter is more difficult to accomplish. When a mother disappoints, the daughter who had expected more of her may rant and rave for a time, whereas when she disappoints her mother, the daughter who cannot accept her own limitations is likely to suffer from overwhelming guilt and reproach herself harshly.

Recently my mother, a widow who lives in a community for the elderly in Florida, asked if she could spend a week or two with me and my family because she was feeling lonely and depressed. Since I was in the midst of my creative work, which would necessarily be disrupted by her visit, I turned down her request. For days I was consumed by guilt and anxiety. Although it has not been easy, I have given myself permission to say "no" to my husband, my children, my friends when their requests clash with my reasonable needs, but I tormented myself with the question, "Do I have the right to say "no" to my aged mother?" What my head knew (and my heart is just now learning) is that the answer is "yes."

A mature, nonexploitative, separated relationship between mother and daughter begins as each accepts the fact that the other cannot be perfectly available or responsive to her *just as she cannot be perfectly available and responsive to the other*. One of the common tragedies of childhood is that the small, dependent child often comes to believe that being herself and for herself alienates the mother on whom her young life depends; to ensure her approval, she believes she must always conform to Mother's standards and even become an extension of her. Many women continue to carry this burden of indebtedness along with the fear of maternal reprisal into their adult lives. When my client Tanya, about whom I wrote at the beginning of this chapter, told me that she anticipated saying "no" to her mother would kill one or the other of them, she was reexperiencing the panic of the child within her who cannot afford to displease Mother for fear of rejection. Similarly, after opposing their mothers, Carol and Natalie—feeling at one level that their acts of defiance warranted punishment—tortured themselves, Carol with a week-long migraine and Natalie with thoughts of suicide.

Returning to the situation with my own mother, allow me to share some observations I made during the weeks that followed her request to visit and my subsequent denial. I noticed that, after expressing some disappointment at not being able to spend time with my family, my mother did not in fact punish me by withdrawing her love or by falling to pieces. Rather, she came up with an alternate plan to meet her needs: a visit to a favorite niece whom she had not seen for years.

Often I forget that my mother—a woman who survived Nazi persecutions in her native Austria; fled alone to war-torn England, then to America, with no more than a few dollars in her pocket; worked for the better part of her life as a sales clerk in a bakery to help support me, her refugee in-laws and mother; and made a long, happy marriage to my father—does not depend on her daughter for well-being. The grandiose child within me, who still thinks of herself as the center of the universe, overinflates her importance as she clings to the illusion that she alone has the power to enhance or devastate Mother's life. Thankfully, the adult that I am for the most part is beginning to know otherwise: Mother can take care of herself and does not resent me when I take care of myself. This is what separation between us allows. What is more, as I come to understand that my mother is strong, vital, and capable of joyful living without my interventions, I am indirectly teaching my daughter that she will not be expected to make me happy when I am old.

In a wonderful collection of letters by mothers and daughters, Karen Payne includes one by the middle-aged Karen Blixen, alias Isak Dinesen, which was written after her divorce and the bankruptcy of her Kenyan coffee plantation. In it she told of her wish to kill herself rather than leave her beloved Africa to return to an anticipated stifling existence in Denmark and a dreaded dependency on her mother, Ingeborg. But, perhaps believing that Ingeborg could not cope with this information or that it might make her too angry, Karen chose not to share it with her and instead revealed it to her brother. Anxious to have news about Karen, however, Ingeborg unsealed the envelope addressed to Thomas and read the enclosed letter, which she guiltily forwarded to him along with an explanatory letter of her own. As the following passages from Ingeborg's letter show, mothers are often more forgiving than their daughters credit them with being. Certainly, Ingeborg's reply is a testament to her autonomy and ability to remain composed in the face of a troubled daughter's rejections.

You know that for the whole of my life with you I have tried my best to understand you, and you may be sure that I understand what Tanne [Karen] is going through now. For I have always known that the environment I offered her was not suited to her character and talents—this has caused me great pain, but it has not been possible for me to change it so much that it would make her happy. Perhaps she has not really been willing to make the attempt to find happiness in this environment; but no matter how much violence she might have done to her nature she would never have been able to feel at home in what she rightly calls a bourgeois existence, and so much value in her would have been wasted.

I know—and I know you believe it to be true—that I will be able to give Tanne complete freedom to do what she thinks is best for herself—I will not hold her back if she thinks life is too hard for her, I will not for one moment put her under an obligation to "be something" to me in these years. . . . The sole consideration for me is that she should live according to her nature—I neither can nor will demand anything else of her. . . .

You know that when I first began to reconsider, after Tanne told me that you wanted to go to war, I was fully aware that it was necessary for you to have my complete approval and blessing before you went—that was what I owed you, the only thing that I have been able to do for all of you is that, to try to understand and help you follow your own natures. Whenever I felt something in you that was alien to me I was always afraid lest it should be impeded if I did not take the trouble to support it. . . .

My own dearest boy, you must not harbor any hard feelings toward Tanne because she despises what I have to offer her. . . . [Tanne] has often caused me anxiety, probably more than any of my other children, but she has filled my life with so much love, so much festivity, I have been—and am—so proud of her, that whatever she may come to do I will always love and bless her. . . ."[11]

Because Karen tried to shield her mother from certain hard facts and because Ingeborg did not want to reveal that she had intercepted her daughter's letter, both women lost the opportunity for honest encounter. Ingeborg's important letter was sent to her son rather than to the daughter who would have been comforted knowing the extent of her mother's support and inspired knowing the depth of her inner strength.

As I continue to struggle toward separation from my mother, I am gradually accepting my limitations as a daughter. Primary among these limitations is my inability to pay her back for all that she has given me. In *My Mother, My Self*, Nancy Friday tells a story ascribed to Sigmund Freud about an eagle that, during a great flood, was about to carry her newborns to safe ground. As she took flight clutching her firstborn in her mighty talons, he promised, "Mother, I will be eternally grateful and devoted to you for saving my life." Naming him a liar, she dropped the eaglet into the raging waters below. The same thing happened with the second child. When the great eagle swept up the third, this wise child said, "When I am grown, I will try to be as good a parent to my children as you are to me," and her mother carried her to safety. Between my mother and me—as between all mothers and daughters—there can never be a quid pro quo. How could I ever pay her back for giving me life? Like the wise eaglet, the best I can do is nurture the lives of my son and daughter (her grandchildren) until they are ready to take full charge of them. As Friday says so well, "The debt of gratitude we owe our mother and father goes forward, not backward. What we owe our parents is the bill presented us by our children." As I come to terms with the fact that I cannot and should not try to meet all my mother's needs, I am increasingly aware that my daughter has the same freedom with me: She need not be eternally grateful and devoted to me. Her debt is also directed forward, not backward.

Unfortunately, in those cases where a mother has not properly prepared for her old age—practically, by setting aside adequate funds for the late years and spiritually, by having developed a rich inner life from which she is able to draw when physical limitations preclude an active life—she may pull her daughter into a depleting caretaking role, expecting the younger woman to support her financially and to nourish her emotionally. At the time that a middle-aged woman's own children are becoming old enough to care for themselves so that she is at last free to pursue personal goals, her mother may call for considerable caretaking.

Just as our culture has tried to force human mothers to transform themselves into their superhuman counterparts—what Virginia Woolf named the Victorian "angels of the house"—so has it imposed unreasonable demands on its daughters. An old proverb, "A son is a son 'til he takes a wife, a daughter's a daughter the rest of her life," suggests that the latter has filial debts that her brothers are spared. Certainly, grown children, sons as well as daughters, must assume reasonable responsibilities for their parents when they can no longer care for themselves. But deciding what is reasonable care and what are unreasonable sacrifices is a complicated, often heart-wrenching moral dilemma.

Until recently, women assumed that giving up their own lives in the service of others—husbands, children, aging parents—was both reasonable and expected of them. The price of their self-sacrifices, however, was high: anger, bitterness, passive aggression, exhaustion, feelings of having wasted themselves. As a therapist, I have yet to meet a woman who has not resented having given up her potentials, her talents, her personal dreams. Virginia Woolf's poignant description of motherly Mrs. Ramsay, the ever-faithful caretaker, comes to mind: "So boasting of her capacity to surround and protect, there was scarcely a shell of herself left for her to know herself by, all was so lavished and spent."[12] Moreover, when the woman who has lived only in the service of others becomes old herself, she may expect her own daughter to become her caretaker—to repeat the pattern of self-sacrifice and to lengthen what Simone de Beauvoir named the "chain of female misery."

Confronted with financial, physical, and emotional responsibilities toward a needy, dependent, and sometimes ailing parent and with the responsibility of living her own precious life, today's woman must strike some kind of balance, but achieving this balance cannot be easy. In his volume *Existential Psychotherapy*, Yalom draws on Rabbi Hillel's questions —which contemporary women must also ask themselves— "If I am not for myself, who will be? And if I am only for myself, what am I?"

So far in my discussion, I have focused on relationships that presuppose a warm, close—sometimes overly close— relationship between mother and daughter in which, if exploitation exists, it is not intentional. Now I will turn to other kinds of relationship, in which instead of goodwill, there is maternal mean-spiritedness. In these cases, mother-daughter separations are necessarily more painful.

In my clinical practice I have treated several middle-aged women with destructive mothers. Leslie, for example, cannot remember an encouraging word or a loving touch from her mother. Instead, Leslie remembers the time when she was beginning puberty and her mother blurted out, "My, you are a homely girl." She also remembers her mother's self-satisfied smile as she stood watching her husband remove his belt to give their daughter yet another beating for some minor transgression. Most stinging of all is Leslie's memory of her mother's remorseless confession that having had a child was her biggest mistake, her ruination.

I once heard an anecdote about a little girl who, upon visiting a cemetery and taking note of the kind tributes engraved on each gravestone, asked, "But where are the bad people buried?" Similarly, we tend to attribute to women who are mothers the quality of goodness. Leslie's previous counselor tried to convince her that she should emphasize the positive about her mother and accept the "shortcomings" because the time had come to mend rather than sever their strained relationship. "Your mother did love you," she assured Leslie, "but just couldn't express it very well. As a middle-aged woman with a daughter of your own, surely you can begin to forgive the old woman and make a peace with her."

My clinical experience teaches me that just as there are bad people buried in cemeteries, there are bad mothers in this world. Victims of some terrible emotional impoverishment, they are deficient as human beings and lack the capacity to love their children because they do not like themselves. I am not speaking about the average mother, who is a combination of personal strengths and failings, and whose daughters need to come to terms with the latter. Here I am speaking of women who are sadomasochistic in their natures. Although their young children are too powerless and dependent to leave them, their grown children can and should. My first therapeutic goal in treating Leslie was to help her become free of, not to forgive, a destructive mother.

Old age had not softened Leslie's mother, who at age seventy continued to criticize and deride not only her daughter but her adolescent granddaughter, Leslie's only child. For it seemed that in these younger women, she saw parts of herself—a self she despised. Moreover, at the same time that she unconsciously condemned them for resembling her, she resented them for having the opportunities to surpass her. Out of her bitterness, the old woman was poisoning her daughter and granddaughter.

When I first suggested to Leslie that she discontinue visits with her mother, because they were inevitably followed by periods of intense despair, heightened feelings of worthlessness, and self-sabotage, Leslie became frightened. "This sounds utterly ridiculous, I know," Leslie confided, "but I have a feeling that if I left her for good, she would do me some terrible harm. When I was a little girl, Mother would take out books from the library on black magic. I worry that if she thinks I'm bad to her, she'll put an eternal curse on me."

Leslie still carried the child's magical conception of an all-powerful mother. In Leslie's case, because of her mother's abusiveness, the image was not of the protective mother but of the evil, omnipresent witch. Eventually, Leslie did terminate the relationship with her. But this "divorce" required a great deal of courage, so entrenched was the belief in the mother's terrible retaliatory powers. What persuaded Leslie to make the physical break was her commitment to her daughter and her determination that the young girl would no longer be humiliated or insulted by the old woman, as she herself had always been. Wanting a better life for her child, Leslie broke the chain of misery that binds generations of sadomasochistic females.

In *The Feminine in Fairytales*, Marie-Louise von Franz addresses this phenomenon in which a woman who might ordinarily be quite passive and do little to change her own miserable conditions becomes heroic for the good of her child. She refers to a Russian tale about a woman without hands. The woman, exhausted and thirsty, wanders through the countryside carrying her little child under her arm, when she comes to a spring. Although she desperately wants to drink from it, she is afraid that the child might fall into the water. And, indeed, as she leans forward she does let the child slip from her arm. In a panic she searches for help and encounters an old man who says, "Well, take the child out!" "But I have no hands," she wails, to which the old man says once more, "Just take the child out!" Then she puts her arm stumps into the water and on them grow living hands. As von Franz comments, "At the moment she was about to lose the child, the last thing she had and the only thing she loved, but by saving it from drowning she is helped."[13] So it is with Leslie: By sparing her daughter from her grandmother's abusive behavior, she also spares herself. The day she told her mother, "My daughter and I will not be seeing you again. I simply won't subject her to your cruel remarks," Leslie stopped subjecting herself to the same.

I do not want to mislead my readers, however, into believing that in ending her relationship with her mother, Leslie became suddenly happy and carefree. Unloved as she was, Leslie is a deeply wounded woman. Like other women similarly deprived, she still struggles against falling into the states of despair that are so familiar to her. Healing her hands is only the beginning; she must also heal her heart.

A major step in this healing process is to admit to herself that she was not loved by Mother. Such an admission is necessarily painful. Despite Leslie's growing awareness that it is her mother who is deficient as a human being, Leslie is still plagued by the false belief that there must have been something wrong with her that compelled her mother to withhold love. As I often remind her in therapy, however, just like all the other babies born on this planet, she was no doubt absolutely lovable. Her psychological task is to come to appreciate her innate goodness: to see herself through different eyes than her mother's cold ones. At the same time, however, she must also recognize that, through no fault of her own, she has been badly bruised. Trusting people and being open to them will not be as easy for her as it is for the woman who was properly loved.

Because acknowledging that one was not loved by Mother hurts so much, many deprived women fight against this fact. Even when their mothers continue to undermine them, they do not turn their backs on them. Rather, they remain devoted and unseparated daughters, eternally waiting for the maternal validation and approval that never come. Or, even if they distance themselves from their unloving mothers, they recreate in their present lives situations that simulate the early relationship with her.

For example, some may quite unconsciously select lovers or husbands who respond to them the way their mothers did. By trying to soften the hearts of these men and win their love, they are indirectly appealing for mother love. Leslie's failed marriage followed this pattern. As she explained, she responded to her husband's coldness and sarcasm by becoming extra sweet to him, always groveling for the crumbs of love he would sometimes toss out to her.

To her credit, Leslie is determined to give up the false hope of changing what is past, either through a continuing relationship with her mother or one with a lover who is a substitute for mother. In her words,

> At the same time that it is still terribly sad for me to know that I've missed the mother love that practically everyone else in the world had, it is a relief not to delude myself anymore. I used to try so hard to believe my mother was a good mother and that she did love me. But she wasn't good and she didn't love me. That is the truth of it. She hurt me very much, and no one has the right to hurt a child. Because I'm not a saint, I no longer believe I have to forgive her, contrary to what my first counselor said. What I want to do instead is be a good mother to my daughter and heal the wounded places in myself.

Leslie has been in therapy with me for three years now. Together we continue to work toward this healing.

For years I harbored a sense of hopelessness in treating women who, like Leslie, had not experienced adequate maternal loving. I had no confidence that they could overcome their early deprivations. And yet a good number did effectively compensate for them. For some, the healing followed what psychoanalyst Alice Miller calls a "deeply felt mourning" for what one has missed—the loving mother, the happy childhood—and the acceptance that their inadequate mothers would never love them, that the past could not be put right. In the presence of an empathic psychotherapist, these badly treated women were at last able to expose their festering wounds and name their despair. Feeling and talking through the pain—the humiliation of being an unloved child, the anger toward the cold mother, the anxiety of turning into her, the fear of maternal retribution for hating her—became the healing salve. Where therapy was successful, these women came to understand that their mothers, who were unfortunate, inadequate, insecure people, *did not have the power* to hurt them anymore. If their mothers continued to act destructively, they could walk away from them. As important, they learned that by virtue of their growing self-awareness, *they did have the power* to behave differently with their own daughters than their mothers had behaved with them.

In addition to the necessary talking through that goes on in an effective therapy, I think the therapist replaces, to an extent, the Bad Mother with a Good Mother. Instead of being derisive, overcritical, and undermining, as the mother was, the therapist affirms her client's potentials and encourages these. Slowly—over many months or years—the wounded woman internalizes the therapist's belief in her goodness. The Good Mother, first represented in the person of the therapist, becomes a part of her. Several times, Leslie encountered this Good Mother in dreams; personified as a small, wizened, brown-skinned woman in a white hand-spun toga, she would gently take Leslie's hand and smile on her. At other times, Leslie hears from inside her own head the Good Mother's words, "You are a lovely and capable woman who deserves to be happy"—the same refrain she hears so often during our treatment. It is when a woman believes that she is worthy that she also believes her daughter—the one with whom she is most closely identified—is worthy. Then she can also say to her, "You are a lovely and capable girl who deserves to be happy."

For others the healing also came through a communion with Nature, so aptly named Mother Nature. In an earlier chapter, I explained that adopted girls, who have suffered the loss of the birth mother, may be soothed by tender relationships with pets. Similarly, inadequately mothered women may feel nourished in the natural world.

As Marie-Louise von Franz explained, the fairy tales tell

the woman who has been damaged by a negative mother to go completely into nature, into the forest "where things begin to turn and grow again." The literature, for example, is full of accounts of so-called Wood Sisters and Brothers who in making friends with the forest animals are thereby blessed with rich and growing spiritual lives. Also, in certain versions of the tales of the woman without hands, she grows hands and is healed as she wraps her arms round a great tree of the forest. Drawing on her clinical work with women, von Franz wrote,

> Frequently women say that the only way in which they can enjoy life a little and not feel so bad over their difficulties is by taking long walks in the woods, or by sitting in the sun, etc. This is a genuine tendency, for it seems as though only nature in its virgin beauty and essence has the power to heal in such a case. Women have a very deep relationship to nature in its positive form. Relationship to animals can also effect the cure and many women make a relationship to a pet, which at that time may mean more to them than anything else because its unconscious simplicity appeals to the wounds within them. . . . Relationship to an animal is simple, and in feeling for it, the lost tenderness may be discovered.[14]

In her *Journal of Solitude*, May Sarton described the healing powers of flowers. Although I am tempted to include many of Sarton's exquisitely rendered images, I will limit myself to selecting only a few of these:

> When I am alone the flowers are really seen; I can pay attention to them. They are felt as presences. Without them I would die . . . they keep me closely in touch with process, with growth. . . . I am floated on their moments.

> The begonias have thrived remarkably, first as house plants last winter, then outdoors all summer. A sturdy plant is a great comfort.

I woke to the sun on a daffodil. I had put a bunch of daffodils and purple tulips on the bureau and when I woke the sun hit just one daffodil, a single beam on the yellow frilled cup and outer petals. After a bad night that sight got me up and going.

Recently, a colleague lent me a book by Harold F. Searles called *The Nonhuman Environment* in which he explained how even those human beings suffering from the most profound grief and despair can find restitution by re-establishing contact with the natural world. Quoting from W. H. Hudson's love story, *Green Mansions*, Searles reminds us how closely related are a child's experience of Nature and of mother love:

Ah that return to the forest where Rima dwelt, after so anxious a day, when the declining sun shone hotly still, and the green woodland shadows were so grateful! . . . I likened myself to a child that, startled at something it had seen while out playing in the sun, flies to its mother to feel her caressing hand on its cheek and forget its tremors. And describing what I felt in that way, I was a little ashamed and laughed at myself; nevertheless the feeling was very sweet. At that moment Mother and Nature seemed one and the same thing.[15]

When a grown woman turns to everyday relationships for the mothering she herself missed, she inevitably exploits them. Outside of the therapy room, relationships in which one partner continually gives and the other receives are a bad solution; the "giver" feels sucked dry and the "taker" feels guilty. However, when a deprived woman turns to the natural world—its sunlight, trees, flowers, and gentle animals—for nourishment, she does no one an injustice. Mother Nature, who is so bountiful, can afford to nourish the way the real mother never did. And it is only after she is nourished with life's love and goodness that she can thrive and be generous herself.

Several years ago, I treated a middle-aged client, Tess, who suffered from debilitating depression. She had been born to a mother who was herself chronically depressed and for this reason unable to respond to Tess during her infancy and childhood. Despite Tess's history of maternal deprivation, she was intent on becoming whole and vital and proved to be a hard-working client. At the time of our psychotherapy, however, I was puzzled by the fact that before each session Tess watered every plant in my office and, in spite of my preference for cool darkness, pulled up the window shades to let in the strong afternoon sun in which she would luxuriate. Because at the time I could not make sense of her behavior, I dismissed it as idiosyncratic and unimportant. In a final report, at the conclusion of our professional relationship, I made no mention of Tess's small rituals and attributed her new psychological health to my support and her hard work. Now I wonder if the philodendrons, the potted rubber tree, the freshly cut flowers, and the Colorado sunshine that grace my consulting room do not deserve some of the credit for Tess's cure.

In my recent work with emotionally undernourished women, I prescribe, together with the more traditional "talk" therapy, some kind of communion with nature. I suggest that my clients work in their gardens or take walks in the hills or sit at night under the full sky. I suggest that they adopt a pet—if not a dog or a cat, then some goldfish or perhaps a bird. I suggest that they not wait until Mother's Day to receive a bouquet of flowers but treat themselves often to daffodils and daisies and, every once in a while, to a rose.

Nature is healer, and nature is teacher. As I write this chapter, I look out toward the back of my house, where the leaves are turning pink, red, and gold. Four deer in different attitudes of rest, readiness, and activity occupy the lawn: One crouches on the grass; another stands still; and the two remaining nibble crab apples that litter the ground. A while ago my daughter walked across the lawn from the lane in back of our fence. She stopped for a moment to look at the deer, who waited, very still, and then continued to watch and scavenge for food while she walked to the house. The scene speaks of harmony and separateness, continuity and change. Everything is in perfect balance.

I notice that my daughter's cheeks have taken on the peach tones that stripe some of the leaves. And in a cluster of orange-peach-crimson leaves still clinging to the branches of the apple tree, when I squint my eyes, I begin to make out human faces, much the way children find hidden objects in the drawings of their busy books or see funny animals in the clouds. The one that delights me most is the face of a crone. I close my eyes and imagine her smiling, and she becomes as beautiful as the fresh-looking teenage girl who entered the room in which I sit. In my reverie, the beautiful faces of the crone and of my daughter merge to become the face of my mother.

The crone is beautiful when her old age suggests completion rather than incompletion. She is beautiful when the wrinkles of age she presents to us are signs of wisdom—of experience accumulated and sorted through. My own mother is most beautiful when, at her ease, she recalls her young, carefree days in Vienna; her courtship by my father, whose gambling and whose darting eye for women she had to tame; her happiness in being reunited with him in England after each escaped from the Nazis—happiness under the greatest hardships—and the love, encumbered by few regrets, that she still has for this man who died seventeen years ago, when I was pregnant with the granddaughter she cherishes. She is beautiful in moments like the one my husband remembers in which, absorbed in our small talk, we neglected to notice that one of us was putting back into soapy water dishes that the other one had rinsed and put aside. Her laughter with me then was open and alive. She is beautiful when she looks with pleasure and wonder at the accomplishments of her daughter and her granddaughter—academic degrees, journal articles, original stories, drawings—that go beyond her own accomplishments in life. And she is beautiful when, without harping on the fixed ideas that often encumber us as we grow older, she can spontaneously and gently suggest something from her own experience that can help her daughter and granddaughter. As my husband once said, after dancing with my mother at our wedding, my mother is light on her feet. That lightness is often an antidote for her daughter's besetting intellectualism.

The crone is ugly when she has not separated adequately from us or we from her; when she does not validate our experience but debunks it; when she does not gently and generously share her own experience, but imposes fixed laws and ideas on us; when she does not smile at the distance we've covered from the place we have left her but draws us back with the tether of obligation and guilt.

May Sarton observes that when the ash has lost its leaves, it, like everything else in nature, is "honed down to structure." In this rich farewell it goes deep into its roots "for renewal and sleep." That is the lesson of nature—the lesson of its cycles. And it is the crone, in her benevolent aspects, who represents this lesson best. She should not be fearful and ugly, as she is portrayed in our culture, which does not encourage its men and women to grow up and condemns them for growing old. She should be beautiful as she shows us how the struggles and gratifications of youth can yield to more mature pleasures.

"Hold on!" says the ugly old crone of our nightmares—the crone who threatens to devour us.

"Let go!" says the beautiful crone of the crossroads—the crone who smiles and waves us on.

Afterword:

A Letter to Leah

Dear Leah,

This morning, a graduate student (who is about to have her first baby) stopped by my office to chat. She asked me how having a daughter has changed me. Funny, but even though I've spent all this time writing a book about mothers and daughters, I couldn't really give her a quick and easy answer. Anyway, after she left my office I thought for a long time about her question, and I want to share the feelings, memories, and longings that it is bringing up. (Be prepared: I think this is going to be a long letter!)

What I know, Leah, is that without you I wouldn't be the "me" I've become—I'd be a poorer, lesser me. Until you came into my world, I was a timid girl, without much pluck or purpose. But from the first weeks of your life, you moved me to love with a tenderness—and a ferocity— that I had never known. Let me tell you a story about us, one that I don't think I've shared with you before.

Very soon after the doctor told me I was pregnant, Dad's parents offered to treat us to a tour all through

France, where they would take us to famous restaurants and pay for our hotel rooms; it was like a fairy tale come true. I remember how excited I was as the four of us piled into our rented Renault and drove away from Paris. As soon as we reached the lovely green countryside, however, the roads became bumpy, and I worried that you—this precious living being growing inside me—would be jolted about. So, trying to cushion you against the bumps and pits in the road, I sat on my hands. In the kindest way, Grandma explained that you were well protected in my womb and that it was hardly necessary for me to sit on my hands, which, as you can imagine, got pretty numb after a few hours. But, despite Grandma's reassurances, I was bound and determined to protect you this way. And so, for two weeks, four or five hours a day, I held this strange position as the little Renault bumped its way past the Loire Valley, across the Pont d'Avignon, down into Marseilles. Even in the womb, Leah, you were changing me—teaching me to love and care as I had never done before.

After you were born, you moved me to do more than sit on my hands. For your sake, I couldn't stay the timid girl who never asked for things—I had to learn to speak up, to take a stand. Quite out of character for me, I bullied the people at the motor vehicles bureau to put up signs which warned, "Slow, Children at Play" all along the street in Athens, Ohio, where we lived when you were a baby. Sometimes, I admit, my expressions of motherly concern became a bit obnoxious. You may be embarrassed to know that I barred anyone who could not demonstrate perfect health from any contact with you. "Sorry," I told this nice young man with a bad case of the sniffles who had come to our house for a political meeting, "but you'll have to leave right away. I have a baby, and I won't have her catch your cold!" You may also be appalled to know that, without a shred of tact or compassion, I scolded the kindly old gentleman who lived next door for slipping you those yellow, red, and green candy Chuckles each time you toddled past his doorway. You see, when I was a young mother I was absolutely convinced that I had the power not only to prevent you from catching someone's cold but from ingesting so much as a bite of impure, unwholesome food. (Smile about that one the next time you're eating those frozen pizzas fortified with ten thousand chemicals.)

Despite my excesses, Leah, you brought out the best in me. Through your sparkling eyes, I was able to see a newer, fresher world. When you were a little girl, you brought into my everyday adult life Big Bird, Magic Markers, mud pies, balloons, and even mythical unicorns. In your child's wisdom, you once wrote in your book of poems, "Even if this creature—with its slender horn of palest white —is only made up and cannot exist through our minds, it can exist in our hearts," and it has lived in mine ever since.

You also invited a family of leprechauns to live with our family. Their furnished cardboard house, which you made so lovingly, sat on our kitchen table for many, many months. How much lonelier my life would have been without your little, magical, mischievous, friends: You and they taught me how to be playful.

Well, sad to say, the leprechauns left several years ago; I miss them sometimes. I miss little Leah too, sometimes.

But you won't let me cling to the past, or to you. You nudge me forward. With your wide smile, you are the open door that leads me toward new and better directions.

When you told me, a few months ago, that you didn't mind being the very worst in your dance class because you were having so much fun, you taught me that I don't always have to be the best—that there are times when I can just enjoy and relax. When you get excited about art history, especially the impressionist paintings you are studying in school, I see them with fresh eyes and they become luminous and vivid as never before. When you and your girlfriends—Sabra, Nan, Karen (who have replaced the leprechauns)—giggle, imitate teachers (and mothers), or belt out show tunes, you infect me with your exuberance and fill me with music. And when you say nice things about the people who cross your path—as you always seem to do—you teach me to be a little less critical, a little more tolerant too.

Still, Leah, sometimes when I behold you I become afraid. At almost seventeen, you seem too lovely, too innocent, too trusting for this world; and I still want to protect you against it: its crimes, its atrocities, its wars, its pollution, its disasters, its plagues. Rightly, you won't let me shield you anymore; you do not allow me to close you in behind my protective doors. Because you are so insistent on taking your place in the world and because I know that my hands can no longer cushion you against life's bumps and jolts, you are pushing me to find new ways to be a caring mother. I can no longer protect you against the world, but maybe, in my small ways, I can try to make it a better place for all its children. Just as you are beginning to develop a social conscience, I am more ready to act on mine.

So you see, Leah, you bring out the best in me. You always have. And for this I thank you with all my heart.

It has just begun to snow; the year is really coming to its end, and the holidays are upon us. You have always delighted me with your holiday gifts—those wonderful poems and drawings that are your creations and my treasures. But today I have a special gift for you. It is a story—an old Indian folk tale, which I have been saving up to tell you for a long time. Now, at almost seventeen, you are ready for it:

Many, many thousands of years ago, when the earth began, there lived a husband and wife named Smoke and Wild Pony. Walking across the young earth, they were joined by a magical creature, what the Jicarilla Apache people called a hatsin, which taught Wild Pony the art of molding clay into bowls.

Years passed. Wild Pony bore children, who in turn bore their own children. She made many clay bowls, which held the corn and water that the Indian people needed to survive. When Wild Pony became a very old woman, realizing her time on earth would shortly come to an end, she decided to pass on the art of making clay bowls to her daughter's daughter. Just as the hatsin had taught her, Wild Pony tried to instruct the girl to mold the red earth into the shape of a bowl, to dry the bowl in the sun, then to wrap it in the bark of a pine tree, and finally to place it in a smoldering fire. But despite her detailed instructions, each time the girl tried to form the clay into a bowl, it cracked and fell apart in her hands.

That night, Wild Pony, full of sadness that she could not pass on her art to her granddaughter, fell into a deep sleep. In a dream, the hatsin, which had not visited her all these many years, appeared once more. This time, it reminded Wild Pony that when it had instructed her to make the clay bowls, it had kneeled with her on the ground, scooped up a handful of the red earth, and rubbed it into Wild Pony's hands saying, "This clay is yours to use." The apparition of the hatsin advised Wild Pony to do with the young one what it had done with her; then it evaporated from the dream.

When morning came, Wild Pony took her granddaughter to the place of the red clay. Taking a handful of the clay and rubbing it into the child's hands, she said, "Now the clay is yours to use." As the grandmother knelt beside her daughter's daughter, the girl began to work the clay and it did not crack. But she did not turn it into a bowl, as her grandmother had first instructed. Instead she formed the first peace pipe on Earth.

My darling Leah, take the clay I have given you and shape it as you will. Your life is yours to create.

I love you,

Mom

December 1987

Appendix

Appendix

Footnotes

Chapter 1

1. Eleanor Mallach Bromberg, "Mother-Daughter Relationships in Later Life: The Effect of Quality of Relationship upon Mutual Aid," *Journal of Gerontological Social Work*, Vol 6 (September 1983), pp. 75-92.

2. M. Esther Harding, *Woman's Mysteries: Ancient and Modern* (New York: Harper & Row, 1976).

3. Toni Morrison, *Song of Solomon* (New York: New American Library, 1977), pp. 13-14.

4. Mary Jane Moffat and Charlotte Painter, eds., *Revelations: Diaries of Women* (New York: Random House, 1974), pp. 242–243.

Chapter 2

1. M. Esther Harding, *The Way of All Women* (New York: Harper & Row, 1970), p. 187.

Chapter 3

1. James Anthony, "The Reactions of Adults to Adolescents and Their Behavior," *Adolescence: Psychosocial Perspectives,* eds. Gerald Caplan and Serge Lebovici (New York: Harper & Row, 1969), p. 63.

2. Louise Kaplan, *Adolescence: The Farewell to Childhood* (New York: Simon & Schuster, 1984), p. 133.

3. Rosetta Reitz, *Menopause: A Positive Approach* (New York: Penguin Books, 1979.)

4. Karen Horney, *Feminine Psychology* (New York: W.W. Norton, 1967), p. 185.

5. Guadalupe Valdes, "Recuerdo," *Between Mothers and Daughters: Stories Across a Generation,* ed. Susan Koppelman (New York: The Feminist Press, 1985), pp. 192-196.

6. *Ibid.,* p. 195.

7. Alice Miller, *For Your Own Good* (New York: Farrar, Straus, Giroux, 1984).

8. May Sarton, *Journal of a Solitude* (New York: W.W. Norton, 1977), p.80.

9. Tori DeAngelis, "Nurture-or-assert Conflict Often Erupts As Depression," *The APA Monitor,* January 1987, p. 21.

10. Grace Baruch, "The Psychologocial Well-being of Women in the Middle Years," eds., Grace Baruch & J. Brooks-Gunn, *Women in Midlife* (New York: Plenum, 1984), pp. 161-180.

11. Audre Lorde, from *A Land Where Other People Live* (Detroit: Broadside Press, 1971).

12. Merlin Stone, *Ancient Mirrors of Womanhood: A Treasury of Goddess and Heroine Lore from Around the World* (Boston: Beacon Press, 1984), pp. 78-79.

Chapter 4

1. Moffat and Painter, op. cit., p. 364.

2. Sir Edwin Arnold, "Mothers," Stanza 6.

3. Jerome Kagan, *The Nature of the Child* (New York: Basic Books, 1984), p. 265.

4. Kim Chernin, *In My Mother's House* (New York: Harper & Row, 1983), p. 192.

5. *Ibid.*, p. 192.

7. Chernin, *op. cit.*, p. 195.

8. Chernin, *op. cit.*, p. 192.

9. Irene Claremont de Castillejo, *Knowing Woman* (New York: Harper & Row, 1973), p. 29.

10. Henry Harbin and Denis Madden, "Battered Parents: A New Syndrome," *American Journal of Psychiatry*, Vol. 136, 1979, pp. 1288-1291.

11. Adrienne Rich, *Of Woman Born* (New York: W.W. Norton, 1976), p. 247.

12. Moffat and Painter, *op. cit.*, p. 364.

13. Alice Miller, *op. cit.*, p. 275.

Chapter 5

1. Brody, Jane E., "One Word of Advice for Dieters: Eat," *New York Times*, March 22, 1987, p. 19.

2. Angelyn Spignesi, *Starving Women: A Psychology of Anorexia Nervosa* (Dallas, TX: Spring Publications, 1983), p. 59.

3. Excerpt in Tillie Olsen, *op. cit.*, p. 29.

4. Geneen Roth, *Feeding the Hungry Heart: The Experience of Compulsive Eating* (New York: New American Library, 1982), pp. 185–187.

5. Kim Chernin, *The Obsession: Reflections on the Tyranny of Slenderness* (New York: Harper & Row, 1981), pp. 17–18.

6. Evelyn Bassoff & Gene V. Glass, "The Relationship Between Sex Roles and Mental Health: A Meta-analysis of Twenty-six Studies," *The Counseling Psychologist*, Vol. 10, 1982, pp. 105–112.

7. Kim Chernin, *The Hungry Self: Women, Eating, and Identity* (New York: Harper & Row, 1986), p. 33.

8. Geneen Roth, *op. cit.*, p. 130.

9. Tillie Olsen, *Yonnondio from the Thirties* (New York: Dell, 1974), pp. 118–119.

Chapter 6

1. Diane di Prima, "A Poem in Praise of My Husband (Taos)," *Selected Poems, 1956–1975* (Berkeley, CA: North Atlantic Books, 1975).

2. Robert A. Johnson, *We: Understanding the Psychology of Romantic Love* (New York: Harper & Row, 1983), p. 164.

3. *Ibid.*, p. 164.

4. *Ibid.*, p. 195.

5. Jeanette and Robert Lauer, "Marriages Made to Last," *Psychology Today*, June 1985, p. 26.

6. Robert A. Johnson, *She: Understanding Feminine Psychology* (New York: Harper & Row, 1976), p. 57.

Chapter 7

1. Bernice L. Neugarten, "Dynamics of Transition of Middle Age to Old Age," *Journal of Geriatric Psychology*, Vol. 4, 1970, pp. 71–87.

2. Tillie Olsen, "I Stand Here Ironing," *Tell Me a Riddle* (New York: Dell, 1960), p. 12.

3. Claire Weekes, *Hope and Help for Your Nerves* (New York: Bantam Books, 1978), p. 203.

4. *Ibid.*, p. 204.

Chapter 8

1. May Sarton, "Of Grief," *Collected Poems of May Sarton, 1930–1977* (New York: W.W. Norton, 1977).

2. Brothers Grimm, *Grimm's Fairy Tales,* trans. E. V. Lucas, Lucy Crane, and Marian Edwards (New York: Grosset & Dunlap, 1945), p. 156.

3. May Sarton, *op. cit.*

4. Alexina M. McWhinnie, *Adopted Children: How They Grow Up: A Study of Their Adjustment As Adults*. (New York: Humanities Press; Routledge & Kegan Paul, 1967), p. 122.

5. Herbert G. May and Bruce Metzer, eds., *The New Oxford Annotated Bible* (New York: Oxford University Press, 1973).

6. Edward Albee, *Who's Afraid of Virginia Woolf?* (New York: Atheneum, 1975), p. 222.

7. May Sarton, *op. cit.*

8. Kahlil Gibran, *The Prophet* (New York: Alfred A. Knopf, 1960), p.17.

Chapter 9

1. Margaret Draughon, "Step-mother's Model of Identification in Relation to Mourning in the Child," *Psychological Reports,* Vol. 36, 1975, pp. 187–188.

2. Anne Morrow Lindbergh, *Gift from the Sea* (New York: Random House, 1978), p. 104.

3. Michel Radomisli, "Stereotypes, Stepmothers, and Splitting," *The American Journal of Psychoanalysis,* Vol. 41, 1981, p. 122.

4. Anne Morrow Lindbergh, *op cit.*, pp. 72–73.

5. Bruno Bettelheim, *The Uses of Enchantment: The Meaning and Importance of Fairy Tales* (New York: Random House, 1977), p. 221.

6. Laurence Steinberg, "Bound to Bicker," *Psychology Today,* September 1987, pp. 36–39.

Chapter 10

1. Adrienne Rich, *op. cit.*, p. 232.

2. Quoted in Adrienne Rich, *op. cit.*, p. 231.

3. Quoted in Adrienne Rich, *op. cit.*, p. 232.

4. Toni Morrison, *Sula* (New York: New American Library, 1973), pp. 71–72.

5. Alice Brown, "The Way of Peace," *Between Mothers and Daughters: Stories Across a Generation,* ed. Susan Koppelman, *op. cit.*, p. 47.

6. Alice Brown, *op. cit.*, p. 47.

7. Toni Morrison, *Sula, op. cit.*, p. 28.

8. Virginia Woolf, *To the Lighthouse* (New York: Harcourt Brace Jovanovich, 1927), p. 294.

9. Virginia Woolf, *op. cit.*, pp. 309–310.

10. Grace Baruch, Rosalind Barnett, and Caryl Rivers, *Lifeprints: New Patterns of Love and Work for Today's Women,* (New York: New American Library, 1983), p. 238.

11. Isak Dinesen, *Letters from Africa, 1914–1931* (Chicago: University of Chicago Press, 1984), pp. 426–428.

12. Virginia Woolf, *op. cit.*, p. 61.

13. Marie-Louise von Franz, *The Feminine in Fairytales* (Dallas, TX: Spring Publications, 1972), p. 87.

14. Marie-Louise von Franz, *op. cit.*, p. 86.

15. Harold F. Searles, *The Nonhuman Environment: In Normal Development and Schizophrenia* (New York: International Universities Press, 1960), p. 96.

Bibliography

Albee, Edward. *Who's Afraid of Virginia Woolf?* New York: Atheneum, 1975.

Anthony, James. "The Reactions of Adults to Adolescents and Their Behavior," in Gerald Caplan and Serge Lebovici (eds.) *Adolescence: Psychological Perspectives*. New York: Harper & Row, 1969.

Arendell, Terry. *Mothers and Divorce: Legal, Economic, and Social Dilemmas*. Berkeley: University of California Press, 1986.

Baruch, Grace. "The Psychological Well-being of Women in the Middle Years," in Grace Baruch and J. Brooks-Gunn (eds.) *Women in Midlife*. New York: Plenum Press, 1984.

Baruch, Grace, Rosalind Barnett, and Caryl Rivers. *Lifeprints: New Patterns of Love and Work for Today's Women*. New York: New American Library, 1983.

Bassoff, Bruce. "Tables in Trees: Realism in *To the Lighthouse*," *Studies in the Novel* XVI (Winter 1984): 424–434.

Bassoff, Evelyn Silten. "Mothering Adolescent Daughters: A Psychodynamic Perspective," *Journal of Counseling and Development* 9 (1987): 471–475.

Bassoff, Evelyn Silten and Gene V. Glass. "The Relationship Between Sex Roles and Mental Health: A Meta-analysis of Twenty-six Studies," *The Counseling Psychologist* 10 (1982): 105–112.

de Beauvoir, Simone. *A Very Easy Death*. Harmondsworth, England: Penguin Books, 1969.

————. *The Second Sex*. New York: Random House, 1974.

Benedek, Therese. "Parenthood As a Developmental Stage: A Contribution to Libido Theory," *Journal of the American Psychoanalytic Association* 23 (1959): 389–417.

Bernadez, Teresa. "Prevalent Disorders of Women: Attempts Toward a Different Understanding and Treatment." Paper presented at the Michigan Department of Mental Health, Women's Task Force Public Forum: Lansing, Michigan. (Published by Hawthorne Press, 1980)

Bernard, Jesse. *The Future of Motherhood*. New York: Penguin Books, 1974.

Bettelheim, Bruno. *The Uses of Enchantment: The Meaning and Importance of Fairy Tales*. New York: Random House, 1977.

Boer, Charles. *The Homeric Hymns*, translated by Charles Boer. Chicago: Swallow Press, 1939.

Bolen, Jean Shinoda. *Goddesses in Every Woman: A New Psychology of Women*. New York: Harper & Row, 1984.

Bowlby, John. *Attachment and Loss*, Vol. 1. New York: Basic Books, 1969.

Brody, Jane E. "One Word of Advice for Dieters: Eat," in *The New York Times*, March 22, 1987, p. 19.

Bromberg, Eleanor Mallach. "Mother-Daughter Relationships in Later Life: The Effect of Quality of Relationship upon Mutual Aid." *Journal of Gerontological Social Work*, 6 (1983): 75–91.

Brown, Alice. "The Way of Peace," in Susan Koppelman (ed.), *Between Mothers and Daughters*. New York: Feminist Press, 1985.

Brown, Thomas Harold. *La Fontaine and the Psyche Tradition*, doctoral dissertation. Urbana: University of Illinois, 1960.

Bruch, Hilde. *The Golden Cage: The Enigma of Anorexia Nervosa*. Cambridge, Mass.: Harvard University Press, 1978.

de Castillejo, Irene Claremont. *Knowing Woman*. New York: Harper & Row, 1973.

Chernin, Kim. *In My Mother's House*. New York: Harper & Row, 1983.

———. *The Hungry Self: Women, Eating, and Identity*. New York: Harper & Row, 1986.

———. *The Obsession: Reflections on the Tyranny of Slenderness*. New York: Harper & Row, 1981.

Cohen, Rebecca S., Bertram J. Cohler, and Sidney H. Weissman (eds.). *Parenthood: A Psychodynamic Perspective*. New York: Guilford Press, 1984.

DeAngelis, Tori. "Nurture-or-Assert Conflict Often Erupts As Depression," *The APA Monitor* (January 1987).

Deutsch, Helene. *The Psychology of Women: A Psychoanalytic Interpretation, Volume Two: Motherhood*. New York: Grune & Stratton, 1945.

Dinesen, Isak. *Letters from Africa, 1914–1931*. Chicago: University of Chicago Press, 1984.

Di Prima, Diane. "A Poem in Praise of My Husband (Taos)," in *Selected Poems, 1956–1975*. Berkeley, CA: North Atlantic Books, 1975.

Draughon, Margaret. "Step-Mother's Model of Identification in Relation to Mourning in the Child," *Psychological Reports* 36 (1975): 183–189.

von Franz, Marie-Louise. *The Feminine in Fairytales*. Dallas, TX: Spring Publications, 1972.

Freud, Sigmund. "Family Romances" (1909), in *Collected Papers, (5)*, J. Strachey (ed.). New York: Basic Books, 1959.

Friday, Nancy. *My Mother, My Self: The Daughter's Search for Identity*. New York: Dell, 1977, 1987.

Fulmer, Richard H. "A Structural Approach to Unresolved Mourning in Single Parent Family Systems," *Journal of Marital and Family Therapy* 9 (1983): 259–269.

Garner, David M. and Paul E. Garfinkel (eds.). *Handbook of Psychotherapy for Anorexia Nervosa and Bulimia*. New York: Guilford Press, 1985.

Gibran, Kahlil. *The Prophet*. New York: Knopf, 1965.

Gilligan, Carol. *In a Different Voice: Psychological Theory and Women's Development*. Cambridge, Mass.: Harvard University Press, 1982.

Glenwick, David S. and Joel D. Mowrey. "When Parent Becomes Peer: Loss of Intergenerational Boundaries," *Family Relations* 35 (1985): 57–62.

Grayson, H. "Grief Reactions to the Relinquishing of Unfulfilled Wishes," *American Journal of Psychotherapy* 24 (1970): 287–295.

Brothers Grimm, *Grimm's Fairy Tales*, translated by E. V. Lucas, Lucy Crane, and Marian Edwards. New York: Grosset & Dunlap, 1945.

Hall, Nor. *The Moon and the Virgin*. New York: Harper & Row, 1980.

Harbin, Henry and Denis Madden. "Battered Parents: A New Syndrome," *American Journal of Psychiatry* 136, 1979: 1288–1291.

Harding, Esther M. *The Way of All Women*. New York: Harper & Row, 1970.

————. *Women's Mysteries: Ancient and Modern*. New York: Harper & Row, 1976.

Hazelton, Lesley. *The Right to Feel Bad: Coming to Terms with Normal Depression*. New York: Ballantine Books, 1984.

Heilbrun, Carolyn G. "Middle-Aged Women in Literature," in *Women in Midlife*, Grace Baruch and Jeanne Brooks-Gunn (eds.). New York: Plenum Press, 1984.

Herman, Judith Lewis and Lisa Hirschman. *Father-Daughter Incest*. Cambridge: Harvard University Press, 1981.

Horney, Karen. "The Overvaluation of Love," in *Feminine Psychology*, New York: W. W. Norton, 1967.

Inge, William. *Four Plays*. New York: Grove Press, 1958.

Jacoby, Mario. *The Longing for Paradise: Psychological Perspectives on an Archetype*, translated by Myron B. Gubitz, Boston: Sigo Press, 1985.

Johnson, Robert A. *She: Understanding Feminine Psychology*. New York: Harper & Row, 1976.

————. *We: Understanding the Psychology of Romantic Love*. New York: Harper & Row, 1983.

Jung, Carl Gustav. *Man and His Symbols*. Garden City, NY: Doubleday, 1964.

———. *Memories, Dreams, and Reflections*. New York: Pantheon Books, 1963.

Kagan, Jerome. *The Nature of the Child*. New York: Basic Books, 1984.

Kaplan, Louise. *Adolescence: The Farewell to Childhood*. New York: Simon and Schuster, 1984.

Kierkegaard, Soren. *The Concept of Dread*, translated by Walter Lowrie, Princeton, NJ: Princeton University Press, 1944.

Klaus, Marshall and Kennel, John. *Maternal-Infant Bonding*. St. Louis, Mo.: Mosby, 1976.

Kohut, Heinz. *The Analysis of the Self*. New York: International Universities Press, 1971.

Kollwitz, Käthe. *Diaries and Letters*, Hans Kollwitz (ed.). Chicago: Regnery, 1955.

Lauer, Jeanette and Robert. "Marriages Made to Last," *Psychology Today* (June 1985): 22–26.

Lawrence, D. H. *Sex, Literature, and Censorship*. Harry T. Moore (ed.) New York: Viking Press, 1953.

Lindbergh, Anne Morrow. *Gift from the Sea*. New York: Random House, 1978.

Lorde, Audre. "Black Mother Woman," in *From A Land Where Other People Live*. Detroit, MI: Broadside Press, 1971.

Luria, Zella and Robert G. Meade. "Sexuality and the middle-aged woman," in *Women in Midlife*, Grace Baruch and Jeanne Brooks-Gunn (eds.), New York: Plenum Press, 1984.

De Maupassant, Guy. *Short Stories of the Tragedy and Comedy of Life*, vol. XV11, New York: Dunne, Publisher, 1903.

McWhinnie, Alexina Mary. *Adopted Children How They Grow Up: A Study of Their Adjustment as Adults*. New York: Humanities Press, 1967.

May, Herbert G. and Bruce Metzger (eds.). *The New Oxford Annotated Bible*. New York: Oxford University Press, 1973.

May, Rollo. *The Meaning of Anxiety*. New York: Washington Square Press, 1977.

Miller, Alice. *The Drama of the Gifted Child,* translated by Ruth Ward. New York: Harper & Row, 1981.

———— *For Your Own Good*. New York: Farrar, Straus, Giroux, 1984.

————. *Thou Shalt Not be Aware: Society's Betrayal of the Child*, translated by Hildegarde and Hunter Hannum. New York: New American Library, 1984.

Mishne, Judith Mark. *Clinical Work with Adolescents*. New York: The Free Press, 1986.

Moffat, Mary Jane and Charlotte Painter (eds.). *Revelations: Diaries of Women*. New York: Random House, 1974.

Morrison, Katalin and Airdrie Thompson-Guppy. "Cinderella's Stepmother Syndrome," *Canadian Journal of Psychiatry* 30 (1985): 521–529.

Morrison, Toni. *Song of Solomon*. New York: New American Library, 1977.

————. *Sula,* New York: New American Library, 1973.

Moss, Miriam and Sidney Z. Moss. The Impact of Parental Death on Middle-aged Children," *Omega* 14 (1983–1984): 65–75.

Mucklow, Bonnie M. and Gladys K. Phelan. "Lesbian and Traditional Mothers' Response to Child Behavior and Self-concept," *Psychological Reports* 44 (1979): 880–882.

Neugarten, Bernice L. "Dynamics of Transition of Middle Age to Old Age," *Journal of Geriatric Psychology* 4 (1970): 71–87.

Neumann, Erich. *The Great Mother: An Analysis of the Archetype*, translated by Ralph Manheim, Bollingen Series, XLVII. Princeton, NJ: Princeton University Press, 1963.

Offer, Daniel and Melvin Sabshin. *Normality and the Life Cycle*. New York: Harper & Row, 1984.

Olsen, Tillie. "I Stand Here Ironing," in *Tell Me a Riddle*. New York: Dell, 1960.

———. *Yonnondio from the Thirties*. New York: Dell, 1975.

———. *Mother to Daughter, Daughter to Mother Mothers on Mothering: A Reader and Diary*. New York: Feminist Press, 1984.

Orbach, Susie. *Hunger Strike: The Anorectic's Struggle as a Metaphor of Our Age*. New York: W. W. Norton, 1986.

Payne, Karen (ed.). *Between Ourselves: Letters Between Mothers and Daughters*. Boston: Houghton Mifflin, 1983.

Plath, Sylvia. *Letters Home*, Aurelia Schober Plath (ed.). New York: Harper & Row, 1975.

Radomisli, Michel. "Stereotypes, Stepmothers, and Splitting," *The American Journal of Psychoanalysis* 41 (1981): 121–127.

Reitz, Rosetta. *Menopause: A Positive Approach*. New York: Penguin Books, 1979.

Rich, Adrienne. *Of Woman Born*. New York: W. W. Norton, 1976.

Richardson, N. J. (ed.). *The Homeric Hymn to Demeter*. Oxford: Clarendon Press, 1974.

Ritter, Michael. "Maternal Deprivation, 1972–1978: New Findings, New Concepts, New Approaches," *Child Development* 50 (1979): 283–305.

Rosewell-Jackson, Susan. *A Research Model Designed to Assess Women's Developmental Issues and Tasks: A Focus on Women in Early Midlife*, doctoral dissertation, Boulder: University of Colorado, 1987.

Roth, Geneen. *Feeding the Hungry Heart: The Experience of Compulsive Eating*. New York: New American Library, 1982.

Sager, Clifford J., Hollis Steer Brown, Tamara Engel, Evelyn Rodstein, and Libby Walker. *Treating the Remarried Family*. New York: Brunner/Mazel, 1983.

Sarton, May. "Of Grief," in *Collected Poems of May Sarton, 1930–1973*. New York: W. W. Norton, 1974.

————. *Journal of a Solitude*. New York: W. W. Norton, 1977.

Searles, Harold F. *The Nonhuman Environment: In Normal Development and Schizophrenia*. New York: International Universities Press, 1960.

Schecter, Marshall D., Paul V. Carlson, James Q. Simmons, and Henry W. Work. "Emotional Problems in the Adoptee," *Archives of General Psychiatry* 10 (1964): 109–118.

Schneider, Stanley and Esti Rimmer. "Adoptive Parents' Hostility Toward Their Adopted Children." *Children and Youth Services Review* 6 (1984): 345–352.

Scott-Maxwell, Florida. Excerpts from *The Measure of My Days in Revelations: Diaries of Women*. Mary Jane Moffat and Charlotte Painter, eds. New York: Random House, 1975.

Seuss, Theodor. *Horton Hatches the Egg*. New York: Random House, 1940.

Sorosky, Arthur D., Annette Baran, and Reuben Pannor. "Identity Conflicts in Adoptees," *American Journal of Orthopsychiatry* 45 (1975): 18–27.

Sorosky, Arthur D. "The Psychological Effects of Divorce on Adolescents," *Adolescence* 12 (1977): 123–136.

Sorrels, Rosalie. "Apple of My Eye," in *What, Woman, and Who Myself, I Am*. New York: Wooden Shoe, 1974.

Spignesi, Angelyn. *Starving Women: A Psychology of Anorexia Nervosa*. Dallas, TX: Spring Publications, 1983.

Steinberg, Laurence. "Bound to Bicker," *Psychology Today* (September 1987): 36–39.

Stone, Merlin. *Ancient Mirrors of Womanhood: A Treasury of Goddess and Heroine Lore from Around the World*. Boston: Beacon Press, 1984.

Sullivan, Harry Stack. *Conceptions of Modern Psychiatry*. Washington DC: William Alanson White Psychiatric Foundation, 1947.

———. "The Meaning of Anxiety in Psychiatry and Life," *Psychiatry* 2 (1948): 1–15.

Suzuki, D. "East and West," in *Zen Buddhism and Psychoanalysis*, Erich Fromm and R. De Martino (eds.). New York: Harper & Row, 1960.

Vaillant, George E. *Adaptations to Life*. Boston: Little, Brown, 1977.

Valdes, Guadalupe. "Recuerdo," in *Between Mothers and Daughters: Stories Across a Generation*, in Susan Koppelman (ed.). New York: Feminist Press, 1985. (First published in *De Colores Journal*, 1974.

Visher, Emily and John Visher. *How to Win as a Stepfamily*. New York: Dembner Books, 1982.

———. *Stepfamilies: A Guide to Working with Stepparents and Stepchildren*. New York: Brunner-Mazel, 1979.

Wallerstein, Judith S. and Joan Berlin Kelly. *Surviving the Breakup: How Children and Parents Cope with Divorce*. New York: Harper & Row, 1980.

Weekes, Claire. *Hope and Help for Your Nerves*. New York: Bantam Books, 1978.

Winnicott, Donald W. *Collected Papers*. New York: Harper & Row, 1956.

Wiseman, Adele. Excerpt from *Old Woman at Play*, in *Mother to Daughter, Daughter to Mother Mothers on Mothering: A Reader and Diary*. Tillie Olsen (ed.). New York: Feminist Press, 1984.

Woodman, Marion. *Addiction to Perfection: The Still Unravished Bride*. Toronto: Inner City Books, 1982.

———. *The Owl Was a Baker's Daughter: Obesity, Anorexia Nervosa, and the Repressed Feminine*. Toronto: Inner City Books, 1980.

Woolf, Virginia. *To the Lighthouse*. New York: Harcourt Brace Jovanovich, 1927.

Yalom, Irwin D. *Existential Psychotherapy*. New York: Harper & Row, 1980.

Young-Eisendrath, Polly. "Demeter's Folly: Experiencing Loss in Middle Life," *Psychological Perspectives* 15 (Spring 1984): 39–63.

Bibliography

Visser, Emily and John S. Major. *How to Wrap a Dragon in the Mist.* Sentinel Books, 1975.

——. *To Summon a Castle: Adventures in the Imagination and Brush Pen.* New York: Braziller, Mazel, 1978.

Waldenses, John S. and Joan Irwin Kelly. *Sharing the Brush: Poor Karma and Power.* Upper Saddle Street. New York: Harper & Row, 1980s.

Weshler, Claire. *Hope and Glory for Your Nerves.* New York: Bantam Books, 1975.

Winet, ed. *Writers' Market Place.* Paper. New York: Harper Row, 1976.

Williams, Ashley. *European Women artists with Watercolor Paintings: The Lives of Mother Watson on Watercolor, A Reader and Diary.* Ill. Photo. 1983. New York: Pantheon Press, 1984.

Wiseman, Marion. *Addison's Collections.* The Still Edition of Early Renaissance City Block 1952.

——. *The Old Witch's Tale: a Dangerous Garden. Aboriginal and the Increased Fountain.* London: Pantheon City Books, 1980.

Woolf, Virginia. *To the Lighthouse.* New York: Harcourt, Brace Javanovich.

Yalom, Irwin. *Existential Psychotherapy.* New York: Harper & Row, 1980.

Young, Beautiful Folk. *The Power of Folly Experienced Love.* Mother Jones. *Psychotherapist's responses.* 16 (Spring 1986): 16.

Index

INDEX